ADORNO AND EXISTENCE

Adorno and Existence

PETER E. GORDON

HARVARD UNIVERSITY PRESS
Cambridge, Massachusetts & London, England / 2016

Library of Congress Cataloging-in-Publication Data

Names: Gordon, Peter Eli, author.
Title: Adorno and existence / Peter E. Gordon.
Description: Cambridge, Massachusetts : Harvard University Press, 2016. |
    Includes bibliographical references and index.
Identifiers: LCCN 2016011712 | ISBN 9780674734784 (alk. paper)
Subjects: LCSH: Adorno, Theodor W., 1903–1969. | Kierkegaard, Søren,
    1813–1855. | Frankfurt school of sociology. | Existentialism.
Classification: LCC B3199.A34 G67 2016 | DDC 193—dc23
LC record available at http://lccn.loc.gov/2016011712

For L.

. . . you must say words, as long as there are any

—SAMUEL BECKETT, *The Unnamable*

Contents

Preface

For many years my ambition of writing a book-length study of Adorno remained unrealized, chiefly because it seemed to me improper to devote attention to a thinker for whom I felt such admiration. Some scholars no doubt prefer the celebratory mode. They write books about those they consider heroes, and they draw nourishment from the feeling of narcissistic union with their subjects. If they write about villains, their antipathy is no less intermingled with pleasure. All too often prosecution is a photographic negative for self-affirmation. In either case, one knows where one stands. I have rarely permitted myself this kind of moral rectitude, nor have I longed for the terra firma of absolute certainty in matters of philosophical argument. Critical of all immediacy, and suspicious—on both moral and political grounds—of intellectual cathexis, I did not feel I could permit myself to write a sustained monograph about Adorno because (to play upon the obvious pun) I feared that I adored him rather too much. Criticism is a scholarly virtue; love is not.

My reluctance was no doubt overdetermined by an important bond between teacher and student: Martin Jay, the scholar who served as a major guide at the University of California–Berkeley into modern European philosophy and social thought, made his academic debut as an expositor of critical theory. In 1984 Jay dedicated a monograph to Adorno in the Modern Masters series (then edited by Frank Kermode), a work that only extended a reputation that was at that point already well established. Jay's very first book, *The Dialectical Imagination,* was first published in 1973, and it now occupies a canonical place in the Anglophone world; it remains the most judicious and reliable introduction to the ideas and history of the Institute for Social Research. It is a remarkable fact that Jay's book first took shape as a doctoral dissertation (submitted, as it happens, to the very institution where I now hold a professorial appointment). The enduring strength of that early work only compounds my admiration for its author, but it may also help to explain my reluctance to write an independent monograph on similar themes. Prudence counseled me long ago to avoid playing the role of apprentice to an acknowledged master; we all know how Goethe's story ends. Rather than risk a similar fate, I sought fallow ground instead, and tilled the soil there.

In two previous monographs, and in various published essays, I have focused my attention on themes of existentialism and religion. I have also written about Martin Heidegger, though never as a philosophical partisan and never from a position of identification or advocacy. But for some time now the urge to work on Adorno has grown more powerful, and, after many years of avoiding the inevitable, the inevitable could no longer be avoided.

My aim in this book is to examine the ways in which Adorno became preoccupied with not only Heidegger but also the broader tradition that often goes (misleadingly) by the name "existentialism." It is well known that Heidegger in particular was a constant presence throughout Adorno's philosophical career. In Adorno's inaugural lecture in May 1931 as a professor of philosophy at the University of Frankfurt, the German philosopher is singled out for special criticism, and from that point forward Heidegger was rarely absent from Adorno's reflections. But Heidegger was not the only one. Kierkegaard, often considered the founder of existentialism, was the subject of Adorno's habilitation, which the young philosopher completed in early 1933 just as the Nazis were coming to power. Adorno would revisit Kierkegaard's philosophy at significant junctures in his career, first in exile and once again after his return to Germany. Nor can we neglect Edmund Husserl, whose phenomenology was the topic of two major efforts, Adorno's first dissertation in the 1920s, and a second major philosophical work that he first undertook at Oxford University in the mid-1930s and published with significant revision in 1956. Although the inclusion of Husserl in this philosophical constellation may strike the reader as somewhat surprising, a careful examination of Adorno's critique demonstrates that transcendental and existential phenomenology stood together as variants of the same bourgeois-idealist tradition. This book unites into one study Adorno's readings of three philosophers: Kierkegaard, Husserl, and Heidegger. All three, I suggest, were exemplars of what I will call "the philosophy of bourgeois interiority."

Just what this term signifies and how exactly it applies to the aforementioned philosophers will be addressed later in the book. For the time being it should be acknowledged that Adorno's readings may tell us less about these three authors than they do about Adorno as a philosopher and social theorist. The reconstruction of his critical engagements may therefore serve as a *via negativa* toward a better understanding of Adorno himself. To explain this point will be the chief burden of my book. To anticipate, I will argue that Adorno saw in existentialism a paradigmatic but unsuccessful attempt to realize what would become his own philosophical ambition, to break free of the systems of idealism and to turn—in the phrase made famous by Jean Wahl—"toward the concrete." In his 1931 inaugural lecture Adorno already announced the themes that would remain his abiding philosophical concerns: the polemic against idealism and an appeal to "what is irreducible." Toward the end of his career, in the preface to *Negative Dialectics,* Adorno affirmed this continuity in his thinking: "To use the strength of the subject to break through the fallacy of constitutive subjectivity—this is what the author felt to be his task ever since he came to trust his own mental impulses." The similarity is remarkable: what philosophers in the opposed tradition had called the "leap into existence" might be compared to what Adorno called "the primacy of the object." To be sure, these two themes are not identical. But understanding their differences may alert us to a remarkable philosophical proximity that continued to be a source of both inspiration and provocation for Adorno throughout his life.

This project has awakened the old anxiety: Could I write about Adorno without lapsing back into scholarship in the celebratory mode? Could I devote a monograph to Adorno without reducing myself to the role of a mere amanuensis for his ideas? Could a scholar in the school of critical theory ever be other than an eternal student or an uncritical advocate? Such questions cannot be lightly dismissed. And yet, as this project has further developed, I have come to understand that my admiration for Adorno, however strong, is hardly absolute. It serves not as a resting place but as a *point d'appui* for thinking in a more critical mode about both existentialism and critical theory. Critical theory, after all, is not a homeland but a method. It is a strategy of reflection that aims to trouble all forms of untroubled cathexis—even the cathexis with critical theory itself.

Originally written for pedagogical aims, this book is chiefly confined to philosophical exposition. Only seldom have I ventured into the more forbidding terrain of criticism. Too little is understood about Adorno's own perspectives on the philosophies of existence, and I have therefore tried here to elucidate what he thought, only occasionally touching upon the question as to whether his thoughts were philosophically defensible. To be sure, the task of philosophical elucidation already demands some understanding of what it would mean for Adorno to be right, and the reader will no doubt discern those moments where rational reconstruction must navigate between skepticism and interpretative charity.

This book originated in a shorter series of lectures that I first delivered in June 2013, under the title "Quatre conferences sur: Adorno et l'existence," during my monthlong service as a *professeur invité* in the department of philosophy at the École Normale Supérieure. My visit coincided with the Kierkegaard bicentennial—he was born in May 1813—so the question of Adorno's relation to Kierkegaard and other strands in the "philosophy of existence" immediately presented itself as a suitable theme. My visit to the ENS was made possible by two extraordinarily generous colleagues and friends, Marc Crépon and Jean-Claude Monod, and I am very much in their debt for the warm reception in Paris. Thanks chiefly to the excellent comments and insights of colleagues and students who followed the Paris lectures, the present volume has been completely reworked and substantially expanded. I do not imagine that a single sentence remains from the original lectures, though one may detect, here and there, stylistic gestures that recall the original format of oral presentation. My warm thanks, too, extend to Philip Nord and all of his colleagues at the Davis Center at Princeton University, where I spent the academic year 2012–2013 as a visiting fellow while working on a rather different project. It is a familiar occurrence in an academic's schedule of work that one book will temporarily displace another, and this is what happened to me in my final month at Princeton, when I had to put the other book on hiatus to begin writing the Adorno lectures for the ENS.

I am enormously grateful to the generous remarks of three anonymous readers for Harvard University Press, and, finally, I am especially grateful to Lindsay Waters, my editor at the Press, along with his editorial assistant, Amanda Peery. Both have been wonderful: sensitive to my concerns and tolerant of my idiosyncrasies. I am grateful, too, to the design department at HUP for creating a cover whose aesthetic characteristics Adorno, I suspect, would have found congenial. For their scrupulous and keen-eyed copyediting my sincere thanks to Brian Bendlin and Pamela Nelson. The index for this book was prepared by Lev Asimow.

Following the lectures in Paris, I presented shorter papers on related themes in many venues, at the University of Sydney, the University of California at Berkeley, the Université de Montréal, and others. I cannot name all of the participants at each institution, but I would especially like to thank Daniela Helbig and Dalia Nassar in Sydney, Sheer Ganor in Berkeley, and Till van Rahden and Iain MacDonald in Montréal. Finally, for their willingness to offer comments on an earlier draft, I am deeply grateful to a handful of esteemed colleagues and friends, all of them accomplished and sensitive scholars in the tradition of critical theory. They are listed here in alphabetical order: Jay Bernstein, Espen Hammer, Axel Honneth, Martin Jay, and Michael Rosen. Specialists will of course understand why the critical insights offered to me by these five tremendously gifted individuals have left me with a debt of gratitude I can never fully repay. But it is my duty to save each of them any further embarrassment by registering the usual caveat: Although the book has been greatly improved thanks to their suggestions, its failings—its *Schründen* and *Rissen*—are wholly my own. To discern such flaws would hardly require a messianic light. Everyday illumination will suffice.

ADORNO AND EXISTENCE

A Philosophical Physiognomy

. . . car c'est moi que je peins.

—MICHEL DE MONTAIGNE, *Essais*

Of one thing we can be certain: Adorno was not an existentialist. From his earliest years as a philosophical reader, his attitude toward the movements associated with "existence" was that of unsparing criticism. In Kierkegaard, Adorno found a paragon of bourgeois interiority; in Heidegger, he saw a purveyor of pseudoromantic depth and a "jargon of authenticity" that served as an ideological ruse for fascism and political regression. And yet, the philosophy of existence was for Adorno what the Rorschach test is for the psychologist's client—a screen on which to project both antipathy and desire. It is a shopworn analogy, but it is not imprecise: those who find their own dreams reflected back at them from inkblots on paper will remark on the fact that those strange shapes are split in two by the fold of the page that runs from top to bottom, like the gutter of a book. All reading is projection. But, of course, it is not *only* projection. Reading in the highest sense promises new insight, an awakening to commonality but also a sharpened awareness of difference. Adorno's readings of the modern philosophical canon, we might say, were laboratories for critical experimentation; they were occasionally polemical and often exhilarating. And we can look over his shoulder and read *with* him so as to gain a deepened understanding of who Adorno was as a philosopher.

Existentialism, the philosophy of existence, existential ontology: these terms are not interchangeable. But in the aggregate, they designate a tradition of philosophical discourse that drew inspiration from the mid-nineteenth century writings of Søren Kierkegaard and then flourished in the twentieth century in the work of such philosophers as Martin Buber, Martin Heidegger, Karl Jaspers, and Jean-Paul Sartre, among many others. What should rouse our interest is the fact that Adorno, throughout his career, remained caught in a troubled yet *productive* bond with this tradition. He did not agree with it, nor did he care for its stylistic register (even if, at times, he indulged in gestures of irony and paradox that would seem to place him in Kierkegaard's company). He excoriated even the great lyric poet Rainer Maria Rilke for impostures of vacuous devotion that harmonized all too well with existential needs. Yet although Adorno professed little sympathy for the philosophy of existence, the fact remains that he could not stop writing about it. Adorno's study of Kierkegaard, submitted in 1931 to Paul Tillich in Frankfurt for his habilitation at the age of twenty-seven, was his very first published work of philosophy. His final book, *Negative Dialectics,* which appeared in late July 1966 when Adorno was nearing his sixty-third year, consists of a critical confrontation with Heidegger as well as with Hegel; it was the very last major work of philosophy to appear during the author's lifetime. (His *Aesthetic Theory* was published posthumously.) Between these two dates we can span the entirety of Adorno's intellectual development—from his earliest years of philosophical apprenticeship when he was not yet certain of his views, to the late works of an acknowledged master whose *Denkstil* was now definitive.

This enduring preoccupation, one could argue, was symptomatic, the sign of an intellectual complicity that Adorno could not and did not wish to undo, since he would succeed in defining his own ideas only in the endless working through of his own troubled investment in the tradition he subjected to relentless criticism. The title of the present volume—*Adorno and Existence*—is therefore neither a mere dualism nor a *coincidentia oppositorum*. It describes neither an abstract negation nor a full reconciliation. Borrowing from Adorno himself, one might characterize it as a negative dialectic.[1] In following his philosophical *Auseinandersetzung* with the philosophies of existence we learn less, perhaps, about those bodies of thought than we do about their critic. Indeed, in tracing the lineaments of this encounter one develops a philosophical portrait of Adorno himself. To borrow a term from Adorno's book on Gustav Mahler, such an exercise might be described as a "philosophical physiognomy."[2]

My chief aim in this book is to trace the complex history of Adorno's critical engagement with existentialism, a history through which the author came to understand his own philosophical purposes. The book begins with Adorno's encounter with Kierkegaard, and it then turns to the major confrontation with Heidegger, the philosophical contemporary who—perhaps more than any other—appears and reappears in Adorno's postwar writings as the bête noire of critical theory and the exemplar sine qua non of both philosophical and political regression. Along the way, however, I will also examine Adorno's assessment of Edmund Husserl, whose appearance in this book may seem counterintuitive. But it will be my task to show why the logical rigor and extravagant idealism of transcendental phenomenology deserves its very own chapter in the story of Adorno's confrontation with existentialism.

The general argument of this book is as follows. Adorno, from the beginning to the end of his career, sustained a troubled but enduring bond with existentialism and phenomenology—a bond that casts his own philosophical commitments in an unexpected light. At first glance, it may seem tempting to characterize Adorno's attitude as one of unsparing criticism verging on polemic. Yet his continued fascination with the philosophical canons of existentialism and phenomenology suggests a connection far more complicated and productive than that of mere antipathy. Indeed, the complexity of this bond merits closer scrutiny. When we pause to consider what unites his disparate philosophical writings on Heidegger, Husserl, and Kierkegaard, we come to see that Adorno assigns to this trio a singular importance: they stand as exemplars for an orientation that I will call "the philosophy of bourgeois interiority."

In the chapters that follow, this term will serve as a heuristic and merely provisional name, the precise meaning of which will come into focus only when we examine seriatim the details of Adorno's various interpretations. Generally speaking, what distinguishes the philosophy of bourgeois interiority is a tendency to esteem the contents of isolated consciousness over and against the material world.

Such an esteem typically places greatest stress on an interior realm (defined as the province of authentic selfhood, transcendental subjectivity, or incorrigible belief), and it withdraws as much as possible from what it considers the degraded phenomena of the exterior (identified variously as everydayness, the natural attitude, or mere publicity).

The use of the term *bourgeois* to characterize this interior demands some explanation, since it is typically deployed as a mere *Schimpfwort*, or term of abuse, in the antiquated discourses of vulgar Marxism. If we wish to understand Adorno's philosophical criticism, the term is instructive insofar as it serves as a helpful reminder that for Adorno, as for Hegel, "philosophy is its own time comprehended in thought [*Die Philosophie ist ihre Zeit in Gedanken gefaßt*]."[3] To Adorno this meant that the immanent critique of a given philosophical doctrine is best conceived as one moment within a larger critique of the social whole. Those who insist otherwise (that is, those who would prefer to believe in the possibility of philosophical interpretation wholly dissociated from social reality) subscribe to the fantastical notion of an undamaged mind split off from the

† see above

damaged world. However consoling this notion may seem, to grant its truth would be to condemn philosophy to stale academicism. At the same time, Adorno also rejected gestures of crude historicism or sociologism that would regard philosophy as "nothing more than" a reflection of social reality. For Adorno, such gestures appear as premature acts of intellectual capitulation: they betray not the tough-mindedness of the *engagé* militant but rather the critic's readiness to surrender even the hope—however unlikely—of resistance against the way things happen to be. In bourgeois society "the network of the whole" is drawn ever tighter, such that the individual consciousness finds "less and less room for evasion." And yet, subjective consciousness still persists in the belief that it is free, and it thereby inhibits a proper grasp of objective conditioning. As Adorno explains, "the semblance of freedom makes reflection upon one's own unfreedom incomparably more difficult" today than it once was "when such reflection stood in contradiction to manifest unfreedom."[4] Among the many difficulties in reading Adorno is that of acceding to *both* moments of this dialectic without permitting either of them an unqualified priority. Adorno's philosophical criticism always conceives of the relation between mind and world as an unresolved tension that forbids to the mind any confidence in its own transcendence even as it resists the demand that it conform to the world.

As creations of the mind, philosophical texts are therefore, for Adorno, always part of the social whole even while they cannot be reduced to that whole. To read a work of philosophy properly is never simply a matter of exposing its ideological function, its scandalous politics or social complicity, for any philosophical text must be understood to contain within itself critical potentialities—possibilities, however faint, that point beyond its debased moment of social use. This may help to explain why Adorno's interpretations of the modern philosophical canon remain so instructive even today: they are interpretations that expose both conformity *and* resistance, both ideology and the critique of ideology. If it is true that philosophy is its own age comprehended in thought, then precisely *as thought* philosophy retains for itself the power of comprehending its age, where such comprehension implies at least some measure of critical leverage against the world to which it remains nonetheless bound. My specific claim in this book will be that Adorno did not and could not blithely reject the philosophies of bourgeois interiority, since the idea of mere rejection fails to convey what he considered most instructive in this canon. From his first published book on Kierkegaard's aesthetic to the mature studies in negative dialectics, Adorno was forever returning to the philosophies of bourgeois interiority to seek in them a paradoxical simultaneity, between their manifest failure and their real—if unrealized—promise.

The suggestion that Adorno saw any promise whatsoever in this philosophical tradition may invite skepticism, especially among readers who find in Adorno's writing about existentialism and phenomenology only the most unremitting hostility. A chief task of this book will be to introduce greater nuance into this commonplace opinion by exploring the ways that Adorno developed his own ideas in a kind of contestatory dialogue with the philosophers of bourgeois interiority. An inspiration for this argument is a remarkable passage from *Negative Dialectics,* in which Adorno writes that "Heidegger reaches the very borders [*gelangt bis an die Grenze*] of the dialectical insight into the non-identity in identity."[5] Those who come to critical theory burdened with customary opinion may be taken aback at Adorno's readiness to admit that existential ontology was not entirely without merit. But we do a serious injustice to Adorno if we fail to grasp the nuance in his argument. The crucial thought, on which I will elaborate at far greater length later in this book, is that Adorno saw in Heidegger's philosophy an important statement of "ontological need [*ontologische Bedürfnis*]" even though this need went unfulfilled.[6] Existential ontology promises the satisfaction of concrete materiality, but remains stuck at a level of idealistic abstraction. I am pleased to note that I am not the first to stress this important nuance in Adorno's critique of Heidegger. In his fascinating contribution to the essay collection *Adorno and Heidegger: Philosophical Questions,* Iain Macdonald emphasizes the significance of this very same passage, with its intriguing allowance that Heidegger approached the "borders" of materialism. Macdonald considers this passage a key for reading Adorno's interpretation of Heidegger. While my own argument goes in a somewhat different direction, I share with Macdonald and his coeditor Krzysztof Ziarek a general interest in dissolving some of the inherited prejudices that have obstructed our understanding of this philosophical *Auseinandersetzung.*[7] The present book, however, does not confine itself exclusively to the Adorno-Heidegger complex; rather, it treats that encounter as only one chapter within the broader history of Adorno's confrontation with the philosophies of bourgeois interiority.

Stepping back from the details, it is important to note that my purposes in this book are largely expository. Although much has been written about Adorno's critique of Heidegger, only a few scholars have given Adorno's texts on Kierkegaard the attention they merit, and even less has been written about Adorno's work on Husserl. The criticism of Heidegger is typically addressed in isolation, not as the concluding chapter in his lifelong engagement with *Existenzphilosophie.* I am convinced, however, that the story of this engagement deserves to be told, and in a manner that does not tax the patience of readers who may not possess the prior knowledge of specialists in the field.

My justification for telling this story is threefold. Most specifically, the story provides us with a new way of considering Adorno's own intellectual development, and in this respect the present book charts not only the philosopher's thought but also his life, from his early dissertation to his final years. Occasionally the work of philosophical exegesis comes to a pause so that the reader might appreciate the mutual entwinement of philosophy and personal existence. Adorno, after all, was first and foremost a philosopher, and whatever fascination we may find in his life, this external appeal must pale when measured against the interest of his ideas. Montaigne's *Essais* begin with the confession that in each of his writings he offers a portrait of himself: "car c'est moi que je peins." Like Montaigne, Adorno left a distinctive imprint on everything he wrote. The present book thus makes a modest contribution to Adorno's intellectual biography.

More generally, the story of Adorno and existence provides us with a new vantage point on the history of European thought in the later twentieth century insofar as existentialism and critical theory are rightly considered two of the largest camps whose interrelations were rarely cordial. I am only too aware that specialists who identify themselves with existentialism and phenomenology will consider much of what Adorno wrote unfair or simply ill informed. It is also true that Adorno failed to acknowledge other tendencies and implications of phenomenology. He appreciated neither its gestures toward realism nor its potential to inspire movements of political emancipation, themes amply discussed elsewhere—especially, for example, in the excellent studies by Michael Gubser and Dan Zahavi.[8] It is an acknowledged limitation of this present book that it confines itself to Adorno's own perspective and takes little notice of such realist or emancipatory alternatives.

By this point a large and still growing body of scholarship addresses both the contestation and the complicity between critical theory and existential ontology. Much of this literature concerns the deep imprint left by Heidegger's thought on Herbert Marcuse, who had studied in Freiburg with Heidegger between 1928 and 1933 and whose own *Habilitationsschrift,* titled *Hegel's Ontology and Theory of Historicity,* reflects his teacher's philosophical influence.[9] More controversial, however, is the critical literature that demonstrates lines of affinity between Heidegger and Walter Benjamin, notwithstanding the latter's well-known critique of Heidegger that first appears in fragments written in 1916. In a letter to Gershom Scholem that year, Benjamin wrote of Heidegger's essay "The Concept of Time in the Science of History" that "it shows precisely how not to deal with the matter. A terrible piece of work, which you should perhaps look at, if only to confirm my suspicion, that most of what the author says about historical time is nonsense." And yet, as Howard Caygill has argued, "this categorial rejection of Heidegger's early work on time conceals the extent of Benjamin's critical engagement, and indeed the several points of agreement between them."[10]

The present study addresses neither Benjamin nor Marcuse, nor the other Frankfurt school affiliates, central or peripheral, who may have encountered the European tradition of existentialism in manifold ways.[11] Nor do I take a direct stand on the continued controversy surrounding the extent of Heidegger's political engagement with national socialism, a shameful episode that obviously remains of great importance for those who wish to grapple in a serious way with Heidegger's philosophical legacy. While I am by no means an apologist for Heidegger and do not wish to minimize the extent to which his work is obviously contaminated by fascism, neither do I feel it should be permitted to dominate or invalidate the many other concerns that may arise in connection with his philosophy.[12] In sum, this book makes no pretense of offering a comprehensive study of critical theory and existentialism, though it is my hope that it contributes to the extant literature on this and related themes.[13] My task here is limited to understanding Adorno's own intellectual development, with a specific focus on his confrontation with those various forms of existential phenomenology and fundamental ontology that played such a powerful role in twentieth-century thought on the European Continent. I will briefly address the existentialism of Jean-Paul Sartre, whose work, as David Sherman notes in his very thoughtful study *Sartre and Adorno,* received only a "rather attenuated" response from critical theory. But my treatment of Sartre will surely strike many readers as inadequate, and I would recommend that they turn to Sherman's book for a full assessment.[14] To be sure, one might plausibly enlarge the category of existentialism to include nineteenth-century thinkers such as Nietzsche, and perhaps even Schelling. However, even while acknowledging the merits of a more capacious inquiry, I have found it prudent to omit other philosophers from the present study so as to preserve a narrower argumentative line.

Finally, the following account has a broader purpose that exceeds the requirements of mere exposition. Its aims are critical and, one might even say, redemptive. My critical purpose is to offer a reading that elucidates Adorno's own philosophical argumentation in such a way as to lend those arguments renewed force. Underlying the existentialist tradition is a certain justifiable skepticism regarding the limits of reason. But this is not the only recent trend in European philosophy to nourish such skepticism. Similar sentiments of skepticism can be found in Schelling as well as Nietzsche, both of whom played a considerable role in Adorno's philosophical development.[15] More recently, the broad movement of poststructuralism in philosophy and the human sciences has also had the effect of radicalizing the existentialist pathos of finitude, slackening our confidence in the critical potentialities of human reason. But it pursued this impulse with such zeal that the spirit of critique was generalized into an aesthetic of irony that could no longer account for its own critical ambitions.[16] Some scholars discern lines of philosophical affinity between Adorno and the poststructuralists, and they are not entirely mistaken: Adorno's own genealogical critique of modern rationalization drew chiefly from Nietzsche, also one of the main resources for the poststructuralist turn of the last half century. Nor should we forget that Kierkegaard's theological rebellion against idealism partakes of this broader mood of skepticism. In certain respects Adorno, too, belongs to this skeptical tradition, and denying such affinities would gravely distort our vision of Adorno's philosophical project.

And yet, a crucial difference remains, and to neglect this difference would be to commit a far more serious distortion: Notwithstanding the hidden and not-so-hidden points of contact between Adorno and existentialism, the traditions diverge insofar as the one sustains the bond with reason that the other abandons. The rational critique of reason becomes unreasonable when it severs its bond with the critical energies that make thinking itself a possibility. It is true that Adorno's critical orientation can appear relentlessly negative, and many readers fail to see that his negativity still glows, however faintly, with a rationalist's hope for a better world. Too much has been written about Adorno's melancholy spirit and, especially in the United States, expressions of regret concerning his exacting aesthetic standards and mandarin sensibility have become de rigueur. The redemptive purpose that guides these chapters is to defend Adorno against such prejudices and to reconfirm his place as one of the very few truly indispensable minds in the philosophical discourse of modernity.

1

Starting Out with Kierkegaard

Open thinking points beyond itself

—THEODOR W. ADORNO, "Resignation"

An Unlikely Cathexis

Adorno once called Søren Kierkegaard "the grandfather of all existential philosophy."[1] But to Adorno he was even more. Only a moment's glance will suffice to show us that in his record of intellectual development Adorno would remain intimately bound to the Danish philosopher in ways that suggest an enduring complicity and even something like an affinity of ideas. It is true, of course, that this complicity must strike us today as highly improbable, most of all because Kierkegaard is remembered primarily for a burning antipathy toward Hegelian dialectics that set him apart from the major streams of critical theory. And yet even this opposition to Hegel helped to solidify Kierkegaard's philosophical appeal for Adorno, whose own conception of negative dialectics also entailed a principled resistance to Hegel's philosophy of reconciliation. One of my purposes in this book is to demonstrate the affinity between Adorno and Kierkegaard, even while acknowledging the estrangement that runs through all of Adorno's writings on the first philosopher of existence.

A passion for Kierkegaard is traceable to Adorno's earliest years.[2] In a winter of 1923 letter to Leo Löwenthal, the cultural critic Siegfried Kracauer described his young friend, then just past his twentieth birthday, as a scholar nearly disabled by his own intellect: "If Teddie ever decides to make a declaration of love so as to escape from the sinful state of bachelorhood," Kracauer wrote, he would "be sure to phrase it so obscurely that the young lady concerned . . . will be unable to understand what he is saying unless she has read the complete works of Kierkegaard."[3] A casual reference, no doubt, and one might object that *any* philosopher might have served to illustrate the travails of "Teddie" Wiesengrund Adorno in matters of romance. But the choice is not without significance. We should recall that during the mid-1920s, not only Adorno but a great many intellectuals in German-speaking central Europe found themselves in the throes of a Kierkegaard renaissance.

Adorno would in fact write his second dissertation, or *Habilitationsschrift,* on Kierkegaard. The topic was first suggested to him by the theologian Paul Tillich, who had succeeded Max Scheler in the chair of philosophy at the University of Frankfurt (previously held by Hans Cornelius, Adorno's early mentor in philosophy). Originally written in the years 1929–1930, the Kierkegaard dissertation served as Adorno's passport to a teaching position; a year later it was accepted by Tillich at Frankfurt, thereby conferring on its author the *venia legendi.* Adorno would later characterize the original manuscript as "thick" and "meandering," and he would spend 1932 reworking it extensively for publication.[4] The final version appeared in early 1933 with the new title *Kierkegaard: Construction of the Aesthetic.*

The very first review of the book was published by Adorno's friend and mentor, Walter Benjamin, in an April 1933 edition of the *Vossische Zeitung.* "The book contains much in a small space," Benjamin observed. "The author's subsequent writings may someday emerge from it. It is, in any case, one of those rare first books in which inspiration manifests itself in the guise of criticism."[5] This statement, like many by Benjamin, proved unusually clairvoyant, for this was not the only text on Kierkegaard that Adorno would write. He would return to the Danish philosopher in 1940 with the essay "On Kierkegaard's Doctrine of Love," and yet again in 1963, just six years before his death, with an essay dedicated to Tillich, "Kierkegaard noch einmal" (Kierkegaard once more).[6] These three texts mark the developmental joints of Adorno's career. They allow us to pursue his thought across the stages of his life, from his days as a young student of philosophy in Frankfurt, to the exile in New York, to his time as an aging émigré, both reviled and revered, who returned to Frankfurt after World War II. Alongside these three texts are the many comments and asides on Kierkegaard that can be found throughout Adorno's written work, especially in *Negative Dialectics* and *The Jargon of Authenticity*, major texts to which I will return in later chapters. There are also two noteworthy reviews, one in German, the other in English, in which Adorno evaluated contemporary scholarship on Kierkegaard by Jean Wahl and Walter Lowrie. Such frequent revisitings only confirm the general impression that Adorno felt himself continually drawn back to the Danish philosopher, in whose works he found ideas that both troubled and fascinated him, demanding constant reconsideration.[7]

What were the grounds for this cathexis? One should not dismiss the simple phenomenon of biographical mirroring. Kierkegaard, the son of a wealthy Danish wool merchant, matured into a bookish and brilliant critic of his time, not unlike Adorno, the son of a financially secure German-Jewish wine merchant who was born nearly a century later. Throughout this book I will entertain the possibility that—even in the image of Kierkegaard as the philosopher of bourgeois interiority—Adorno saw his own reflection, however distorted or inverted. But all facts of biography seem to pale in significance when one considers the political and philosophical differences between the two thinkers. The greatest temptation when interrogating Adorno's bond with the philosophy of existence would be to reduce it to a merely political antagonism, as if critical theory and existentialism were little more than rarefied and philosophical names for an essentially political standoff between two opposing ideologies of the mid-twentieth century, socialism and fascism. Although the memory of Jean-Paul Sartre's antifascism immediately challenges such reductive mappings of philosophy onto politics, it is of course true that the political struggle left no one innocent: it magnetized the rarefied world of intellectuals no less than the world of politicians and nation-states. Alliances of philosophy took on a weight and significance disproportionate to their modest shape, to such a degree that even today we have difficulty separating the actual meanings of philosophical debate from their politicized interpretations.[8] Adorno himself later wrote of his *Kierkegaard: Construction of the Aesthetic* that from the very beginning its impact on German letters was compromised, if not wholly eclipsed, by "political disaster [*Unheil*]. The book was not forbidden and continued to be sold, even while the author had been denaturalized. Perhaps it was protected by the censors' inability to understand it. *The critique of existential ontology that the book works out was meant already at that time to reach opposition intellectuals in Germany.*"[9] To be sure, we should not permit this retroactive description wholly to determine our own reading of the book. After all, Adorno's own philosophical reflections proceed at a level of negative-dialectical complexity that obviates any such reduction. And yet the political moment of the book's composition merits our attention.

The Kierkegaard Reception in Germany

Kierkegaard has long occupied a contested and symbolically over-determined place in the German philosophical imagination. The relative neglect of the Dane until the close of the nineteenth century is due to the obvious fact that for many years his work was not available in German translation, a situation only remedied thanks to the efforts of the Protestant theologian and pacifist Christoph Schrempf, whose biography and translations of the complete works of Kierkegaard were available for German readers by 1925.[10] But even before this date Kierkegaard had become a cultural touchstone, celebrated not only as a philosopher and theologian but also as a source of literary inspiration for the circle of expressionist and neo-romantic authors associated with the journal *Der Brenner* (founded in 1911), which Karl Kraus called "the only honest review in Austria."[11] The Brenner Kreis (Brenner Circle) attracted not only writers such as Hermann Broch, Thomas Mann, and Georg Trakl but also a young philosopher named Martin Heidegger.[12]

Yet Kierkegaard's name spread beyond the circle as well. In his 1911 collection of literary and philosophical essays, *Soul and Form,* the young Georg Lukács included an essay on Kierkegaard that suggested that the entirety of the Dane's life could be made intelligible on the basis of a single gesture: the decision to cancel his anticipated marriage to Regine Olsen.[13] Kierkegaard's writings also made their way into the so-called Prager Kreis (Prague Circle), a name Max Brod used to describe the handful of writers that included, most notably, his friend Franz Kafka, who first encountered Kierkegaard around 1913 and began to study his writings in earnest during the final years of World War I.[14] Although Kakfa initially confessed that he found Kierkegaard "inaccessible," his parables, stories, and personal diaries all testify to the enormous power that Kierkegaard came to exert over his literary and philosophical imagination.[15] In Brod's 1937 biographical memoir of Kafka, the influence of Kierkegaard plays a disproportionate role, especially in the interpretation of his friend's religious sensibility.[16] As we shall see, the question of an "inverted" theology, uniting both Kierkegaard and Kafka, would become a decisive theme in Adorno's mature philosophical work.

Although it was primarily thanks to the Brenner Kreis that Kierkegaard first received serious attention in Germany, his appeal

✳ "wholly other"

gained special intensity only with the emergence of dialectical theology after the war.[17] Beginning with *Der Römerbrief* (The epistle to the Romans), first published in 1918 and extensively revised in a second edition in 1922, the Swiss theologian Karl Barth ignited a firestorm of controversy and religious enthusiasm for a new species of antihistoricist theology that broke sharply from the "culture Protestantism" of the later nineteenth century. Invoking Kierkegaard's idea of an "infinite qualitative distinction" between time and eternity, Barth insisted on the radical separation between humanity and God. This separation—or *Krisis,* in the Greek sense—also served as a political corrective to the nationalist strain in central European Protestant theology (associated chiefly with Barth's teachers, the Marburg theologian Wilhelm Hermann and the Berlin-based theologian Adolf von Harnack). In Kierkegaard Barth found the conceptual tools for a critique of cultural and political conformity, notwithstanding the rather inconvenient fact that the Dane himself had been in most obvious respects a political conservative. The Barthian revolution of "crisis theology" injected a new passion for Kierkegaard into the religious controversies of the 1920s. Alongside Barth, the primary representatives of dialectical theology included both Emil Brunner and Friedrich Gogarten, and it sent shockwaves through nearly all of the major philosophies of the day, awakening fervent themes of Lutheran individualism and conscience that would come to prominence in the earlier efforts from philosophers such as Karl Jaspers and Martin Heidegger. For our purposes here, it is especially important to recall the enormous impact of the Kierkegaardian and Barthian revolution on Paul Tillich, who recommended the topic of Kierkegaard's philosophy to the young Adorno.[18]

The political implications of dialectical theology proved highly labile. Although Barth himself radicalized into a vehement critic of the Third Reich (a criticism he made explicit in his June 1933 "Theological Existence Today," and in the famous "Barmen Declaration," which he helped to draft the following year). But in the era of political crisis other exponents of the Kierkegaard revival would turn sharply to the right. Gogarten, for example, actually embraced the Nazi regime and the evangelical movement of so-called German Christianity. Nor should we neglect the case of the Lutheran theologian Emanuel Hirsch, who ranked among the most accomplished Kierkegaard scholars of the interwar era and between 1930 and 1933 authored a highly regarded three-volume work, *Kierkegaard-Studien*. Following a pattern already set by Carl Schmitt (who cited the Kierkegaardian theme of radical decision in his 1922 treatise *Political Theology*), Hirsch himself made the fateful decision in 1934 to publicly endorse the Nazi regime as the worldly incarnation of divine will. A blatant act of political accommodation, his manifesto prompted a searing condemnation from Tillich, who by that time was already living in exile at New York's Union Theological Seminary and who accused his former colleague of equating the Nazi *Machtergreifung* with the crucifixion: "You have moved the year 1933 so close to the year 33 that for you it has now acquired salvation-historical significance [*Damit hast Du das Jahr '1933' dem Jahre '33' so angenährt, daß es für Dich heilsgeschichtliche Bedeutung bewonnen hat*]."[19]

Adorno's Kierkegaard Book

Such episodes will suffice to remind us that Adorno's *Kierkegaard: Construction of the Aesthetic* made its debut in a moment fraught with theological and political controversy.[20] Although it was Tillich himself who apparently first encouraged the young Wiesengrund-Adorno to write his second dissertation on Kierkegaard, Adorno's esteem for Tillich was counterbalanced from the very beginning by marked differences in intellectual temperament.[21] During the 1920s, Tillich had developed the foundations of a religious existentialism inflected by an increasingly principled commitment to social democracy, culminating with the 1933 manifesto, *The Socialist Deci-*

sion.[22] Although Adorno felt only the most qualified admiration for Tillich's own contributions to existential religious philosophy, he shared Tillich's broadly socialist perspective on contemporary politics. In his autumn 1965 lectures on negative dialectics, Adorno opened the first with a eulogy to his former professor who had died just a few weeks before: Tillich had combined a "genuinely irenic temperament" with "the greatest resoluteness" in personal conduct. "His open-mindedness," Adorno recalled, "did not prevent him from drawing the necessary conclusions when what was at stake was the need to show whether or not he was a decent human being. And in that particular historical context, the plain statement that a person is a decent human being gains an emphasis that it perhaps does not otherwise possess."[23]

By the time Adorno began to revise the dissertation for publication, the political scene was beginning to show signs of serious fracture and "decency" grew increasingly rare. Seeking a place of relative quiet for his efforts, in the spring of 1930 he retreated to the town of Kronberg, just to the northwest of Frankfurt, where he worked day and night in a state of "complete isolation." By the beginning of August (as he confessed in a letter to Alban Berg) he had suffered a "complete breakdown," something that, he hastened to explain, had "never happened to me in the whole of my life."[24] By 1932, however, the book was nearly complete. In a letter to the composer Ernst Krenek he wrote that "in three weeks I've dragged eighty pages out of myself."[25] He dedicated the finished book to his friend Siegfried Kracauer, and it was published with J. C. B. Mohr (Siebeck) in the winter of 1933. We now know that it appeared in bookstores on February 27 since, as Adorno would later observe, this was "the same day that Hitler seized dictatorial powers."[26] It is also worth noting that in the very same year Tillich published his book "The Socialist Decision," an attack on the new regime that led to his dismissal from the university and, soon thereafter, his flight into exile. With this history in mind, we can readily understand why Adorno would later characterize his own *Kierkegaard* as a message to the "intellectual opposition" in Nazi Germany. Whether this is truly the case, and in what respects the book might be construed as a gesture of philosophical or political resistance, remains to be seen.

Reading Kierkegaard against the Grain

Not all readers were impressed by Adorno's book, even while they acknowledged the difficult circumstances of its author. In a letter to Walter Benjamin, Gershom Scholem wrote, "I have thus far read about two-thirds of the book on Kierkegaard by Wiesengrund [Adorno]—whose name I just read next to 50 others on the official list of people dismissed from Frankfurt—and to my mind the book combines a sublime plagiarism of your thought with an uncommon chutzpah, and it will ultimately not mean much for a future, objective appraisal of Kierkegaard."[27] In sharp contrast to Scholem, Benjamin himself offered a more favorable response. In a published review of the book for the *Vossische Zeitung* he alluded to the Barthian movement in dialectical theology as "the last attempt to take over or develop Kierkegaard's intellectual world" and further noted, "At their outer limits the waves of this theological movement [also] make contact with the concentric circles set in motion by Heidegger's existentialist philosophy." But while Barth had seen in Kierkegaard an unabashedly *religious* rebel, Heidegger had exploited Kierkegaard for his own *non*theistic and purely existential analytic of being-in-the-world. Meanwhile, Benjamin wrote, Adorno's interpretation broke with existential convention in exposing "the hidden elements of idealism" that lay buried in Kierkegaard's work. "All the arrogant pretensions of his [Kierkegaard's] existentialist philosophy," wrote Benjamin, "rest on his conviction that he has found the realm of 'inwardness,' of 'pure spirituality,' which had enabled him to overcome appearance through 'decision,' through existential resolve— in short, through a religious stance."[28]

On this point Benjamin was a discerning reader indeed. The governing claim of Adorno's book is that one can only unlock the true mystery of Kierkegaard's philosophy if one resists both its theistic appeals to a transcendent God and its protoexistentialist meditations on the anxiety of finite life. To dwell upon such themes only serves to camouflage and does not reveal the true meaning of Kierkegaard's philosophical legacy. One properly understands that legacy only if one comprehends the category it simultaneously constructs and condemns as the antithesis of religious existence: the aesthetic.

It should be immediately apparent that Adorno's reading of Kierkegaard proceeds *gegen den Strich* (against the grain). The book's paradoxical message is that one can penetrate to the true core of Kierkegaard's philosophical significance only if one attends to the outermost or "poetic" register of his writing and the metaphors or images it deploys so as to convey its secrets. Kierkegaard himself, we should recall, conceives of the aesthetic as merely the first and lowest of the three "stages" (as portrayed in *Stages on Life's Way*): The individual passes from the aesthetic to the ethical and finally to the religious as the last and highest stage of life. Adorno's interpretation refuses to accept this stadial architecture and its manifest subordination of the aesthetic to both ethics and religion. In a gesture of "materialist" inversion, Adorno seeks to show how the aesthetic serves in Kierkegaard's writing as the hidden though debased infrastructure for philosophical argument. In this sense the aesthetic is a *philosophical* construct and not merely a realm of mere semblance or metaphor. That Adorno was himself a musician and a lover of the theater may further suggest that he took personal umbrage at the low status assigned to the aesthetic in Kierkegaard's work. Indeed, it is worth noting that only once in the book does Adorno betray overt disdain for Kierkegaard; this is when he pauses to write that the religious philosopher's opinions about music were "absurd" and that the Dane would have been incapable of appreciating "a single phrase of Beethoven."[29]

Adorno's further justification for exploring the construction of the aesthetic in Kierkegaard's work has to do with the very conception of philosophy as a discipline. "All attempts to comprehend the writings of philosophers as poetry," Adorno writes, "have missed their truth content." Nineteenth century philosophy conceived of itself as a discipline modeled after or even equated with science. It followed that thinkers of a "subjective" character were demoted to the status of mere poets. But such a verdict on the merely aesthetic character of subjective philosophy can hardly be justified, especially if we consider the dialectical conception of philosophy as a mode of reasoning that strives to integrate all partial perspectives into a rational totality. In a footnote, Adorno refers to Lukács' 1923 study *History and Class Consciousness* as an illustration of the neo-Hegelian model in which totality serves as the highest idea for philosophical reasoning. Once we adopt this dialectical conception, Adorno explains, we are hardly free to dismiss a thinker as a mere poet and exempt him from philosophical consideration only because he rejects totality and cleaves instead to subjectivity. This was the dismissive stance, for example, of Hermann Gottsched, a cotranslator with Christoph Schrempf of Kierkegaard's collected works, who in an afterword praises Kierkegaard as a philosopher and a poet but fails to relate the two. A proper interpretation of philosophy, Adorno insists, will treat it neither as a mere "manifestation of the thinker's subjectivity" nor as the formal and systematic coherence of concepts. Rather, a work achieves the rank of philosophy where "the real has entered into concepts." To understand the philosophical import of what Kierkegaard deems "the aesthetic," we must therefore avoid Hermann Gottsched's error of celebrating Kierkegaard merely as a poet, and we must instead recognize the place of this aesthetic category within the whole of Kierkegaard's philosophy. Most important, we must make this effort even if Kierkegaard himself would have rejected such an interpretative strategy.[30]

Needless to say, Kierkegaard himself was hardly prepared to acknowledge the higher philosophical import of the aesthetic. Adorno reminds us that Kierkegaard saw aesthetic existence only as "the location of depravity" in human life, and deemed poetry "the mark of the deception borne by all metaphysics in the presence of positive revelation." Against Kierkegaard's own verdict, then, Adorno sets out to show how Kierkegaard's aesthetic categories in fact serve as "primitive" signs for philosophical concepts that may not have received sufficient philosophical elaboration. This is true even of the most fundamental metaphysical distinctions in Kierkegaard's writing: the diary of the seducer, for instance, appears as a "parody" of the philosophical idea that in divine revelation time and eternity come into momentary contact: "the seducer possesses the beloved once, in order to abandon her at once forever." Moreover, such aesthetic categories reflect the social and historical situation of the author himself and thus reveal the historical conditioning of a philosophy that would deny to history any genuinely philosophical meaning. Consider, for example, the figure of the nonreligious sensualist, or, alternately, the literary aesthete or flâneur (as Kierkegaard later characterized his own situation when writing *Either/Or*), both of which function throughout Kierkegaard's work as antitypes to the integrity of religious existence. These figures obviously represent a determinate social type, whose appearance coincides with an earlier phase of bourgeois city life: "It is there, like artificial street lighting, in the twilight of incipient despair, that this strange, dangerous, and imperial form emits its beam to eternalize, garishly, life as it slips away."[31]

The governing argument of Adorno's book is that just as Kierkegaard's philosophy reveals itself in his aesthetic categories, those aesthetic categories in turn reveal the historical determinants of Kierkegaard's thought. These hidden entanglements show us that even while Kierkegaard declared himself opposed to Hegel and thus "developed no philosophy of history," the very attempt to retreat from historical conditions reveals those very conditions; they are nothing less than the disavowed objective and material foundations for Kierkegaard's subjectivist philosophy.[32]

The chief illustration for this self-subverting problem is Kierkegaard's idea of inwardness (*Innerlichkeit*), which "attempts to still the external world that crowds in on it by anathematizing history." Kierkegaard wants to believe that "internal history is the only true history." But this subjective desire lacks the power to undo its own historical conditions, just as the events of 1848 did not succeed in dismantling bourgeois society. In an explicit rejoinder to Barthian dialectical theology, Adorno concludes that, despite its express aim of rejecting Hegel, Kierkegaard's philosophy actually remains caught within Hegel's horizon and its logic of dialectical reconciliation: "The doctrine of the 'real dialectic', which contemporary Protestantism reads out of Kierkegaard and opposed to the idealist dialectic, remains unconvincing."[33] Kierkegaard, concludes Adorno, did not "overcome" Hegel's system of identity. Notwithstanding Kierkegaard's reputation as a critic of Hegelian identity theory, Kierkegaard only succeeded in projecting Hegel's drama of reconciliation from the outer contest between spirit and world into the inner realm of the soul. Cleaving to the eternal, the finite subject thereby gained a kind of interior serenity that resembles the self-satisfaction of Hegelian *Geist*. But whereas spirit was driven outward from itself and into dialectical union with the world, the Kierkegaardian soul was driven inward from the world and fell into a changeless space of a nondialectical solipsism. It is in this sense that Adorno characterizes Kierkegaard's philosophy not as an overcoming of Hegel but rather as an "inverted" or "interiorized" Hegelianism.[34] With this rather striking argument, Adorno sought to reveal an unlikely resemblance between Kierkegaard and the great architect of nineteenth-century philosophical systematicity.

Aesthetics and Interiority

To develop this interpretation of the material and historical under-pinnings of Kierkegaard's work, Adorno offers an extensive analysis of the poetic-metaphoric figure of the mid-nineteenth-century bour-geois dwelling, or *intérieur,* images of which recur throughout Kierkegaard's early writings. For Adorno, this quintessentially nineteenth-century ideal of bourgeois privacy figures as the aesthetic and historical precondition for the philosophical idea of inwardness itself.[35] Adorno admits that this claim is not entirely original; in his 1909 biography of Kierkegaard, Olaf Peder Monrad had already observed that "the parlor" lay at the symbolic center of Kierkeg-aard's thought. "Everywhere one looks in Kierkegaard," Monrad wrote, "one finds something undeniably shut in; and out of his pro-digious oeuvre there comes to us the smell of the hothouse."[36] But Adorno pursues this claim with greater vigor, since he considers it the key for unlocking the inner secret of Kierkegaard's entire philosophy. Thus Adorno takes special note of a revealing passage from "The Diary of a Seducer" in *Either/Or:* "Environment and setting still have a great influence upon one; there is something about them which stamps itself firmly and deeply in memory, or rather upon the whole soul, and which is therefore never forgotten. However old I may become, it will always be impossible for me to think of Cordelia amid surroundings different from this little room. . . . The living room is small, comfortable, little more than a cabinet [*klein, gemüt-lich, eigentlich nur eine Kabinett*]."[37]

In such passages, Adorno claims, the *intérieur* functions as "the incarnate image" of Kierkegaard's philosophical concept of a "point" or the temporal "instant." It is an aesthetic-material sign in Kierkeg-aard's writing for the "simultaneity" to which everything external and historical has been reduced so as to secure immunity against all historical conditioning. The bourgeois apartment thus serves as a sign of the "subjective thinker" who wishes to isolate him- or herself from society. But the impossibility of this isolation reveals itself as an aesthetic construction: "Just as external history is "reflected" in internal history, in the *intérieur* space is semblance."[38]

But the *intérieur* for Kierkegaard is not only the scene of seduction and bourgeois interiority. It is "the prototypical cell of abandoned inwardness" and the "melancholy" realm of a "domesticity" whose artificial light is "more beneficial than the subdued light of evening to weak eyes." Ironically, as a construct of bourgeois property that offers an illusory dream of existence without semblance, the *intérieur* itself remains a realm of pure artifice, even while it offers itself as a realm where all artifice will fall away. The bourgeois dwelling thus typifies "the contours of his doctrine of existence itself."[39] Dialectically conjoined to this philosophical meaning, however, a distinctively sociological meaning emerges in Adorno's analysis of the *intérieur,* a meaning Kierkegaard himself would not have disavowed. The *intérieur,* writes Adorno, is a space of asocial *inwardness* that contrasts with the external realm of the "crowd" and its "untruth."[40] Kierkegaard conceives of public space as the realm of bourgeois inauthenticity where the incommensurable truth of inward subjectivity dissolves into a currency of universal exchange. In this sense Kierkegaard flees the public world as a space of "reification [*Verdinglichung*]." The religious individual eschews the realm of exchange just as he avoids the crowd. "Fleeing precisely from reification, he withdraws into 'inwardness.' "[41] As such, the *intérieur* promises the appearance of unreified truth. Although it is admittedly a "metaphor of technical life," the apartment serves as the figure of the "temporal present" and as nothing less than the setting of "eternal preparedness" for Christian redemption. Thus a quotidian element of nineteenth-century existence reveals itself in Adorno's interpretation as a key to Kierkegaard's entire philosophical doctrine. The *intérieur* is nothing less than bourgeois property transfigured into metaphysics, the privileged site in Kierkegaard's writing where history and eternity reveal their dialectical complicity.[42]

Needless to say, this kind of social and materialist criticism suggests a strong divergence of philosophical perspective between Adorno and Kierkegaard. It is hardly surprising, then, that some readers have characterized Adorno's *Kierkegaard* as "unfair" or "misleading."[43] In her exceptionally insightful study, *Kierkegaard and Critical Theory*, Marcia Morgan even writes that it is crucial "to debunk Adorno's *Kierkegaard* as an outlier beyond any possible congruence with Kierkegaard's oeuvre."[44] One should note, however, that such statements presuppose Adorno's unrestrained hostility toward Kierkegaard, reading the dissertation as little more than a sustained polemic. As we read further in the dissertation, however, we can detect a barely disguised bond of sympathy that stretches across the century and connects the critic to his predecessor. As an early opponent of bourgeois reification, Kierkegaard anticipated a line of criticism that would preoccupy Adorno himself throughout his life. "Kierkegaard recognized the distress of incipient high-capitalism," Adorno avers. "He opposed its privations in the name of a lost immediacy that he sheltered in subjectivity."[45]

I will return to this sympathetic bond shortly. But before doing so it is important to acknowledge that in Adorno's eyes Kierkegaard did not and in fact *could not* turn his complaint concerning reification onto the path toward sociohistorical emancipation. This is because the individual who announces this complaint remains trapped in a state of asocial dissociation. In Kierkegaard's philosophy, Adorno explains, "the knowing subject can no more reach its objective correlative than, in a society dominated by exchange-value, things are 'immediately' accessible to the person."[46] The polemic against society thus remains *doubly* asocial, both at the level of metaphysical preconditions and at the level of social consequences.

As an illustration, Adorno explores the social and historical meaning of the "window mirror [*Reflexionsspiegel*]," which would seem at first glance to be nothing more than "a characteristic furnishing of the spacious nineteenth-century apartment." Such a mirror projects "the endless row of apartment buildings into the isolated bourgeois living room" in such a way that by a trick of optics, the living room "dominates the reflected row at the same time that it is delimited by it." As a consequence, the interior space always looms larger than the exterior world beyond the apartment, "just as in Kierkegaard's philosophy the 'situation' is subordinated to subjectivity and yet is defined by it." Like the *intérieur,* the mirror serves as the perfect symbol of Kierkegaardian inwardness that, when looking beyond itself, only discovers a repetition of its own solitude. "He who looks into the window mirror," Adorno writes, "is the private person, solitary, inactive, and separated from the economic process of production. The window mirror testifies to objectlessness—it casts into the apartment only the semblance of things—and isolated privacy." The mirror symbolizes a subjectivity that remains caught in its own melancholy. In its shining surface, the bourgeois subject confronts only his own isolation and sees nothing else but "the imprisonment of mere spirit in itself."[47]

Wahl's *Études kierkegaardiennes*

During the years that followed the dissertation, Adorno turned his attention to other matters, and the consolidation of the Nazi dictatorship left him increasingly uncertain about the chances for a secure career in Germany. An official notice from the new government informed him that his license to teach was no longer valid, and for the next four years he entertained the possibility of a new career in England, devoting the greater share of his time there to a new study of Husserlian phenomenology (as will be discussed in Chapter 2). Adorno and his wife Gretel left Europe, and in February 1938 their transatlantic steamship landed in Manhattan, where the Institute for Social Research had secured temporary offices in the vicinity of Columbia University. But Kierkegaard was never far from his mind. In 1939 and once again in 1940, Adorno published two separate critical reviews of the massive 1938 work *Études kierkegaardiennes,* by the French scholar of Kierkegaard and existentialism, Jean Wahl.[48] In a March 1938 letter to Benjamin, Adorno expressed his discontent with Wahl's book:

> What we can expect to hear one day from an eighty-year-old Jean Wahl is already abundantly revealed by his 745-page book on Kierkegaard. It is a solid scholarly work, but also an indescribably tedious one. Nothing more than a lot of interpretation, exposition and existential bridge-building, with special chapters on Kierkegaard and Jaspers and Kierkegaard and Heidegger; there is no attempt to develop a critique or a theoretical elucidation of the philosophy of existence, but simply the desire to fortify the latter with a kind of "standard work" or textbook. I have the task of reviewing the work twice: in an American journal and in our own. I cannot possibly force myself to express any great show of friendship. I would therefore, be grateful, if you could let me know how you think we should proceed tactically with regard to Wahl. Incidentally I do believe that my David is just as unattractive to him as his Goliath is to me.[49]

Despite this confession, Adorno did not keep his discontent a secret for long. In the first review, he took strong exception to Wahl's interpretation chiefly because it had failed to mention the reactionary appropriation of Kierkegaard's ideas. Kierkegaard, Adorno complained, "is not even defended against the abuse of his notions for the sinister purposes obtained by the present sacrifice of conscience for the sake of a cult of powers, which Kierkegaard certainly would have condemned as demonic."[50]

In the second review, Adorno carried on in a similar vein, expressing his discontent that Wahl's studies remained "exegetical and mostly apologetic" while avoiding any philosophical analysis of Kierkegaard's "concept of the subject." More troubling still for Adorno was Wahl's effort of rendering harmless (*Verharmlosung*) those facets of Kierkegaard that earlier interpreters such as Heidegger and Jaspers had bent toward "conformist and ideological" ends. Wahl left unexamined what any faithful exegesis of Kierkegaard should have revealed: the "protests against the misuse of the Kierkeg-aardian sacrifice of the unhappy consciousness into a festive cult of darkness [*zum festlichen Kult der Finsternis*]." Only once, Adorno wrote, had it occurred to Wahl to ask whether the modern parti-sans of existence had properly understood their predecessor: "'On peut se demander si l'effort philosophique de Heidegger et de Jas-pers ne consist pas à montrer dans certains concepts de Kierkegaard les présuppositions nécessaires de toute étude phénoménologique et si leur oeuvre n'est pas une sécularization et une généralisation de celle du penseur danois.' In other words: whether this ambitious effort has not had the effect of flattening him out. After all, with Kierkegaard himself in the 'Concluding Unscientific Postscript,' the concept of ontology is expressly avoided." Adorno reserved the greatest venom, however, for Walter Lowrie's study, *Kierkegaard* (1938) which he found philosophically imprecise and "wholly lacking in erudition." Adorno granted that, notwithstanding the su-perficiality of his book, Lowrie was "not wrong that Kierkegaard, via Barth's presentations, strengthened that spine of the Protestant opposition in Germany." Adorno saw no sign, however, that Lowrie grasped the true impact of that resistance, and he went even fur-ther, noting darkly that "it would not be idle to pose the question to Lowrie whether his own book, not to mention that of Emmanuel Hirsch, could acquit itself as well."[51]

Both of Adorno's reviews betray a stubborn refusal to consider the possibility that Kierkegaard might inspire new philosophical tendencies that could *oppose* the conservative and fascist reception of the 1920s and 1930s. Adorno saw little merit in apologetic inter-pretations of Kierkegaard's legacy that avoided a forthright reck-oning with its modern political reception. Very soon, however, he would revisit the question of Kierkegaard's philosophical signifi-cance. Contesting his earlier, single-minded emphasis on its affirmative political message, Adorno would discover unexpected resources in Kierkegaard's work for strengthening the powers of critical resistance.

Kierkegaard on Love

Two years later, in February 1940, Adorno gave a lecture at Columbia, "On Kierkegaard's Doctrine of Love." Apart from the reviews, this was the first time since the early 1930s that Adorno had permitted himself the opportunity to revisit the Danish philosopher, and in the intervening years much had changed. The critical and even polemical spirit of the *Habilitationsschrift* was mostly gone, and so too was the image of Kierkegaard as a bourgeois thinker of impotent interiority. Rather than reading Kierkegaard with a materialist's eye for aesthetic signs of ideology and social position, Adorno now seemed ready to entertain at least the possibility that Kierkegaard's apparent retreat from the present social order might also contain an implicit critique of that order. "Kierkegaard's misanthropy," Adorno observed, "the paradoxical callousness of his doctrine of love enables him ... to perceive decisive character features of the typical individual in modern society." Even if there were moments where love for Kierkegaard remained indistinguishable from "demonic hatred," the author's "gloomy motives" might be dialectically redeemed if one interpreted his arguments as "social critique."[52]

Significantly, this revaluation of Kierkegaard's critical potential arose from Adorno's new readiness to consider precisely the theological qualities his earlier analysis had ignored. Focusing his attention most of all on the 1847 *Works of Love*, Adorno noted how in one passage Kierkegaard "actually intends to warn us against Christianity." This is because Kierkegaard conceived of history as bound to Christianity, but only in an inverted fashion. The Hegelian idea of history as the self-realization of spirit was turned upside down.

For Kierkegaard, "the history of Christianity is . . . the history of an apostasy from Christianity." With his rebellious attitude toward the increased stereotyping of religion in the modern age, Kierkegaard now appeared to Adorno as a thinker who anticipated later critics of cultural modernity such as Karl Kraus, for whom "the criticism of progress and civilization" was "the criticism of the reification of man." In *Works of Love,* for example, Kierkegaard inveighed against the incipient tendencies of "mass society" that during his own era still remained at an embryonic stage. Such tendencies included "the substitution of spontaneous thinking by 'reflectory' adaptation taking place in connection with modern forms of mass information." Some of this diagnostic language would reappear in *The Authoritarian Personality,* the 1950 social-psychological study of fascist and conformist styles of thought in contemporary society for which Adorno served as coauthor. But we should not neglect the philosophical continuities with Adorno's earlier work. The metaphor of reflection (the bourgeois mirror) that in Adorno's dissertation had once revealed Kierkegaard as an ideologue of helpless interiority was now a feature of the very society against which Kierkegaard rebelled. This shift of perspective meant that even Kierkegaard's antidemocratic sensibility might be assigned a critical meaning. As Adorno explained, "Kierkegaard's hatred of the mass, however conservatively it styles itself, contains something of an inkling of the mutilation of men by the very mechanisms of domination which actually change men into a mass." Adorno now went so far as to imply that in his reaction to the mass meetings of 1848, Kierkegaard was not merely a conservative but instead a clairvoyant critic of future events: Kierkegaard, he wrote, "seems to have heard those loudspeakers which filled the Berlin Sportspalast one hundred years later."[53]

It is perhaps easy to understand why Adorno, recently displaced from Germany, would have felt moved to see in Kierkegaard an anticipation of his own condition as a critic of modern society. Perhaps more intriguing and paradoxical, however, is the fact that by

1940 Adorno also saw in Kierkegaard an *antagonist* of existential philosophy itself. Because Kierkegaard embraced the absurdity of Christian truth against worldly knowledge, he represented the intellectual's capacity to think *against* mere existence and against the empirically given. The norms of public life that Kierkegaard disdained were those that conspire against the possibility of "anything radically new." For the task of the genuine Christian, Adorno argued, was to sustain *hope,* a hope which Kierkegaard had defined as "the sense for . . . possibility." But insofar as the role of the critical intellectual according to Adorno is to hold open *possibility* against existence, then Kierkegaard's idea of hope preserved not only a critical but even a utopian meaning: "Fundamentally (and this reveals an Utopian tendency aided even by his conservatism which denies it) [Kierkegaard] cannot even imagine that one could breathe for one moment without the consciousness of possibility, that is to say, without hope of the transfiguration of the world."[54]

Such arguments may suggest a certain affinity between Adorno and Ernst Bloch, whose three-volume *Principle of Hope* (1938–1947) also invoked Kierkegaard in its complex history of utopian thought.[55] Whether or not we find such a resemblance persuasive, however, the 1940 essay clearly marks a new and more generous phase in Adorno's encounter with Kierkegaard, who now appeared as an emissary of future possibility and critical resistance. With only the mildest acknowledgment of Kierkegaard's notorious political conservatism, Adorno now identified a utopian tendency in Kierkegaard that eschewed both hopelessness and world-affirmative "sobriety." This resistance marked the great distance between Kierkegaard and later existentialists such as Heidegger: "The worldliness that Kierkegaard wants to 'remove,' Adorno wrote, "is actually the stage of despair. Kierkegaard has introduced the concept of the existential seriousness into philosophy. In the name of hope, he becomes the foe of seriousness itself, of the absorption by practical aims which is not suspended by the thought of what is possible.

[Such a view] could very well be used against Kierkegaard's present successors, the German existential philosophers, particularly against Heidegger."[56]

This was a surprising change. Already in the dissertation Adorno had distinguished Kierkegaard's thought from recent trends in existential ontology. But now Adorno no longer cared to associate Kierkegaard with the recent philosophers at all. Instead it was the theological element in Kierkegaard that came to the fore, and with a surprising consequence, for even as this new and more sympathetic reading drew Kierkegaard away from contemporary existentialism it brought him into a horizon of thought with which Adorno felt a far greater affinity.

The newfound sense of philosophical identification with Kierkegaard became most legible in a passage from the end of Adorno's 1940 essay, in which he offered an interpretation of Kierkegaard's sermon, "Wie wir in Liebe Verstorbener gedenken" (How we think in love of those who have passed away). In this sermon the Dane meditated upon the paradox that to preserve the memory of someone who has died, one must defend oneself *against* reality; otherwise the dark fact of death may efface the memory of the deceased. Death, Kierkegaard concluded, does not merit the "insipid seriousness" that too often surrounds it like a shroud. According to Kierkegaard, such solemnity would permit the mere fact of a mortal's demise to eclipse the higher truth of immortality. Clearly, however, the first is of lesser moment than the second; "the seriousness of death is not the seriousness of the eternal." To recall with love those who have died requires that we do so while keeping in mind their resurrection; but this motivates a turn *against* seriousness and, surprisingly, it may even awaken a mood of levity. As Kierkegaard explained,

If it would not sound so merry (as it can sound only to him who does not know what seriousness is) I should say that one could put this inscription over the door of the cemetery: "Here no one is urged" or:

"We do not urge anybody." And yet I shall say so and shall firmly stick to what I have said. For I have thought so much about death that I know well: no one can talk seriously about death who is incapable of utilizing the cunning lying in death, the whole deep-thinking roguishness of death—the roguishness to resurrection. The seriousness of death is not the seriousness of the eternal. To the seriousness of death belongs this particular awakening, this deep-thinking jesting overtone. Of course, apart from the thought of eternity, it is often an empty, often cheeky jest, but in connection with the thought of eternity, it is what it ought to be; and then, indeed, something radically different from that insipid seriousness. The latter is least of all capable of conceiving and maintaining something of the tension and bearing of the thought of death.[57]

Commenting on the passage above, Adorno concluded his own essay with the remark, "The hope that Kierkegaard puts against the "seriousness of the eternal" is nothing but *the hope of the reality of redemption.*"[58]

This conclusion is especially remarkable insofar as it points toward a concept that would only grow in significance for Adorno himself over the coming years. The famous concluding passage from *Mimima Moralia* (dated 1947) tells us, "*The only philosophy which can be responsibly practiced in the face of despair is the attempt to contemplate all things as they would present themselves from the standpoint of redemption.*" Although this passage does not invoke Kierkegaard by name, its governing conceptual contrast—between despair and redemption—reminds us that Adorno was still drawing upon a philosophical lexicon that Kierkegaard had helped to create. Indeed, the passage recapitulates what is, at the very least, a paradox of which Kierkegaard would have approved: Adorno writes that "perspectives must be fashioned that displace and estrange the world, reveal it to be, with its rifts and crevices, as indigent and distorted as it will appear one day in the messianic light." To achieve such a

perspective is "the simplest of all things" because "consummate negativity, once squarely faced, delineates the mirror-image of its opposite." But at the same time "it is also the utterly impossible thing, because it presupposes a standpoint removed, even though by a hair's breadth, from the scope of existence."[59]

Repeating an argument from the 1940 lecture, this famous passage from *Minima Moralia* suggests that mere *existence* must never claim our highest allegiance and that the "mirror" of philosophical reflection must not trap us in a repetition of this existence but should instead reveal its negativity, thereby awakening hope for an unrealized possibility existence denies. The penultimate and often cited phrase from *Minima Moralia* reads as follows: "Even its own impossibility it must at last comprehend for the sake of the possible." In reading such a paradoxical statement, one may feel tempted to imagine that the name Theodor Wiesengrund Adorno was only one among the many pseudonyms under which Kierkegaard had published his own work a century earlier.

2

Ontology and Phenomenology

> The person who interprets instead of unquestioningly
> accepting and categorizing is slapped with the charge of
> intellectualizing as if with a yellow star.
>
> —THEODOR W. ADORNO, "The Essay as Form"

Reading Philosophy in the 1930s

With his habilitation on Kierkegaard complete, Adorno secured a
post as professor of philosophy at the University of Frankfurt, and
he delivered his inaugural lecture, "The Actuality of Philosophy,"
before the assembled faculty in early May 1931. In the history of
critical theory this was an auspicious moment. The former head of
the Institute for Social Research, Karl Grunberg, had just stepped
down, and Max Horkheimer, at just thirty-five years of age, had recently been promoted to professor of social philosophy at Frankfurt; in 1930 he was appointed director of the institute, a position
he would retain until Adorno replaced him in 1953. The philosophical friendship between them was already well established—
Adorno and Horkheimer had first met in the early 1920s—and it
was a partnership that would remain the animating heart of critical theory well into the postwar era. Adorno's inaugural lecture
may therefore be read as a founding document in his own intellectual career as well as an important milestone in the history of

critical theory (though its canonical status is doubtless eclipsed by Horkheimer's no less programmatic essay from 1937, "Traditional and Critical Theory"). Significantly, Adorno hoped his own lecture would be published with a dedication to his friend Walter Benjamin, whose influence throughout the lecture one can easily detect.[1]

Notwithstanding its many sources of inspiration, "The Actuality of Philosophy" also marks an important milestone in Adorno's own emergence as an independent thinker. Already it bears many of the characteristic themes that would remain at the fore of Adorno's negative thinking throughout his career: the critique of bourgeois idealism, an aesthetic and formal preference for the essay as against the system, a complaint against the positivistic and reified prestige of the noninterpretative "given," and—perhaps most of all—the constant and repeated assault on the doctrine of constitutive subjectivity. Indeed, it is hardly an exaggeration to say that is it this last philosophical theme that would most consume Adorno's attention, as he would confess much later in the preface to *Negative Dialectics* (1966): "To use the strength of the subject to break through the fallacy of constitutive subjectivity—this is what the author felt to be his task ever since he came to trust his own mental impulses."[2]

Considered as a matter of philosophical doctrine, it seems fair to say that the problem of constitutive subjectivity is associated most of all with the legacy German idealism. For Kant the entire field of possible experience gains its intelligibility only insofar as it is structured in advance by the pure forms of intuition and the categories of the understanding: the world discloses itself as an objective realm for empirical inquiry only on the condition that it is first constituted as such in virtue of the spontaneous work of the human mind. In this sense Kant ranks as the theorist of constitutive subjectivity sine qua non. The further development of German idealism, from Fichte onward, only elaborates and extends this doctrine until, with Hegel, subject and object achieve a mediated unity under the aegis of "absolute knowing." Adorno's polemic against the Hegelian idea

Kant

of a seamless reconciliation between subject and object is well documented.[3] More perplexing, however, is the question as to why Adorno would also find a thesis of constitutive subjectivity in the philosophers of existence such as Kierkegaard and Heidegger. The charge is controversial, and to many readers counterintuitive. Kierkegaard is more typically reputed to be the thinker who opens the subject to an always paradoxical encounter with the alterity of the divine. Heidegger, meanwhile, enjoys an enduring prestige as the philosopher who brought the era of humanist-metaphysical subjectivity to an end: what Heidegger called the project of a "destruction" begins as early as *Kant and the Problem of Metaphysics* in 1929 and reaches its completion in the later 1930s with the assault on Nietzsche's metaphysics of the will.

Both Kierkegaard and Heidegger, in other words, would seem to be overtly *hostile* to the inflationary doctrines of German idealism that see the self as either the creator or ground of the world. We are therefore faced with a significant challenge: How can it be that in the 1930s Adorno would commence his critique of existentialism by describing its foremost philosophers not as opponents but rather as partisans of constitutive subjectivity? We can best answer this question if we follow Adorno as he develops the critique of existentialism from the inaugural lecture of 1931 through the early years of exile in Oxford, when his distinctive interpretation of Heidegger's crypto-idealism took on added sophistication. This critical interpretation first emerged, however, within the framework of the so-called meta-critique of Husserlian phenomenology. First published in 1956, the book known in English as *Against Epistemology* (originally titled *Zur Metakritik der Erkenntnistheorie*) is considered by many a recondite and merely academic work whose connection to the larger history of critical theory is at best remote. But this reputation is undeserved. In the preface Adorno offers the illuminating remark that Husserl's philosophy is merely "the occasion [*Anlaß*] and not the point [*Ziel*] of this book."[4] The larger thesis is that Husserlian phenomenology remains of interest chiefly because it signifies the general "crisis of idealism" that Adorno saw as the endgame in modern bourgeois philosophy. It is therefore a crucial text if we wish to understand Adorno's claim that existentialism failed to escape the gravity well of German idealism. In this chapter, we will follow Adorno's philosophical trajectory through the 1930s and beyond— from the inaugural lecture at Frankfurt to the metacritique of Husserl, fastening our attention on the intriguing moments when Adorno diagnosed the antinomies of bourgeois philosophy.

Philosophy and Actuality

It is a major conceit of "The Actuality of Philosophy" that academic inquiry has entered an endgame in which the obsolete ambitions of philosophical idealism must at last be set aside. The "crisis of idealism" corresponds to a "crisis in philosophy's pretensions to to-tality." Animating idealism in all its forms, Adorno claims, was the thesis of the *autonome ratio,* the principle that thought can generate all of reality from out of itself. This principle has begun to disinte-grate even though the illusory belief that "the power of thought is sufficient to grasp the totality of the real" still holds much of aca-demic philosophy in its grip. Adorno therefore feels he must first provide a survey of the general academic terrain, touching briefly upon both the Vienna and Marburg schools. Marburg neo-Kantianism struggled to uphold the basic premise of constitutive subjectivity in its most extreme form insofar as it sought "to gain the content of reality from logical categories," but if it managed to retain "its self-contained form as a system" it thereby "renounced every right over reality" and had withdrawn into mere formalism. Adorno devotes the greater share of his attention to Husserlian and Heideggerian phe-nomenology as the most contemporary manifestations of the present crisis in idealism.[5]

In Husserl's work Adorno sees an ironical attempt to resurrect the spirit of idealism notwithstanding the historical fact of its disintegration: "It is the deepest paradox of all phenomenological intentions that, by means of the same categories produced by subjective, post-Cartesian thought, they strive to gain just that objectivity which these intentions originally opposed. It is thus no accident that phenomenology in Husserl took precisely its starting point from transcendental idealism, and the late products of phenomenology are all the less able to disavow this origin, the more they try to conceal it."[6] For Adorno the key problem of Husserlian phenomenology is that it seeks to discover the foundations of objectivity within the *horizon* of the subject, and it therefore remains locked within the constitutive thesis of transcendental idealism. This original (if disavowed) commitment to the primacy of the subject cannot be escaped even by Heidegger, no matter how much he wishes to conceal it.

Heidegger, too, like his mentor in phenomenology, strives to break free of idealism so as to secure "a trans-subjective, binding order of being." But Heidegger no less than Husserl remains shackled to an idealist point of departure precisely because "the question of Being" that is to serve as the constitutive framework for all of reality remains accessible only from within the privileged confines of human understanding. The question of being thus enjoys the sham-prestige of an ostensibly radical inquiry even though in fact it is "really the least radical of all." Heideggerian ontology betrays its idealist character insofar as it cleaves to the premise that "thinking about Being" retains a disclosive power vis-à-vis the totality. But Adorno insists that notwithstanding its bold promise to at last unlock the ultimate secrets of the real, this disclosive premise has disintegrated into a vacuous formalism: "The idea of being," he writes, "has become powerless in philosophy; it is nothing more than an empty form-principle whose archaic dignity helps to cover any content whatsoever."[7]

"Being"

For Adorno this is the great irony of Heidegger's philosophy. Although it advertises itself as breaking free of phenomenological idealism for the sake of a nonsubjective realism, its turn toward reality involves little more than an external "pathos" that leaves intact an idealist and subject-centered core. The new ontology masquerades as the "self-revocation of phenomenology," but at a deeper level it remains faithful to the crypto-idealism and subjectivism of its founder. "With Heidegger, at least in his published writings, the question of objective ideas and objective being has been replaced by the subjective. The challenge of material ontology is reduced to the realm of subjectivity, within the depths of which it searches for what it was not able to locate in the open fullness of reality." Adorno's characterization takes aim specifically at the *early works* of Heidegger—his critique addresses chiefly *Being and Time* but perhaps also "What is Metaphysics," "On the Essence of Ground," and *Kant and the Problem of Metaphysics*—since these retain the strongest attachment to the doctrine of constitutive subjectivity. The persistence of this transcendental doctrine in Heidegger's earlier philosophy (a doctrine that we can summarize as the grounding of the object in the subject) may also help to explain why Adorno discerns in the new ontology a late repetition of Kierkegaard's earlier experiments in *subjective* ontology. It is no accident, Adorno notes, that "Heidegger falls back on precisely the latest plan for a subjective ontology produced by Western thinking: the existentialist philosophy of Sören Kierkegaard."[8]

Adorno is naturally aware of the gulf that separates Kierkegaard from Heidegger. Although both thinkers advocate a "leap" and an "undialectical negation of subjective being," Heidegger's analysis of everyday existence "avoids the transcendence of belief which is grasped spontaneously with the sacrifice of subjective mind," and instead it embraces nothing more absolute than "the transcendence of a vitalist 'thus being' *(Sosein):* in death." The fact that even in Heidegger's philosophy the old principle of a *memento mori* continues to play such a pivotal role as the disclosure of authentic life suggests that "phenomenology is now on the verge of ending in "precisely that vitalism against which it originally declared battle." The resemblance is profound; both bespeak a turning from theism to death as the phenomenon that most reveals the authenticity of the subject. "The transcendence of death with Simmel is distinguished from Heidegger's solely in that [Simmel's vitalism] remains within psychological categories whereas Heidegger speaks in ontological ones."[9]

For Adorno this unexpected resemblance between existential phenomenology and vitalism is especially suggestive, since it means that phenomenology remains vulnerable, like vitalism, to the aporias of a full-blown historicist relativism. Just as Husserlian phenomenology reacted sharply against historicism (for instance, in the founder's 1911 manifesto "Philosophy as a Rigorous Science") so too Heideggerian phenomenology retreats onto the higher plane of a timeless ontology: in place of historicism, Heidegger responds by "ontologizing time." But insofar as it has been transformed into a neutral field of ontological constitution, time itself becomes no less timeless than the Husserlian reason it has displaced, and temporality undergoes an apotheosis into the "eternal." Heidegger's formalistic model of historical being thus brings modern academic philosophy to an ironic conclusion: if the concept of "throwness [*Geworfenheit*]" appears as "the ultimate condition of man's being," then "life by itself becomes as blind and meaningless" as it was for the partisans of life philosophy. In neither case can death or life generate a "positive meaning" beyond the sheer facticity of an existence that was always already there.[10] With this critique Adorno begins to develop a comparison between existentialism and scientific reification as twin structures of affirmation. Ideological to the core, both abandon themselves to the merely given. Unlikely as the resemblance may seem, existentialism is thus revealed as a philosophical cousin to positivism.

✳ "merely" ?!

* see p. 41 contradictions?

In the "Actuality" lecture Adorno did not develop this point at great length; it would emerge as a major theme in his critique of existentialism only in the writings of the postwar era, especially in *Negative Dialectics* and *The Jargon of Authenticity*. The inaugural lecture sounds only the more general complaint, that Heideggerian ontology bears an ironic resemblance to positivism insofar as both furnish an uncritical "justification for that which exists." No less than the Vienna school, phenomenology pretends that its aim is little more than faithful *description* and therefore imagines that it can convert philosophy into a purely descriptive science. Their shared premise is that reality makes itself available to the researcher as a coherent field, governed either by the overt rules of empiricism or by the more elusive existential categories of an all-pervasive being. In both cases, however, Adorno suggests that their efforts must fail once they reckon with the discomfiting truth of a "fragmentation in being." The reality which philosophers wish to explore does not exhibit the smooth perfection of a meaningful whole; rather, it is as fragmented as society itself, a landscape of "crevices" and "rifts."[11] Its broken texture defeats the intellectualist ambitions of positivism and phenomenology alike, both of which remain captive to the fantasy of a knowledge that could penetrate to the heart of seamless and all-encompassing being.

Adorno denies that philosophy should confine itself to the task of either positivist or phenomenological description. The fatal error that afflicts all of Heidegger's earlier and explicitly phenomenological studies is the belief that the question of being admits of a single and decisive answer (the *Sinn von Sein*); this answer is supposed to emerge from the experience of questioning as if it were little more than a "discovery" of a datum that was half forgotten or partially obscured. This ambition characterizes not only Heideggerian philosophy; it also animates most bourgeois philosophies—from Kant to Schopenhauer—in which the primacy of the subject remains unchallenged: "He who interprets by searching behind the phenomenal world for a world-in-itself which forms its foundation and support, acts mistakenly like someone who wants to find in the riddle of reflection of a being which lies behind, a being mirrored in the riddle, in which it is contained." For Adorno philosophy must abandon this expectation of philosophical discovery since it encourages a misleading model of thought as mere "research" that is borrowed illicitly from the natural sciences. It must embrace instead the more volatile and historically contingent self-conception as an *interpretative* activity. "The idea of science is research," he concludes; "that of philosophy is interpretation."[12]

The new trend in existential ontology, however, retains its plausibility only because it feeds upon the false hope that the question of "being" admits of a definitive and permanent answer. Adorno, however, considers this belief mistaken, as it disallows any awareness of historical contingency. He thus proposes an alternative agenda that will seek *constellations* rather than fixed meanings or intentions: "Authentic philosophic interpretation," he declares, "does not meet up with a fixed meaning which already lies behind the question, but lights it up suddenly and momentarily, and consumes it at the same time. . . . So philosophy has to bring its elements, which it receives from the sciences, into changing constellations." This alternative formula clearly draws upon Walter Benjamin's model of interpretation as presented in the study of the German *Trauerspiel* (or "mourning play"). Philosophy, Adorno says, should not seek "concealed and manifest intentions of reality," but should rather commit itself to the task of interpreting "unintentional reality" as it reveals itself in figures or images. This is the task of the "interpretation of the unintentional," which best corresponds with "the thinking of materialism."[13]

Such an interpretive method will abandon the traditional philosophical search for "metahistorical" and symbolic "ideas" and must instead turn its attention to the nonsymbolic, a realm of objectivity that is constituted in an "inner-historical" fashion. This approach (which Adorno identifies with historical materialism) contrasts strongly with the Heideggerian strategy of "ontologizing history as totality" in which the abstract theme of historicity dissolves every particular "tension between interpretation and the object." In taking note of this tension the historical materialist both interprets a given reality and (following Marx's "Theses on Feuerbach") also demands its transformation: "The interpretation of given reality and its abolition are connected to each other," Adorno explains, "not, of course, in the sense that reality is negated in the concept, but that out of the construction of a configuration of reality the demand for its [reality's] real change always follows promptly." The new style of materialist criticism directs itself to "historical images" that are "not simply self-given" and "do not constitute the meaning of existence [*Dasein*]." Such images "do not lie organically ready in history" and to recognize them requires no Husserlian strategy of "showing" [*Schau*] or intuition [*Anschauung*]. Nor are they "magically sent by the gods to be . . . venerated." Historical materialism finally differentiates itself from the merely contemplative philosophy insofar as—unlike historical ontology—it abandons the idealist ambition to comprehend the totality: abandoning "invariant general concepts" and "all ontological questions in the traditional sense," it embraces the "liquidation of philosophy."[14]

Heidegger's Crypto-Idealism

The concluding portion of Adorno's "Actuality" lecture brings the specific polemic against Heidegger into sharper focus, perhaps because it is phenomenology in its distinctively Heideggerian form that best exemplifies the errors of traditional philosophical speculation. As an "essentially undialectical philosophy," historical ontology ironically seeks to establish an "ahistorical truth" even while it disparages the Cartesian and Husserlian attempt to raze traditional structures of philosophy so as to build it anew on apodictic foundations. The irony is that Heideggerian phenomenology declares itself more "historical" than its Husserlian antecedent because it abjures "the deception of beginning."[15] But such an appeal to historicity proves highly unsatisfactory, insofar as the historical tradition for Heidegger appears chiefly as a field of distortions and misunderstandings that must be destroyed and eventually carted away like rubble that obstructs genuine speculation. It is worth adding that when Adorno offered this criticism he did not yet know that in the mid-1930s Heidegger would turn to a new task of thinking an "other beginning" for philosophy beyond the errors of Western metaphysics (an attempt that might have given further substance to Adorno's critique).

The inaugural lecture concludes with a noteworthy attempt to entertain possible rejoinders that Adorno imagines might be raised against him by "the representatives of fundamental ontology."[16] Especially striking is the way that Adorno actually permits himself to adopt the language of his opponents:

> The central objection is that my conception, too, is based on a concept of man, a blueprint of Being [*Entwurf des Daseins*]; only, out of blind anxiety before the power of history, I allegedly shrank from putting these invariants forth clearly and left them clouded; instead I bestowed upon historical facticity, or its arrangement, the power which actually belongs to the invariant, ontological first principles, practiced idolatry with historically produced being, destroyed in philosophy every permanent standard, sublimated it into an aesthetic play of images *(Bilderspiel)*, and transformed the *prima philosophia* into essayism.[17]

This passage surely belongs among the more polemical moments in Adorno's early philosophical writing (exceeded, perhaps, only by the extended cri de coeur of the habilitation on Kierkegaard). Atypical for Adorno, it adopts a tactic of ventriloquism that verges on parody: he imagines himself charged, presumably by Heidegger, with adopting a foundationalist humanism, a certain ontology of "man" that he nonetheless keeps hidden; his imagined opponent further suspects him of succumbing to a "blind anxiety" before history, while also practicing "idolatry" with "historically produced being," thereby destroying "every permanent standard," abandoning philosophy for mere aestheticism and "essayism." But these imagined charges only prepare the way for Adorno's retort:

> In response, I can relate to these objections only by admitting of their content, but I defend it as philosophically legitimate. I will not decide whether a particular conception of man and being lies at the base of my theory, but I do deny the necessity of resorting to this conception. It is an idealist demand, that of an absolute beginning as only pure thought by itself can accomplish. It is a Cartesian demand, which believes it necessary to raise thinking to a form of its thought presuppositions and axioms. However, philosophy which no longer makes the assumption of autonomy, which no longer believes reality to be grounded in the *ratio*, but instead assumes always and forever that the law-giving of autonomous reason pierces through a being which is not adequate to it and cannot be laid out rationally as a totality—such a philosophy will not go the entire path to the rational presuppositions, but instead will stop there where irreducible reality breaks in upon it.[18]

This final rejoinder to an imagined representative of fundamental ontology is noteworthy in at least two respects. First, it once again charges the Heideggerian with crypto-idealism, since by impugning Adorno for neglecting his own foundationalist "conception of man and being" fundamental ontology betrays its own Cartesian expectation that all philosophical inquiry proceed from first principles that reside in "pure thought." Heideggerian ontology is therefore a species of rationalism *malgré lui*. Second, it suggests that due to this crypto-idealist commitment fundamental ontology refuses to acknowledge the "irreducible reality" that "breaks in" upon the arrogance of an idealist consciousness. What Adorno here calls the "irreducible" is more powerful than any "blueprint of being" that could anticipate this reality or serve as its constitutive horizon. Reality intrudes upon the presumed sovereignty of consciousness in specific instances, in "concrete" and "historical" events: indeed, it is *history itself* that "retards the movement of thought in its [ontological] presuppositions."[19] This argument, with its strongly materialist overtones, prepares the way for the cardinal theme of Adorno's *Negative Dialectics*, where the emphasis on "irreducible reality" would reappear under the title of the "primacy of the object."

Finally, in a last rejoinder to an imagined ontological critic, Adorno simply accepts the reproach of "essayism." The form of the essay admits of experimentation, he explains, and it therefore enjoys at least one distinctive advantage over the philosophical system—namely, it disables the pretension of thought to form a closed totality and instead admits "the power of freshly disclosed reality." Anticipating arguments from his later meditation, "The Essay as Form," Adorno argues that with the turn from system to essay philosophy must surrender its "security" and open itself to the "real," even if this encourages a species of interpretation that is "limited, contoured, and unsymbolic." Aesthetic essays, too, Adorno avers, will prove instructive "provided that the objects are chosen correctly." Forsaking the formalism and abstraction of traditional philosophy, interpretation must countenance the disorder of things. "For the mind [*Geist*] is indeed not capable of producing or grasping the totality of the real, but it may be possible to penetrate the details, to explode in miniature the mass of merely existing reality."[20]

Historicizing Nature

As we have seen, a great many of the themes that were to preoccupy Adorno in his later encounter with existentialism already made their appearance in the inaugural lecture on the actuality of philosophy. Such themes would receive further elaboration in the lecture

"The Idea of Natural History," which was presented on July 15, 1932, before an assembly of the Kant-Gesellschaft in Frankfurt. Although the lecture was never published in this form during his lifetime, Adorno would later incorporate its materials into *Negative Dialectics* in the section "World-spirit and Natural History."[21] The lecture's express purpose is to dismantle the reified antithesis of nature and history, where "nature" signifies all that is changeless or endowed with the timeless qualities of myth. What appears in this lecture under the name of myth thus anticipates the argument in *Dialectic of Enlightenment,* where Adorno and Horkheimer trace the ironic reversal of reason's emancipatory promise as instrumental reason assumes the quasi-mythic character of fatalism and unreflective repetition. In the natural history lecture, however, Adorno leaves the comparison to myth undeveloped, and instead he pursues a line of analysis that places greater stress on the polemic against phenomenology as represented by Husserl and his successors (Scheler and Heidegger). This is immediately clear from Adorno's opening definition of nature as "what has always been" and "as fatefully arranging predetermined being [*als schicksalhaft gefügtes, vorgegebenes Sein*]." Such an understanding of Being as what-has-always-been or as the-always-already imprints ontology with a distinctive fatalism, with the ironic consequence that Being becomes indistinguishable from a changeless substratum or *hypokeimenon:* Being appears as that which "underlies history and appears in history," although it is not itself *of* history and it remains a mythic substratum unperturbed by historical change. Adorno therefore concludes that Being in this Heideggerian sense is "substance in history." Surprisingly, this means that Being occupies the role of changeless and ahistorical *nature.*

Such a claim is no doubt controversial. To identify Being with a changeless nature or ahistorical substratum gravely understates Heidegger's bold attempt to absorb all of reality into the historical continuum, leaving behind nothing that could qualify as a changeless or metaphysical ground. Adorno no doubt recognizes that his definition cuts against this ambition, but he insists that, pace Heidegger's stated aims, existential ontology actually disallows the thought of history as a space for "the occurrence of the qualitatively new." The paradoxical consequence of Heidegger's argument is to transform actual history *(Geschichte)* into the existential category of mere *historicality (Geschichtlichkeit)*; ironically, however, this is a constitutive and timeless condition that serves as little more than a theater for the constant reappearance of "mere identity" and for the "mere reproduction of what has always been." It is in this sense that "Being" corresponds to what Adorno (in a gesture of interpretive malice) calls "nature." Genuine history, by contrast, would be defined as a temporally defined movement that "gains its true character through what appears in it as new." These opening definitions prepare the ground for Adorno's general task in the essay: to destabilize the conventional dualism between ahistorical nature and history so as to better understand "the interweaving of historical and natural being."[22]

The opening thesis of Adorno's essay is that "post-Husserlian phenomenology," despite its own intentions, lapses back into the idealist doctrine of constitutive subjectivity. It is true that Heidegger and other phenomenologists such as Max Scheler thought of themselves as opposing the transcendental motifs in Husserl's own project (motifs that become most explicit in his *Ideas*). For Adorno this opposition explains the self-described turn from subjectivism to a "transsubjective" theory of being. And yet this apparent rejection of subjectivism ended in what Adorno calls the "fundamental paradox of all modern ontological thought"—namely, "the means with which the attempt is made to establish transsubjective being is none other than the same subjective reason that had earlier erected the infrastructure of critical idealism." The paradox is due chiefly to the fact that the "question of being [*Seinsfrage*]" can be construed in two distinctive ways: It can be raised in a pre-Kantian mode as the question of "being itself [*Sein selber*]," where being resides in the inaccessible realm of the thing-in-itself; or, alternatively, it can be raised in the epistemological mode as what Heidegger calls "meaning of being [*Sinn des Seins*]" or what Adorno calls "the meaningfulness of the existing [*Sinnhaftigkeit des Seienden*]." In the first instance meaning remains as a "transcendent content" that lies behind the manifest world; in the second instance meaning requires the "interpretation of the existing itself." The ambiguity in the Heideggerian *Seinsfrage* shows that existential ontology remains bound despite itself to the terminus a quo of traditional epistemology, where subjective consciousness confronts an external world as something "foreign and lost." Heidegger's concern to answer a question of this generality is therefore a symptom of the crisis in bourgeois philosophy as it awakens to the truth that consciousness cannot comprehend the whole of what there is. For the ontological question can arise only when "reality is no longer immediately accessible and reality and reason have no common meaning."[23]

Whereas Husserlian phenomenology accepts the conventional dualism of nature and history, Heidegger in his much-vaunted rebellion against all such metaphysical conventions claims to abolish the distinction altogether: "The question of being no longer has the significance of the Platonic question of the extent of the static and qualitatively different ideas that stand in contrast to the existing, the empirical." Instead, the existing itself now becomes the site of meaning, and "a grounding of being beyond history is replaced by a project *(Entwurf)* of being as historicity." With this rebellion, however, history itself loses its character as a plenum of openness, while contingency transforms into a "basic ontological structure." On the one hand, this gesture is supposed to abolish the false antithesis between history and being, thereby absolving Heidegger of the taint of mere formalism. On the other hand, the possibility of actually thinking historically is lost, since history is "reduced to a philosophically based structure of historicity as a fundamental quality of human existence *(Dasein)*." History alone (with "its most extreme agitation") loses its innovative dynamism and ossifies into a fixed and ahistorical ground. The problem of abstract formalism thereby returns. Although Heidegger has a great deal to say about the historical character of existence and the incorrigible historicity of worldly possibilities, his arguments cannot descend from the arid plane of "ontological formalism" that bears only the most arbitrary connection to concrete historical events. "The problem of historical contingency cannot be mastered by the category of historicity," Adorno observes. "One can set up a general structural category of life, but if one tries to interpret a particular phenomenon, for example, the French Revolution, though one can indeed find in it every possible element of this structure of life . . . it is nevertheless impossible to relate the facticity of the French Revolution in its most extreme factual being to such categories."[24]

For Adorno this indifference to concrete facticity is disingenuous, since ontology borrows its formal categories precisely *from* the concrete world it neglects. The categorial analysis of existence is therefore an exercise in tautology. As a formal structure, "historicity" is no different in this respect than "being-toward-death" or, presumably, any of the other fundamental categories of the existential analytic that contain nothing but "qualities of being have been first "subtracted [*weggenommen*] from human existence" and then "transposed [*transponiert*] into the sphere of ontology." In a final gesture of tautological self-affirmation, these categories are then deployed as mere instruments for the interpretation *(Auslegung)* of that which is "said once again." Hence the self-affirmative or tautological character of ontological argument, which first abstracts from existence only to explain existence. The vicious circle that Heidegger apologetically characterizes as "hermeneutics" cannot be avoided because it arises from the very structure of the *Seinsfrage*. The question is supposed to hold itself open to concrete experience, but it only abstracts this experience into themes that it can answer without difficulty and without leaving the self-enclosed dwelling of the idealist *ratio*. Trapped in its own creations, Heideggerian philosophy offers only an illusory reconciliation between nature and history: everything that appears *as* history is merely an idealist category dressed up in the language of historical existence. The tautological problem is thus a sign that the new ontology has merely acquired "new camouflage" for the "old classical thesis" of an identity between subject and object.[25]

Anticipations of the Hegel Studies

It is not hard to see how Adorno's critique of the identity theory that underwrites existential ontology closely resembles the later critique of Hegel's identity theory, especially as found in the 1957 essay "Aspects of Hegel's Philosophy," a lecture first given in 1956 at the Free University in Berlin to commemorate the 125th anniversary of Hegel's death. In that lecture Adorno would attempt to redeem Hegel from the distortions of Heidegger's interpretation by noting that what Hegel calls "being" is an "essentially negative, reflected, and criticized moment of the dialectic" and it is therefore "incompatible with *the contemporary theologization of being.*" According to Adorno, Hegel "denies being the very absoluteness, the very priority over all thought or concept, that the most recent resurrection of metaphysics hopes to secure." And yet Adorno ultimately condemns Hegel for asserting the same false identity between being and thought: "The linguistic expression 'existence,' which is necessarily conceptual, is confused with what it designates, which is nonconceptual, something that cannot be melted down into identity."[26] The critique of Hegel's identity theory is even more pronounced in "Skoteinos, or How to Read Hegel" (the last of the *Three Studies on Hegel* published together in 1963), where Adorno notes that Hegel initially appeared ready to acknowledge nonidentity as an independent moment in the system, only to retract this recognition and demote nonidentity to the status of a mere "instrument" for affirming identity. By defining *nonidentity within* a concept, "the dialectic imagines itself to have gone beyond nonidentity and to be assured of absolute identity." But this is a mistake; "one cannot move from the logical movement of concepts to existence." The *truly* nonidentical, Adorno writes, is that which exceeds its own concept and therefore belies the totalizing pretensions of idealist philosophy. As he explains in *Minima Moralia*, "The Whole is the Untrue [*Das Ganze ist das Unwahre*]."[27]

Adorno goes on to explain that Heidegger's neo-ontology subscribes to idealism in two key respects. First, much like the conciliatory promise of the Hegelian dialectic, neo-ontology, too, is captive to the fantasy of holism. In subsuming all that allows for phenomenological description under the master concept of "being," neo-ontology conceives the existential world as "a structural whole, a structural unity or totality," and then claims the right to "know adequately the existing in itself." Second, neo-ontology stresses "possibility" over "reality," since it describes existence primarily as a "project [*Entwurf*]" that presses forward into the future.[28] This emphasis on the individual's self-understanding as projecting itself into future possibilities betrays the fact that existential ontology still subscribes to a species of "subjectivistic" idealism where the cogito stands unchallenged as the coordinating principle of all reality. In these two respects, Adorno concludes, Heidegger's philosophy does not resolve the dualism between nature and history but only shifts nature onto the occluded plane of "being," from which position the thinking subject can then declare itself identical with objectivity. To overcome this dualism, Adorno claims, it would be necessary to overcome the reified conception of nature that persists in existential ontology so as to recognize nature itself as historical through and through.

Lukács and Benjamin

In the concluding portion of the 1932 lecture, Adorno appeals to both Lukács and Benjamin to develop the proposed reconciliation between nature and history. Such a reconciliation must proceed in both directions: "No being underlying or residing within historical being itself is to be understood as ontological, that is, as natural being," he writes. But it is no less imperative to "comprehend nature as an historical being" even where "it seems to rest most deeply in itself as nature." The first task, inspired by Lukács, requires that we critically dismantle our image of the social world as a place of "petrified" and "estranged" convention. Forgetting that our world is "historically produced," we may come to experience its "all-embracing power" as something irresistible: a "second nature." When we naturalize society in this fashion and neglect its sociohistorical origins, it confronts us as a "dead world" of alienated and reified meaning or, in Adorno's striking phrase, as a "charnel-house of rotted interiorities." A genuinely *critical* philosophy of history must undo the false naturalization of the social world and restore it to the volatile space of a genuinely *historical* consciousness. The second task, inspired by Benjamin, would demand that we resist any conception of nature that would seek to isolate it from historical time. For nature, too, bears the imprint of human consciousness as it has unfolded historically through labor and cultural expression. The Platonist's dream of a higher nature uncontaminated by change is a patent falsehood, for even nature bears "the mark of transience."[29]

This twofold analysis of Lukács and Benjamin may confuse the reader since at first glance it may appear as if Lukács contributes an important insight to the interpretation of natural history.[30] Adorno does not take sufficient care to explain that the concept of a "second nature" (borrowed from Lukács' diagnosis of social convention in his *Theory of the Novel*) does not provide a critical-emancipatory route from nature and back to history but instead only thinks of the problem in terms of "theological resurrection."[31] According to Adorno, Benjamin alone offers the proper solution to the puzzle of natural history, in that he brings the resurrection of second nature out of its "infinite distance" and makes it an object of philosophical interpretation. Specifically in Benjamin's reading of the German *Trauerspiel*, allegory becomes a "secular exposition of history as the passion of the world."[32] In allegory, history appears as a "petrified primordial landscape." It presents itself as a *facies hippocratica* (the sickened face of one about to die). Indeed, the more history seems "meaningful" the nearer it approaches death. It is therefore crucial to resist the allure of historical "meaning [*Sinn*]" in the manner of historical ontology for which the historical continuum offers an undamaged and mythical image of reconciliation. The very same could be said of works of art: only inferior artworks are rich with emotion. The true promise of reconciliation, however, "is most perfectly given where at the same time the world is most firmly immured from all 'meaning.'"[33]

Rather than venturing further into the details of the discussion of Lukács and Benjamin, it will suffice here to note that Adorno ends the lecture by recalling the sharp distinction between natural history and historical ontology. The polemical thrust of this distinction is especially evident in the concluding remarks on "meaning" in both history as in art. Anticipating his later remarks on Beckett's *Endgame* (which I will examine in Chapter 3), Adorno condemns the very notion of "meaning." From the materialist perspective, he claims, any appeal to an uncontaminated plenitude of meaning would only encourage an unreflectively mythic and naturalistic affirmation of the social world as it is given. Hence Benjamin's advantage over historical ontology: whereas historical ontology naturalizes history and thereby disables criticism, Benjamin does away with the ideology of a changeless realm (being, nature, the Platonic idea) and thereby helps us to grasp "the interweaving of historical and natural being."[34] With this argument, the terms were set in place for Adorno's formidable critique of Husserlian phenomenology.

The Metacritique of Phenomenology

The deteriorating political and economic situation in Germany ultimately forced Adorno to emigrate. Decommissioned from his pro-
fessorship by the terms of the newly imposed racial laws, by the
spring of 1934 Adorno had solidified plans to obtain a doctorate at
Oxford University (Merton College) with the aim of qualifying for
a professorial post in Britain. His supervisor, Gilbert Ryle (at Christ
Church) was among the very few British philosophers at the time
who could claim a strong knowledge of contemporary currents in
German philosophy.[35] Ryle had in fact authored a review of *Being
and Time* in 1929, one of the earliest reviews in the entire Anglophone world, and one that anticipates Adorno's interpretation of
Heidegger in noteworthy ways, especially in its reading of existential ontology as "subjectivistic" and still "caught in a kind of idealism."[36] But Adorno's stay in Oxford brought many difficulties. To
a young philosopher who already possessed a doctorate and a *venia
legendi* from the University of Frankfurt, the necessity of securing a
second doctorate seemed, as Adorno confided to Horkheimer and
Berg, nothing less than a "nightmare." And despite his own efforts
to familiarize himself with British idealist philosophers such as
F. H. Bradley, Adorno never managed to acclimate to the British
environment. His tastes for social theory and aesthetics were not
widely shared, nor did his new peers at Oxford extend a warm reception; they were repelled by what they perceived as Adorno's
"dandified manner" and his "anxiety."[37] Closely following upon
the political crisis in Germany, Adorno confronted personal tragedy
as well: his beloved Aunt Agathe died in July 1935, and then, in a
second blow, his instructor in composition, Alban Berg, died in December. The following year Adorno would write a short remembrance that described Berg's "impregnable quality, indeed something uninvolved [*Zuschauerhaftes*], of the kind that Kierkegaard . . .
decried in aestheticism."[38]

It is against this somber background of exile and isolation that we must understand Adorno's readiness to bury himself in the texts of classical phenomenology. He focused his efforts most of all on Husserl's *Formal and Transcendental Logic* and the *Cartesian Meditations*. The fruit of this research, written in Oxford between 1934 and 1937, would be a typescript of more than four hundred pages. Some time later, in the years 1955–1956, Adorno would add an introduction and a new (third) chapter, both of which he included in the book published in 1956 as *Zur Metakritik der Erkenntnistheorie, Studien über Husserl und die phänomenologischen Antinomien*. An English edition of the book appeared under the title *Against Epistemology*. To dismiss the Husserl book as marginal to Adorno's corpus would be mistaken. As late as 1968 Adorno would still characterize the Husserl book as "the most important" of his works alongside *Negative Dialectics*.[39]

Nor was this his only venture into the forbidding texts of Husserlian phenomenology. As early as 1924 Adorno had already devoted great energy to the topic, in the doctoral dissertation he wrote at Frankfurt under the guidance of the neo-Kantian Hans Cornelius. The dissertation, titled "The Transcendent Status of Thing and Noema in Husserl's Phenomenology," scrutinized what Adorno considered a fatal conflict in the Husserlian doctrine, between its ambition to isolate the experiential elements of immanent consciousness from its necessary appeal to the transcendent objects of the world. Notwithstanding the phenomenologist's stated desire to ground philosophy on the "immediate evidence" of pure consciousness alone, Husserl (Adorno argued) could not explain how consciousness as a "ontological sphere of absolute origins [*Seinssphäre absoluter Ursprünge*]" was supposed to retain an intentional bond to the "transcendent" objects beyond that sphere.[40] According to the well-known theory of intentionality, consciousness was always "conscious of . . . ," and this meant that the transcendent objects of intention could not be annulled even for an immanent analysis of meaning. Husserlian phenomenology was therefore caught in a self-contradiction, a split between "being as consciousness [*Sein als Bewußtsein*]" and "being as reality [*Sein als Realität*]."[41] Most readers still agree with critics such as Fred Dallmayr, whose superb grasp of Adorno's encounter with phenomenology did not restrain him from dismissing the 1924 dissertation as "not a very original piece of work."[42] Adorno's biographer Stefan Müller-Doohm characterizes it as a product of a young writer who had not yet moved beyond "the self-enclosed world of academic philosophy."[43] Yet it would be rash to deny its significance for our study of Adorno's encounter with phenomenology, for even this somewhat unoriginal and academic interpretation of Husserl contains *in nuce* an essential complaint about the idealistic tendencies of phenomenology that would reappear in Adorno's later, more mature writings on the philosophies of bourgeois interiority—namely, a critique of the undialectical dualism between subjective consciousness and material reality.

The Oxford study was not the only philosophical work of his later years that Adorno devoted to Husserlian phenomenology; he also wrote a shorter essay, "Husserl and the Problem of Idealism" (first published in English in 1940).[44] For anyone who wishes to understand the grounds for Adorno's general assessment of phenomenology and existentialism as forms of idealism, these essays—especially the 1940 essay and the book from 1956—are of great significance. Indeed, Adorno singled out the introduction to the book as the work that, alongside "The Essay as Form" (from *Notes to Literature*) best contained "a program for his philosophy."[45] It is therefore unsurprising that he reacted with some dismay when Horkheimer rejected a longer essay on Husserl that Adorno had submitted to the *Zeitschrift für Sozialforschung* for publication.[46] In a letter to Horkheimer he offered the explanation that it served as "a kind of critical, dialectical prelude to a materialist logic."[47]

Surprisingly, even *Against Epistemology*, a major work that ranks among the most sustained philosophical studies in Adorno's entire oeuvre, has not always received the attention it deserves.[48] This is no doubt in part due to the fact that its style of analysis oscillates between laborious scholasticism and vigorous polemic. Its occasionally aggressive character comes in for especially sharp criticism from Joanna Hodge, who remarks on the "distasteful" political gestures and even the "brutality" of Adorno's treatment of Husserl: "It ill behooves the philosopher," Hodge writes, "to abandon the name 'rigorous science' in favor of cheap polemics, and it is Husserl, not Adorno, who takes up the task of thinking, not in the name of humanity, or in the name of Auschwitz, or even in the name of truth, but in his own name, painfully signing and owning every twist and turn, every grammatical inflection and hard-won insight."[49] Such charges are not without merit: Adorno's interpretation of Husserl is occasionally overzealous, lapsing into a style of criticism virtually indistinguishable from political vilification. It is therefore all the more crucial that we take seriously the remark in the preface, where Adorno explains that "Husserl's philosophy is *the occasion and not the point of this book*."[50] This is not to propose that we dismiss the technical ruminations on phenomenology as mere distractions (which they surely are not; their insights are often profound). But we should not forget that, just as with *Negative Dialectics* and other exercises in philosophical criticism, Adorno reads even the most recondite philosophical texts with an awareness of the dialectical and nonreductive relation between the internal and the external, the logical and social. This critical strategy holds for the analysis of philosophical texts no less than for the exercises in musicology, where Adorno follows the basic interpretative principle (later formulated in *Aesthetic Theory*) that "unresolved antagonisms of reality return in artworks as immanent problems of form."[51] ⭐

The idea of a *metacritique* thus merits some comment. The term derives from J. G. Hamann, who used it to describe his own critical reflections on Kant's critical philosophy. The implications of the prefix *meta-*, as indicating a critique *beyond* critique, have been

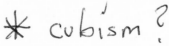 ⭐ cubism ?

lucidly explained by Simon Jarvis, who notes that Adorno wished to develop a self-reflexive examination (in a transcendental mode) of the conditions for the possibility of a critical inquiry.[52] With reference to Adorno's larger project of negative dialectics, Brian O'Connor offers further explanation: "The motivating idea behind the metacritique of epistemology is that every epistemology is determined by a normative commitment to how the world ought to be." The purpose of a metacritique, then, is to bring this normative commitment to light, in part because one can then demonstrate its entanglement in a host of social conditions that would remain otherwise obscured (hence linking the practice of metacritique to the Marxian practice of ideology critique). Thanks to this very demonstration, a metacritique prepares the ground for what O'Connor calls a "rationally articulable account of experience."[53] Within the bounds of the Husserl book, however, this further conception of experience remained largely implicit, and Adorno confined himself to working out the normative implications of phenomenology, which were shown to be deeply ideological.

Following this nonreductive strategy of immanent critique, Adorno anticipates the central lesson of the Husserl book by selecting as its epigram a quote from Epicharmus (who Socrates describes in the *Theataetus* as "the prince of comedy"): "A mortal must think mortal and not immortal thoughts." Husserlian phenomenology thus serves as an occasion for coming to grips with a general problem that afflicts the entirety of the philosophical tradition insofar as it strives to lift itself free of "mortal" (social) conditions for the sake of ostensibly "immortal" insight. Husserl merely instantiates what Adorno calls "the original sin of *prima philosophia*"—namely, the ambition to transcend or merely abolish any contaminant traces of contingency and empirical residue so as to arrive at a higher stage of unconditioned necessity. Any philosophy that strives for "continuity and completeness" finds it necessary to "eliminate everything which does not fit from whatever it judges." The unconditional world fashioned in philosophy appears as a "closed circle" and pretends to "the unbroken illusion of the natural" or, ultimately, "the metaphysical illusion of being."[54]

But such transcendence is at once illusion *and* truth. It is illusion because thought can never achieve the purity it desires; it is truth because the philosophical ideal of thoroughgoing necessity bears witness to a different kind of necessity—namely, the social reality of unfreedom. As Adorno explains, "Thought submits to the real compulsion of societal debt relations and, deluded, claims this compulsion as its own." He denies, however, that this claim leaves him vulnerable to the charge of sociological reductionism. "The real life process of society," he claims, "is not something sociologically smuggled into philosophy through associates. It is rather the core of the contents of logic itself." On this point Adorno adheres to the principle of dialectical mediation, according to which philosophy must foreswear any attempt to arrive at a sphere of untroubled immediacy. For this reason the technique of sociological reduction is no more valid than the technique of transcendental reduction favored by phenomenologists: "The doctrine that everything is mediated, even supporting immediacy, is irreconcilable with the urge to 'reduction.'"[55] The stricture against reduction thus forbids *both* a crude sociologism of philosophical contents *and* an arrogant belief in the philosophical transcendence of society. But this stricture nonetheless leaves the way clear for Adorno to develop a dialectical critique of Husserl's efforts. As in the aesthetic theory, so too in Adorno's critique of phenomenology, social compulsion appears not as an external referent but as an "immanent problem" of philosophical form.[56]

The immanent critique of Husserlian phenomenology involves a far-reaching critique of the self-contradiction in idealist epistemology. But Adorno hastens to explain that such a critique is genuinely dialectical, and that "criticizing epistemology also means . . . retaining it."[57] If phenomenology understands itself as *prima philosophia*, it is precisely this claim to primacy that must be revealed as an illusion—*not in order to refute phenomenology through abstract negation but rather to show how its failure bears within itself a hidden philosophical insight.* "Idealism is not simply untruth," Adorno explains. "It is truth in its untruth."

The Antinomy of Idealism

This dialectical conception of idealism's failure turns out to be a crucial theme in all of Adorno's work on both existentialism and phenomenology. Although idealism assigns false primacy to the monad of subjective consciousness as the *fundamentum* for all philosophical knowledge, this primacy is "the correct appearance of a false world in which men are alien and uncertain to each other." The transcendental ego that organizes all experience as experience *for* consciousness expresses the truth of a social order in which every individual "feels knowledge of himself *(von sich selber)* is more immediate and certain than the same knowledge of all others" and immediately relates only to his "particular interests" even while these interests are considered universal and essential laws. The monadological structure of Husserl's idealism therefore presents us with the candid truth of the bourgeois world, even while it also stands as an indictment of its current untruth. For consciousness does not enjoy the sovereignty Husserl imagines: "The intertwining of illusion and necessity in idealism," writes Adorno, "has seldom become clearer in its history than with Husserl. An enemy of both the necessary illusoriness of induction and the illusory necessity of deduction, he strived to confine idealism in a paradoxical standoff. The ground of the paradox, the monadological constitution of man, could only be sublated if consciousness were at some time finally to rule over being [*wenn einmal endlich Bewußtsein über das Sein geböte*], which it constantly only with untruth asserts is grounded in consciousness."[58]

According to Adorno, then, Husserl not only typifies idealism but brings its defining principles to an unprecedented extremity: "Anxiety

 see above

[*Angst*] over absolute security, even the original Cartesian postulate of indubitable certainty, leads Husserl to surpass the entire idealistic tradition. He points out the dependence on contingent fact in the Cartesian ego and establishes as a true and solely sufficient presupposition the ideal of a fact-free transcendental." But Husserl also wants to affirm the place of this essential ego within the "ontic" sphere, since this will establish the ego's factual power in constituting the world. This desire betrays a contradiction in the concept of "eidetic existence," or what Adorno calls a "phenomenological antinomy," a contradiction that will eventually afflict Heidegger's thought as well.

The irony of this charge deserves our attention, since it bears some resemblance to the dissatisfaction with Husserl that would motivate Heidegger in his efforts to supersede Husserl's transcendental unworldliness.[59] Ironically, however, Adorno resists the consoling thought that Heidegger succeeded where Husserl failed. On the contrary, Adorno faults Heidegger for the very same error. In neither case has phenomenology succeeded in shedding its hidden debt to idealism:

> The contradiction in a concept of eidetic existence tacitly marks the phenomenological antinomy. Husserl attests that essence, which should soar above all the frailty of existence, also has a being independent of thought that can be derived from nowhere else than from an existence with which Husserl's essences will not be contaminated at any price. He qualifies one and the same thing as ontological and ontical—a preliminarily version of the later doctrine of being there *(Dasein)* as the ontical thing which has the priority of being ontological, in which, moreover, no less than in Husserl, the constitutive primacy of subjectivity, the old idealism, lies concealed.[60]

This idealism manifests itself most of all in the method of phenomenological bracketing, or *époché,* according to which (as Husserl writes in the *Cartesian Meditations*), "I grasp myself as pure self *(moi)* with the life of consciousness which is proper to myself, a life in

and by which the entire objective world exists for me, just *as* it exists for me."[61] But the ambition to grasp everything *for consciousness* asserts a reflexive identity between the "pure self [*moi pur*]" as "grammatical subject" and the pure self as grammatical object. This generates the aforementioned antinomy, since "the most rigorous concept of the transcendental cannot get out of its interdependence with the fact. To that extent it remains what Husserl dislikes about the Cartesian ego: a piece of the world [*Stück Welt*]."[62] Despite this contradiction, however, phenomenology nonetheless serves the inflationary ambitions of the ego, since it exemplifies the subject's claim to stand as the constitutive principle for all worldly being. "By furnishing the principle from which all being proceeds, the subject promotes itself."[63] In this respect phenomenology only radicalizes the tendency to domination *(Herrschaft)* that underlies all forms of philosophical idealism.

But it is crucial to note that Adorno injects a dialectical nuance into this critique: anticipating the interpretation of humanity's path toward freedom as simultaneously progress *and* regression (as expounded in the *Dialectic of Enlightenment*), Adorno acknowledges that the subject's claim to primacy hardly meant to achieve total domination. On the contrary, the apotheosis of the subject has its origins in a bid for emancipation. But the idealist inflation of the subject into the principle of world-constituting identity eventually awakens a fear that this principle is merely a new species of subjectivism that has not in fact conquered the world as it had hoped. Idealism therefore finds itself caught in an antinomy, the subjectivistic consequence upon its own apotheosis:

First philosophy has in no sense been pure lordship [*Herrschaft*]. Its initial goal is liberation from the context of nature, and rationality has never entirely given up the memory of autonomy and its actualization. But as soon as it was absolutized, it almost constantly approached the feared dissolution. The philosophy of origins—which through self-consistency, the flight before the conditioned, turns to the subject and pure identity—also fears that it will lose itself in the determinacy of the purely subjective, which, as isolated moment, has precisely never reached pure identity and bears its defect as well as its opposite. Great philosophy has not escaped this antinomy.

Several years later, Adorno and Horkheimer would characterize this ironic denouement as a pathological dialectic in the history of reason. Already in the Husserl book, however, Adorno develops the basic claim that the emancipation of the subject ultimately turns *against* the subject in its effort to establish absolute objectivity: "Thought, which regards itself as the ground of being, is always on the point of prohibiting itself as a disturbing factor in being [*Denken, das sich selbst als Seinsgrund behauptet, ist stets auf den Sprung, sich also Störungsfactor des Seins zu verbieten*]." As the end point of bourgeois philosophy, Husserlianism exhibits precisely this dialectical reversal: taking the subject as its transcendental foundation it has turned against or "desubjectivized" the subject.[64] This self-subverting denouement is evident not just in phenomenology, Adorno concludes; it is found in all forms of idealist thought. Even Hegel, "the metaphysician of absolute spirit," celebrates the principle of the subject's world-constituting power to such a degree that "the world is always right" and, ultimately, despite its own intensions, allies itself with the antisubjectivist stance of positivism.[65]

Intrinsic to the antinomy of phenomenological idealism, then, is the simultaneous inflation of the constitutive subject and the readiness to erase the suffering subject for the sake of objectivity. This apparent contradiction explains why phenomenology in Adorno's view adopts such a conservative stand in its faithful affirmation of "the given." The basic claim, which Adorno will repeat in his later critique of Heidegger, is that such an affirmation of the given reveals an unlikely convergence between phenomenology and positivism. On the one hand, phenomenology installs the ego as the organizing principle of all possible experience; but on the other hand what is given in perception becomes the fulfillment of that experience. For Husserl, as for positivism, the qualifier "real" becomes (as defined in the *Logical Investigations*) "being a possible object of sense-perception."[66] Givenness and inflationary subjectivity therefore belong together: "Superiority to crude facticity does not hinder the acceptance of the thing world 'as it gives itself.' "[67] In obedience to its grandiose slogan, "To the things themselves [*Zu den Sachen selbst*]," phenomenology models itself after the sciences but unwittingly capitulates to a positivism that will suffocate constitutive subjectivity: "As long as philosophy is no more than the cult of what 'is the case,' in Wittgenstein's formula, it enters into competition with the sciences to which in delusion it assimilates itself—and loses. If it dissociates itself form the sciences, however, and in refreshed merriment thinks itself free of them, it becomes a powerless reserve, the shadow of shadowy Sunday religion."[68]

The desire to capture the given so as to realize its pure description prompts Adorno to entertain a rather fanciful analogy between phenomenology and photography, illustrating how the phenomenologist reduces the objective world to a passive, static reality. "Like the photographer of old," he writes, "the phenomenologist wraps himself with the black veil of his *époché,* implores the objects to hold still and unchanging and ultimately realizes passively and without spontaneity of the knowing subject, family portraits of the sort of that mother 'who glances lovingly at her little flock.' " In Chapter 1 we saw that Kierkegaard's philosophy had the mirror as its defining metaphor. Here we see that Adorno likens Husserl's philosophy to a camera. In his devotion to the "given," the phenomenologist does not permit the objects to retain their dynamism and independence. Instead he wishes to seize upon them for the sake of an image *inside* the phenomenological apparatus: "Just as in photography the *camera obscura* and the recorded pictorial object belong together, so in phenomenology do the immanence of consciousness and realism."[69]

The phenomenologist's appeal to a much-vaunted realism is therefore little more than a pretext for fortifying the authority of consciousness over the real, though consciousness in its turn loses all contact with the external reality it wished to master and instead lapses into solipsism. Thoughts "seal themselves off more and more from whatever does not emanate from them and their jurisdiction, the immanence of the subject."[70] Through the phenomenological reduction, phenomenology effects nothing less than a "renunciation of existence *(Dasein)*," that culminates in what Adorno calls "logical absolutism."[71] Phenomenology only *abstracts* from the real and thus fails to grasp the real in its nonsubjective reality. Its failure is a sign that "advanced bourgeois self-consciousness can no longer be satisfied with that fetishizing of abstract concepts in which the world of commodities is reflected for its observer."[72] As in the analogy to photography, the real remains only the real-for-thought, and it retains no more of its reality than is required for it to qualify as the "property" of the bourgeois subject: "nothing more is thinkable which is not subject to this subjectivity and in the strictest sense its property [*Besitz*]."[73] As in the *Dialectic of Enlightenment,* Adorno suggests that the idealist ambition to domination and possession originates in animal fear: "Anxiety [*Angst*] stamps the ideal of Husserlian philosophy as one of absolute security, on the model of private property. Its reductions aim at the secure: viz. the immanence to consciousness of lived experiences whose title deeds the philosophical self-consciousness to which they 'belong' should possess securely from the grasp of any force; and essences which, free from all factical existence, defy vexation from factical existence [*faktischen Dasein*]."[74] Idealism is therefore a retreat into an immanent sphere of protection, and the reality that was supposed to stand as the object of investigation becomes disfigured: Either it is transformed into an object of cognitive possession, or it is banished altogether from the phenomenologist's workshop, where the researcher recalls it with hushed embarrassment as "residue" or "mere existence."

Failure and Nonidentity

The signal failure of phenomenology to make contact with its object first becomes apparent when subjective immanence discovers that it cannot expunge the moment of "nonidentity" that lurks within itself. Indeed, idealism in general (at least as Adorno understands the term) might be defined as the subject's concerted effort to do away with the nonidentical as a threat to its own dream of self-constitution. But Adorno offers the important qualification that among the idealists Kant alone sustained at least the *thought* of nonidentity thanks to his "retreat to formalism," whereas Hegel and later the phenomenologists came to see this formalism as a deficiency. By restraining cognition to the constitution of form rather than metaphysical content Kant left space for a nonidentity that would not be absorbed into the subject "without residue [*ohne Rest*]." In the *Critique of Pure Reason* the concept of the given thus served as "the last refuge of the irreducible in idealism." But this persistent appeal to a nonsubjective exterior would eventually conflict (in Hegel's philosophy) with "the concept of spirit as complete reducibility."[75] In phenomenology, however, the last constraint against such a reduction is finally removed and thought attempts to establish itself as "absolutely first." And yet this ambition ends in failure because "immanence can never completely disentangle the moment of nonidentity within itself, and because subjectivity, the organ of reflection, clashes with the idea of an absolutely first as pure immediacy. Though the idea of philosophy of origins aims monistically at pure identity, subjective immanence, in which the absolutely first wishes to remain with itself undisturbed, will not let itself be reduced to that pure identity with itself. What Husserl calls the 'original foundation' *(Urstiftung)* of transcendental subjectivity is also an original lie."[76]

This attempt to vanquish nonidentity is hardly new. According to Adorno, it originates at the very dawn of philosophical inquiry, specifically in the pre-Socratic fascination with mathematics. Indeed, numbers are "an arrangement for making the nonidentical . . . commensurable with the subject, the model of unity."[77] Seen from a truly critical perspective, however, the nonidentical signifies novelty, that which disturbs the illusion of permanence or total knowledge: "The praise of the unchanging suggests that nothing should be otherwise than it has always been" and "the thought of identity really always already presupposes total surveyability and acquaintance [*totale Überschaubarkeit und Bekanntheit*]."[78] Thus, idealism for Adorno is at once totalitarian and traditionalist: any element of novelty is simply "filtered out," or it must bear the stigma of the "intruder." Idealism looks askance at the very material that could rescue it from solipsism: "What helps the subject out of its self-imprisonment is emphasized as negative." The nonidentical appears as "a danger which must be overpowered and immediately withdrawn into the preserve of the familiar. Thus empiricism agrees with its opponents and is linked to [the] philosophy of origins."[79] This hostility to the new, writes Adorno, is "primally bourgeois [*urbürgerlich*]." Secure only in its own domain, it typifies the bourgeois confidence that its world, untroubled by social change, will endure for eternity. "Out of the familiar nothing unfamiliar, nothing other should possibly arise."[80]

Phenomenology's principled antagonism toward the nonidentical manifests itself even in the peculiar habit of "bracketing" with quotation marks, "a ritual of writing," Adorno notes, that both repeats and suspends all of nonideational reality. In the *Ideen,* Husserl sought to assure the reader that with the phenomenological reduction signified by bracketing "We have properly lost nothing"; but this implied that the reduction was actually powerless, an empty gesture that "leaves everything as it was." The world as it appears in the ἐποχή is nothing but "a tautology of the existing world." And yet, Adorno observes sharply, in using brackets to signal the "purity" of the philosophical investigation, "the rigorous researcher wields some of the fatal humor of the journalist who writes 'lady' when he means prostitute."[81] Bracketing therefore betrays disdain for what it leaves aside, and it believes it has established a sphere immanent to consciousness. Recalling a notorious remark from the *Cartesian Meditations* ("It is I and my culture who form here the primordial sphere with respect to every 'foreign' culture"), Adorno suggests that the phenomenological ἐποχή signifies nothing less than "transcendental xenophobia."[82]

Amusing or merely offensive, such moments of polemic in the Husserl book should not blind us from recognizing the more dialectical moments where Adorno seeks to discover the "truth" in phenomenological "untruth" by means of immanent critique. Especially illuminating on this score is the claim that the very concept of cognition points beyond the confines of idealism. This is chiefly because the very concept of the given implies "a subject to which it can refer." Although idealism wants to imagine this subject as the very foundation for the "thing world," it cannot dispel the fact that givenness contains an "ontic residuum"; in other words, it *presupposes* the thing world that the subject was supposed to establish. Here idealism is caught in a double bind, because in making the subject the constitutive beginning of the world it must suppress awareness of the subject's own natural, mimetic constitution. In a late addition that alludes to the *Dialectic of Enlightenment,* Adorno notes that the mimetic relation between mind and world is indeed a precondition for their separation: "Without mimesis, the break between subject and object would be absolute and cognition impossible." This mimetic relation to nature cannot be done away with entirely: "Cognition can never rid itself of its mimetic moment without some remainder, the resemblance of the subject to nature, which it wants to dominate and which arose out of cognition itself." Idealism may wish to renounce this resemblance as an illusion, but it sublimates the "lost mimesis" into its own yearning for 'the things themselves.' "[83]

As Michael Rosen has observed, the great emphasis placed on *description* helps to explain Adorno's "continuing respect" for the phenomenological method, notwithstanding Husserl's own hostility to the nontranscendental self.[84] But this nontranscendental, natural-embodied subjectivity remains something like the bad conscience of phenomenology; its own descriptions cannot wholly expunge reference to bodily sensation and the sense organs that mediate one's access to the world: "Seeing simply could not be conceived without eyes nor hearing without ears." This is not an opportunistic criticism but rather one that points to a deep contradiction in the way that phenomenology relies on perceptible experience yet also tries to dissociate the naturalistic ground of such experience from "the irreducible *factual* state of the transcendental ego."[85] For Adorno this contradiction already inheres in the idea of the "given" as the boundary line where idealist philosophy both *needs and disavows* the reality of an external world (a point Adorno made the very center-piece of his 1924 doctoral dissertation on Husserl's phenomenology). Just as the naturalistic subject vanishes into the transcendental ego, so too does the external nature by which that subject lives: "The human has value for phenomenology only in its inhumanity, viz. as something completely foreign to man in which he cannot recognize himself. Man becomes immortal through death. Phenomenology mercilessly sequesters meaning and intention *(Meinen und Meinung)* from those who mean and intend; it sequesters the given from the giver and feels it objectively all the more fundamentally secured, the more it forgets existence [*je mehr sie vom Dasein vergessen hat*]."[86]

Husserl's Progress, Heidegger's Regression

Adorno's analysis of the contradictory character of the concept of the given anticipates a major theme of *Negative Dialectics*, where

Adorno will fault phenomenology for its "pseudo-concreteness," a term he borrowed from an essay on Heidegger by Günther (Anders) Stern.[87] In *Against Epistemology*, Adorno wields the similar concept of the "illusory concrete" to explore the antinomies of Husserlian phenomenology in which "the aura of the concrete" carries over into the concept itself. The difficulty is that Husserl imposes a "taboo against facticity" such that the most concrete concepts are "flimsy [*dünn*]." These concepts "feed themselves with ontic elements which are then simply labeled 'pure,' pure consciousness or purely ontological." The Husserlian taboo on all merely empirical elements in epistemology betrays not only a positivistic longing for objectivity but also a philosophical alliance with the antisensualism of the German idealists. "The illusion of the concrete [*Schein des Konkreten*]," writes Adorno, "rests on the reification of results, not unlike positive social science which records the products of social processes as ultimate facts to be accepted. Its metaphysical pathos, however, takes the illusory concrete directly from what is emphatically distant from the fact, viz., that spirituality which is preordained to facticity in ontological idealism as in all German Idealism. No participant in idealism need dirty his hands with those mere entities from which characteristic concepts borrow their tone."[88]

Adorno recognizes that such a "metaphysical pathos" is not unique to modern philosophy. "The illusion of concretization," he grants, "was the *fascinosum* of scholastics, who longed to construe the spiritual as something "intuitable and immediately certain" and who therefore presented concepts as "sensually tinted." But in modern phenomenology this pathos is no longer credible: "The metaphorical, *art nouveau*, purely ornamental quality of such language . . . becomes obvious in Husserl himself in that the sensuousness he claims for thought has no consequences in the philosophical structure." Modern phenomenology thus signifies a crisis stage in philosophy, a final dissolution of the scholastic ambition of understanding worldly incarnation in the concept. Sensual embodiment becomes little more than a language for invoking a prohibited sensuality: "*philosophia perennis* behaves towards undiminished experience as do Unitarians towards religion."[89]

Already in the *Metakritik* (thus well antedating the 1960s) Adorno had coined the now recognizable phrase to characterize this language of "pseudo-concreteness": he calls it "the jargon of authenticity." Phenomenology, writes Adorno, "speaks the jargon of authenticity [*Jargon der Eigentlichkeit*] which meanwhile ruins the whole of cultivated German language and turned it into sacred gibberish. It struck a theological note devoid of theological content, or any other content except self-idolization. It feigns the incarnate presence of the first which is neither incarnate nor present."[90] Adorno's *Jargon of Authenticity,* a book that is chiefly directed against Heidegger and his epigones, was first published in 1964. It is therefore instructive to note that the phrase already makes an appearance in 1956. Beyond any philological interest, however, the use of this polemical phrase in the most capacious sense, embracing not only Husserl but the entire movement of phenomenology (including Heidegger), should remind us that Adorno had philosophical and not merely political motives for his criticism. The jargon of authenticity draws its strength chiefly from the regressive longing to dispense with dialectical mediation and to ground all philosophical speculation in pure immediacy *(Unmittelbarkeit):* "The [Hegelian] doctrine that everything is mediated," Adorno explains, "is irreconcilable with the urge to 'reduction,' and is stigmatized as logical nonsense." This is already the case for Husserlian phenomenology, but "in the schools deriving from Husserl this theme quickly enough turned against all labor and effort of the concept."[91]

Adorno recognizes that according to the "official" and "academic" narrative in Germany ("even before Hitler"), Husserl was condemned as a bourgeois formalist who ignored the pathos of existence and already at the midpoint of his career had grown not just old but obsolete: "Although [Husserl] may have been given credit for the method of the new ontological concreteness, which was supposed to overcome an idealism fallen into disrepute, his service seemed to the condescending estimation as fortuitous as the modest contributions of an empirical scientist to a metaphysical project."[92] It is a major theme of the Husserl book, however, that this official narrative is incorrect, since it inhibits us from seeing the strong continuities between Husserl and his rebellious disciples, and it obstructs our view of those common themes that mark *both* Husserl *and* Heidegger as legatees of idealism. Nor did the pathos of existence, which Heidegger borrowed from Kierkegaard, signal an actual break from the philosophy of consciousness. Although Heidegger ruminates at great length on themes of anxiety, and identifies care among the "pure ways of the being of *Dasein*," such categories make a mere pretense of drawing "close to experience," while in fact they "simply do not connect to the reality of society."[93]

Heidegger no less than Husserl seeks to masquerade themes of contingency as essences, such that nothing impermanent can survive unless it inheres in the very "structure of being." Especially revealing is the term "facticity" itself, which "magically transforms facts into facts that are subsumed under a universal concept" so that the "obstinate facts should no longer resent them." Such alchemy does not achieve an actual breakthrough from idealism to reality; it merely transforms reality into an ideal category. The result is no more convincing than the episode from the Baron von Münchhausen's adventures when he gives himself a yank on his own hair to rescue himself from the swamp. "Drowning phenomenology," writes Adorno, "seeks to pull itself out of the swamp of contemptible mere existence *(Dasein)* by its own essential ponytail [*Wesenzopf*]. Such a fraud provides the factual foundation for the linguistic correspondence with Heidegger. In both, concepts drawn from experience are repeatedly disguised with an antiquated dignity by transplantation into the eidetic realm."[94]

For both Husserl and Heidegger, phenomenology conspires to lift the real into the ideal even when the ideal comes disguised as the real. Yet Adorno nonetheless insists on the distinction between them. Existential ontology (Heidegger) and philosophical anthropology (Scheler) drew instruction from the phenomenological method, but the method's "shipwreck [*Scheitern*]" afforded them space to develop their distinctive philosophical insights: "The fact that pure thought is not the absolutely first in the world, but has its origin in man and corporeal existence, has become a platitude for all those whose 'Anti-Cartesianism' is meant less to analyze concretely the relation between consciousness and being, than to calumniate consciousness itself by appealing to the solidity of the sheer existent [*auf die Härte des bloß Daseienden*]." Adorno does not hesitate to align himself against the rebels and with the founder, whom he extols for keeping "faith [*Treue*]" "despite everything" in "critical [or] 'judicial' reason."[95]

It is one of the neglected ironies in Adorno's critical readings of phenomenology that in the *Metakritik* he adopts a highly polemical tone toward Husserl and yet in the concluding pages when he compares the founder with his student, Adorno credits Husserl for sustaining a certain ideal of progress (however ambivalent) while he condemns Heidegger for regression.[96] It is true, Adorno grants, that in Husserl's thought "reason gets entangled in irresolvable antinomies" because it believes itself "the absolute and total ground of being." The metacritique of idealism annuls the presumptive right of consciousness to rule over being. But the critique of sovereign consciousness does not mean that sovereignty is simply inverted or handed over to existence *(Dasein)*. Rather, "The endless suit which Husserl brings against the absolutely first confutes the very concept of the absolutely first." This is not Husserl's intention, but it is nonetheless *the objective significance of his failure*. "Hence the old guard philosophy of consciousness is, by its objective function, more advanced than *arriviste* philosophers of being [*Seinsphilosophen*]. The latter reverts to the thought of identity, whereas the former ultimately does not of course reach, but does extort [*nicht erreicht zwar, doch erzwingt*] the resolution of the philosophical drive to identity."[97]

Husserlianism, in other words, bears within itself a disavowed truth, the dialectical seed of its own undoing. Heidegger's philosophy, however, seems at first glance to lack this antinomical structure because it willfully abandons reason for the sake of worldly immediacy. Husserlian phenomenology thus pays homage despite itself to the disunity of subject and object and it thereby sustains at least the *possibility* of differentiation. Not so the new ontology, which "casts off the compulsion for system, in order to abruptly appropriate that first for itself which became thoroughly questionable through its universal mediation. Its escape from immanence sacrifices rationality and critique in objective harmony with a society which descends into the darkness of immediate domination." Husserlian phenomenology wishes to make the subjective objective, whereas Heideggerian phenomenology only succeeds in making the objective subjective. Thus "the subjective arbitrariness of the escape avenges itself. It fails." For Adorno this difference is decisive: whereas classical phenomenology advances into contradiction, "resurrected ontology regresses."[98]

The *Metakritik* ends where it began, with a tremendous condemnation of the philosophy of immediacy as a regressive tendency that guarantees an "affinity with domination [*Herrschaft*]." In any philosophical system the subject proclaims power and universality only in contrast to "the enemy, the other, [and] the non-identical." Throughout the history of philosophy the nonidentical has served as the occasion for self-assertion and disdain, "from Plato's curse against ostensibly effeminate musical keys to Heidegger's invective against 'idle talk' (*Gerede*)." The rage against the nonidentical is also a longing for restoration of a primal whole, a nostalgia that authorizes modern persecution. "To its greater glory, the pure concept abuses the more highly developed individual as impure and decay." Modern bureaucratic tyranny is therefore the realization *non plus ultra* of the philosophy of consciousness: "Totalitarian systems have not contrived that saying out of the historical nowhere, but rather brutally executed what ideology for thousands of years had prepared spiritually as the lordship of spirit."[99]

According to Adorno we should not find it paradoxical that fascism as a truly modern political form nonetheless admits of an etiology reaching deep into human prehistory; the awakening of the drive to domination was coterminous with the birth of the human subject. The ambivalent feature of modern tyranny—that it is at once regressive and highly modern—corresponds to the ambivalent meaning of the word *elementary* by which the subject declares itself the origin of the world. "The word 'elementary,'" Adorno observes, "includes both the scientifically simple and the mythologically original. The equivocation is as little an accident as most. Fascism sought to actualize the philosophy of origins." The rise of human subjectivity is therefore, simultaneously, both emancipation *and* unfreedom, both reason *and* unreason. The emergence of the discursive self culminates in an unreflective subjectivism that believes itself immune to rational scrutiny. "With growing demythologization, philosophical concepts become ever more spiritual *and* more mythical."[100] Phenomenology, in other words, is the philosophical sign of a mystified subjectivism; it is but one instance in the broader pattern of reason's regression that Adorno and Horkheimer would later call "the dialectic of enlightenment."

Toward Negative Dialectics

In this chapter we have followed Adorno's path of thinking from the early academic lectures (1931–1932) through the metacritique of phenomenology (completed in 1937, revised and published in 1956). The metacritique itself is especially polemical and one may rightly ask if it does proper justice to Husserl's thought; indeed, Horkheimer himself found its argumentation unconvincing. But this does not wholly explain its relative neglect. These texts are important not least because they reveal much about Adorno's own development as a philosopher, especially at a stage when his own critical insights had yet to reach full maturity. Indeed, we might best think of them as laboratories in which the author conducted a critical testing and experimentation on concepts and arguments that would later emerge in the antisystem of negative dialectics. Already in the methodological introduction of the Husserl book, Adorno insists that his critique strives for "salvation [*Rettung*]" of phenomenology's central ideas.[101]

Such a salvation requires "mindfulness of the suffering that sedimented itself in concepts," and, rather than working for their wholesale destruction, it "waits for the moment of their ruin. It is the idea of philosophical critique. It has no other measure than the ruin of illusion." A critical reading of phenomenology, then, must understand that even its "highest formalisms" and "miscarriages" cannot be dismissed simply as specimens of philosophical error. Rather, a dialectical mode of critical interpretation requires an awareness that "even the decaying concepts of epistemology point beyond themselves [*weisen über sich hinaus*]." Such moments "are to be rescued as a bit of unconscious transcription of history. For they must be helped to procure self-consciousness against what they explicitly mean."[102] As I have already noted in the introduction, immanent critique for Adorno is therefore a form of redemptive criticism: it seeks to discover the signposts in bourgeois philosophy that point toward its own overcoming. In reading Adorno's early philosophical work from the 1930s we must therefore take care to note how it prepares for just such a reversal.[103]

We should pause for a moment to note that Adorno's understanding of a metacritique invites a comparison with Heidegger's idea of a "destruction" (*Destruktion*) of the history of ontology.[104] For Adorno, a metacritique is a method of philosophical interpretation that aims to expose the "unconscious" contradictions and ideological commitments that are hidden within official philosophical doctrines, whereas Heidegger's "destruction" is a method of interpretation that aims to uncover the "unthought" or suppressed insight in official philosophical doctrines of the past. The resemblance is instructive, though it may seem that metacritique and destruction differ in at least one important respect: Adorno's metacritique tends to involve a *materialist* gesture of interpretative suspicion; that is, a given philosophy is shown to have hidden complicities with social and material conditions. Heidegger's destruction, however, avoids virtually any allusion to nonphilosophical social or material conditions—that is, it holds to a strictly philosophical conception of the "unthought" of a given philosophy. Moreover, while both Adorno and Heidegger seek to show that the hidden truth of a philosophical doctrine is precisely the opposite of its manifest claims, for Heidegger this hidden truth only serves to validate his own philosophical perspective. The well-known illustration of Heideggerian destruction is *Kant and the Problem of Metaphysics,* which aims to show that Kant's *Critique of Pure Reason* bears within itself an "unthought" and suppressed insight into a primordial temporality that is deeper than reason itself.[105] For Adorno, however, Husserlian phenomenology suffers from a "self-contradiction" that disables its own philosophical ambitions.

At first glance, the strong language of self-contradiction in *Against Epistemology* might prompt us to conclude that Adorno did not subscribe to anything so extravagant as Heidegger's self-validating idea of an "unthought" thought within a rival philosophy. On closer inspection, however, it turns out that the comparison has considerable merit. Running through the Husserl book from beginning to end is the bold claim that phenomenology wished to break free of constitutive subjectivity and to do so it deployed categories that belong to the subject itself. "In phenomenology," Adorno writes, "the bourgeois spirit strives mightily to break out of the prison of the immanence of consciousness, the sphere of constitutive subjectivity with the help of the same categories [*aus der Gefangenschaft der Bewußtseinsimmanenz, der Sphäre der konstitutiven Subjektivität, auszubrechen mit Hilfe der gleichen Kategorien]* as those implied by the idealistic analysis of the immanence of consciousness."[106]

Now, for those who may feel some impatience with the details of Adorno's metacritique this passage could stand as a summary of its overall complaint: phenomenology, Adorno claims, is symptomatic of an antinomy that afflicts all bourgeois idealist philosophy—namely, a desire to reach out beyond the subject to the object that suffers from self-contradiction since the instruments of this very effort derive from the subject itself.[107] This claim, however, is of great interest insofar as it bears a strong resemblance to a confessional statement from the prologue to *Negative Dialectics*, where Adorno announces his own long-standing ambition to overcome the subject's delusions of absolute mastery without surrendering the subject's own critical energies: "Since the author has trusted himself to follow his own intellectual impulses," Adorno writes, "he felt it to be his task to break through the delusion of constitutive subjectivity by means of the power of the subject [*mit der Kraft des Subjekts den Trug konstitutiver Subjektivität zu durchbrechen*]."[108]

The coincidence between these two passages (the first from Adorno's metacritique of Husserl, the second from *Negative Dialectics*) should not be lightly dismissed. Indeed, the striking resemblance between them may serve as a helpful illustration of my general argument in the present study. Adorno, I am suggesting, would move toward the thought of negative dialectics via a critical reading of phenomenology; and it was precisely the failure of phenomenology to achieve its proposed "breakthrough" from the subject to the object that would help him to grasp "the impossibility of reducing the real to its concept" or "the object to the subject."[109]

The Husserl book, then, merits sustained attention because it represents Adorno's initial attempt both to diagnose the constraints of idealism and to entertain the possibility of breaking through those constraints to reach a new species of materialism. For the purposes of my general argument, this point calls for special emphasis: in striving to break through the illusory power of constitutive subjectivity by means of the subject's own power, Adorno would commit himself to realizing the task at which phenomenology had failed.[110] "To think nonthinking [*Das Nichtdenken denken*]": this was the paradoxical assignment that would lead Adorno to embrace *in thought itself* the thought of what is other than thought. Without abandoning his commitment to philosophy, this adventure would lead Adorno *through* the subject to what he called "the primacy of the object."[111]

3

The Jargon of Authenticity

> The enemy of all illusion, Mahler's music stresses its
> inauthenticity, underlines the fiction inherent in it,
> in order to be cured of the actual falsehood that art
> is starting to be.
>
> —THEODOR W. ADORNO, *Mahler: A Musical Physiognomy*

Existentialism's Aura

In the last years of World War II, Adorno was living with his wife
Gretel in an exotic locale: the Los Angeles neighborhood of Brent-
wood. The environs were unfamiliar but not without solace; the sun-
drenched landscape of Southern California reminded him of Tuscany.[1]
The great number of German intellectuals and artists who had found
refuge in Los Angeles after 1933 earned this community the elegiac
nickname Weimar on the Pacific. In 1945 Adorno was composing the
later sections of his book *Minima Moralia,* which he subtitled *Reflections from Damaged Life.* In a section titled "Gold Assay," he wrote,

> Among the concepts to which, after the dissolution of its religious
> and the formalization of its autonomous norms, bourgeois morality
> has shrunk, that of genuineness ranks highest. If nothing else can be
> bindingly required of man, then at least he should be wholly and
> entirely what he is. In the identity of each individual with himself the

postulate of incorruptible truth, together with the glorification of the factual, are transferred from Enlightenment knowledge to ethics. It is just the critically independent late bourgeois thinkers, sickened by traditional judgments and idealistic phrases, who concur with this view. Ibsen's admittedly violated verdict on the living lie, Kierkegaard's doctrine of existence, have made the ideal of authenticity the centerpiece of metaphysics. In Nietzsche's analysis the word genuine stands unquestioned, exempt from conceptual development. To the converted and unconverted philosophers of fascism, finally, values like authenticity, heroic endurance of the "being-in-the-world" of individual existence, frontier situations, become a means of usurping religious-authoritarian pathos without the least religious content. They lead to the denunciation of anything that is not sufficiently of sterling worth, sound to the core—that is, the Jews.[2]

This passage should hold our attention on several counts. First and most obviously, it is an instructive foray into the speculative history of anti-Semitism. At a time when Adorno and his wife were living amid such a great many refugee intellectuals, both Jewish and non-Jewish, it was altogether natural that he often found himself returning to the question of the place of anti-Semitic prejudice, both in the history of philosophy and in the history of humanity tout court.[3] In *Dialectic of Enlightenment,* the manuscript that Adorno and Horkheimer coauthored during their years of American exile, the phenomenon of anti-Semitism figured as a primary symptom of civilizational repression: because bourgeois rectitude demands both repression and domination of whatever threatens to escape its mastery, the anti-Semite projects the nature he has repressed in himself upon the external figure of the Jew, who is then vilified as a quasi-naturalistic object to be dominated or even destroyed.[4] But anti-Semitism can also invert the contrast between nature and artifice, accusing the Jew of inauthenticity or artful dissimulation. We can therefore understand why the title to Adorno's aphorism in *Minima*

Moralia recalls the technique of a "gold assay," a prospector's test to determine whether gold is true or counterfeit. Adorno concludes the passage (quoted above) with the observation that since at least the nineteenth century anti-Semites have trafficked in an ideologically freighted contrast between nature and artifice: "Did not Richard Wagner already play off genuine German metal against foreign dross," Adorno asks, "and thus misuse criticism of the culture market as an apology for barbarism?"[5]

The attack on artifice or illegitimate currency also alerts us to a second theme that deserves our attention: in the above passage from *Minima Moralia,* Adorno suggests that the anti-Semite's hostility to whatever is not genuine finds ideological justification in the philosophy of existence, which—from Kierkegaard to Heidegger—extols the "authentic" and inveighs against anything that seems to betray even the slightest trace of inauthenticity. It is Kierkegaard most of all who may bear primary responsibility for solidifying the contrast between the authentic and inauthentic. In *The Present Age,* for example, Kierkegaard blamed the "leveling" effect of public life on the dissolution of all difference in an age of "mathematical equality." Though Adorno may have shared Kierkegaard's quasi-sociological lament on the positivistic reduction of quality to quantity, he sharply dissents from Kierkegaard's theological assault on idolatry in the name of the one true faith. For one cannot qualify the unqualified religious commitment that lies at the very core of Kierkegaard's work; after all, Kierkegaard launched the attack on inauthentic Christendom only to defend the honor of an authentic Christianity that Christendom had ostensibly betrayed.[6] But this latter-day assault on idolatry survived the death of God. In "Gold Assay" Adorno proposes that we see the category of authenticity in modern existentialism as a secularized aftereffect of this older, essentially religious contrast. The appeal to authenticity worked only because it has usurped a "religious-authoritarian pathos" while dispensing with any religious content.

The notion of writing an entire study of the cultural significance of existential language seems to have been on Adorno's mind already in the mid-1940s if not well before. His *Kierkegaard: Construction of the Aesthetic* might itself be read as an attempt to dismantle the ideologically fraught contrast between two modes of existence, the merely aesthetic and the genuinely religious. But the robust critique of Heidegger, though implicit in the dissertation, came to the fore only in the postwar era. In his 1951–1952 lecture course, "On the Concept of Philosophy," Adorno referred to the mystifying effects of Heideggerian philosophy when he noted that Heidegger's language "created a theological aura."[7] Adorno was also fond of referring to such language as *Heideggerei* (an insulting term that follows the same form as *Schwärmerei,* or "enthusiasm," which writers of the German Enlightenment used when heaping abuse on religious pietists). In 1959 he wrote to the French literary historian Robert Minder (a specialist on Germany) that "it would be a good idea to tackle the entire phenomenon of 'Heideggerism' for once in a very principled way. In order not to do him an honour that in my view he does not deserve," Adorno explained, "such a critique should not focus on [Heidegger] and his personality, but it should be formulated more as a matter of principle."[8]

Cultural criticism of this sort, of course, was hardly Adorno's primary objective. By 1960 he was already beginning to prepare the composition of what he called "my chief philosophical work," the book that was eventually published in 1966 as *Negative Dialectics.*[9] But during the composition of this larger book Adorno found that its initial sections had grown well beyond their intended proportions, and these early exercises in what he characterized as "linguistic physiognomy" and "sociology" did not suit the chiefly philosophical character of the larger project.[10] Having published some of these sections in *Neue Rundschau* in 1963, he then published a separate book the following year under the title *The Jargon of Authenticity.*[11]

Satire and Secularization

No one could doubt that this little book is an exercise in polemic as much as it is a specimen of philosophical critique. Adorno's biographer Stefan Müller-Doohm notes that, at an evening event in November 1964 when Adorno presented sections of the book before an audience, his reading "was frequently punctuated by laughter and applause."[12] This should not come as a surprise, since the book is composed in a style that often resorts to dry wit—though it is a wit interlaced with poison. Indeed, *The Jargon of Authenticity* belongs to that special genre of essays in cultural critique in which Adorno offered lacerating and often satirical reflections on the debased sphere of the mass commodity. Other works in this same category might include the "Theses against Occultism" and the critique of the *Los Angeles Times* astrology column.[13]

But what distinguishes this book from other exercises in cultural criticism is the zeal with which its author set about demolishing existentialism. The chief explanation for its unusual vigor is that in Adorno's eyes the movement of existentialism, in both its German and French variations, could be properly understood only if it were treated simultaneously as both a philosophical trend *and* a popular fashion. In *The Jargon of Authenticity* he attacked it on both of these fronts and ultimately refused any saving gesture that would might help to isolate the official philosophy from its own debased expression. Müller-Doohm records the fact that the respected Tübingen philosopher Otto Friedrich Bollnow (the author of numerous studies in existentialism and a long-standing student of Heidegger's) felt the sting of Adorno's pen.[14] In a December 1964 letter to Herbert Marcuse, Adorno wrote, "Ernst Bloch phoned to say that because of the 'Jargon' Bollnow is having a nervous breakdown. Let him."[15]

The scandalous memory of Heidegger's support for the Third Reich, along with the readiness of postwar intellectuals to whitewash the German philosopher's record, no doubt helps to explain the vehemence with which Adorno set about dismantling the general phenomenon of postwar *Heideggerei*. But Adorno was not the only critic of authoritarian and pseudomystical trends in the German language. Indeed, *The Jargon of Authenticity* bears a more than superficial resemblance to the 1947 book *LTI—Lingua Tertii Imperii*, the penetrating analysis of National Socialist Party rhetoric that the philologist Victor Klemperer had composed during the war.[16] With anatomical skill, Klemperer had dissected the barbarism of Nazi metaphor and style, taking special note of the regime's antipathy for reason and intellectual abstraction, its preference for concreteness, and its celebration of intuition *(Anschauung)* as a medium for "essence" and "soul."[17]

In the text of *Jargon,* however, direct allusions to the Nazi era were few, and its arrows were aimed at a far broader target than Heideggerian philosophy alone. Its real objective was to expose a certain kind of vulgarized and thoughtless existentialism that had come to pervade too much of postwar German culture, from the university lecture halls to the corporate boardroom. It may be that Adorno exaggerated this point for polemical effect: the greater share of his illustrations for the jargon were drawn not from everyday life but from well-known philosophical works by Heidegger and Jaspers. But Adorno was careful to note that even while the jargon appeared "irresistible," it was in fact remarkably weak, and if exposed would suffer an easy defeat: "The fact that the jargon has become an ideology unto itself destroys this ideology as soon as this fact is recognized." For laughter is often the best weapon against authoritarian sobriety (a Nietzschean truism that gains renewed truth when one recalls Charlie Chaplin's mockery of Hitler in the 1940 film *The Great Dictator*). The book's satirical technique would therefore suffice, or so Adorno hoped, to embarrass those who trafficked in the jargon and thus bring about their downfall. "Even followers who believe in authority," he explained, "will shy away from ridiculous-ness as soon as they feel the fragile nature of that authority to which they look for support."[18]

The technique of satire also carried an echo of an earlier age. Adorno, still committed despite his pessimism to the critical promise of Enlightenment reason, may have modeled his effort after the great satires of the Enlightenment, when humor had once served to puncture the delicate balloons of sacred authority. His own exercise in satire served a similar purpose, since the jargon was quite clearly a species of secularized religion. It carried an unmistakable odor of piety that granted its practitioners the sham dignity of this-worldly priests. But between the traditional religion criticized by the philos-ophes and the pseudoreligion analyzed by Adorno there was an important difference. Over the span of two centuries, an allusive and largely aesthetic *disposition* had supplanted the tangible and historically resonant patterns of religious tradition itself. This shift—from conventional religion to its postconventional simulacrum—distinguished genuine theists such as Kierkegaard from all of his posttheistic epigones. Adorno's book opens with a recollection of such pseudoreligious groups with which he was obviously familiar from his own early years as a philosophy student at the University of Frankfurt:

In the early twenties a number of people active in philosophy, sociology, and theology, planned a gathering. Most of them had shifted from one creed to another. Their common ground was an emphasis on a newly acquired religion, and not the religion itself. All of them were unsatis-fied with the idealism which at that time still dominated the universities. Philosophy swayed them to choose, through freedom and autonomy, a positive theology such as had already appeared in Kierkegaard. However, they were less interested in the specific doctrine, the truth content of revelation, than in conviction. . . . Heretics dubbed this circle the authentics [*Ketzer tauften den Kreis die Eigentlichen*].[19]

A key to Adorno's satirical work, then, is the claim that the jargon could not have been possible were it not for the historical decay of traditional religion. Flourishing only since Kierkegaard and thus coincident with the rise of an increasingly rationalized society, the rise of the jargon followed upon the process of secularization: "The theological freeing of the numinous from ossified dogma has, ever since Kierkegaard, involuntarily come to mean its partial secularization."[20] This process especially touched Kierkegaard's subjectivist model of religion. Ironically, however, the trend of secularization radicalized his subjectivism only to produce an objectified jargon that circulated throughout mass culture, thereby confirming the reified solidity of a mindless consensus. This was subjectivism objectified, a bogus currency that presented itself as genuine experience. A modern culture now highly skilled in the techniques of commercial promotion supplanted traditional piety with its mimetic changeling. To express this historical condition Adorno appended to his book an epigram from Samuel Beckett's *The Unnamable:* "Il est plus facile d'élever un temple que d'y faire descendre l'objet du culte [It is easier to build a temple than to make the object of worship reveal itself within]."[21]

According to Adorno, Heidegger was not the progenitor of the jargon; its seedlings had germinated decades before, in the fin de siècle archaism of *Jugendstil* and in the high-minded rhapsodies of German lyric poetry that culminated with Rilke. But in Adorno's view it was Heidegger alone who was singularly responsible for transposing the jargon's contents from the register of pseudotheology into a this-worldly language of "authenticity":

> Throughout his work [*Being and Time*] Heidegger employed "authenticity" in the context of an existential ontology, as a specifically philosophical term. Thus in philosophy he molded that which the authentics strive for less theoretically, and in that way he won over to his side all those who had some vague reaction to that philosophy. Through him,

denominational demands became dispensable. His book acquired its aura by describing the dark drives of the intelligentsia before 1933—directions which he described as full of insight, and which he revealed to be solidly coercive. Of course in Heidegger, as in all those who followed his language, a diminished theological resonance can be heard to this day. . . . Nevertheless, the sacred quality of the authentics' talk belongs to the cult of authenticity rather than to the Christian cult, even where—for temporary lack of any other available authority—its language resembles the Christian.[22]

These opening remarks on the path of secularization from Kierkegaard to Heidegger furnished the historical background for the polemic that followed. The book's basic conceit was that the jargon only secured a true footing in German culture once Kierkegaard's concept of religion as subjectivity had torn itself free from its theological referent. "What remains after the removal of existential bombast," Adorno explained, "are religious customs cut off from their religious content." The consequence was a repertoire of dispositions—a "mere attitude" and an assortment of terms and allusions that could attach itself to anything so long as the attachment displayed sufficient conviction. "The jargon," he wrote, "secularizes the German readiness to view men's positive relation to religion as something immediately positive, even when the religion has disintegrated and been exposed as something untrue. The undiminished irrationality of rational society encourages people to elevate religion into an end in itself, without regard to its content: to view religion as a mere attitude, as a quality of subjectivity. All this at the cost of religion itself."[23]

The jargon of authenticity thus represented the reduction—or, in other words, an illicit transfer—of sacred predicates from their divine referent to the immanent world: "Once the original theological image has fallen, transcendence, which in the great religions is separated from the likeness by powerful taboos—thou shalt have no graven images of me—is shifted to the likeness. This image is then said to be full of wonder, since wonders no longer exist." Animating this argument, however, was Adorno's own barely stated and persistent investment in the theistic categories he considered obsolete. To be sure, Adorno felt that in the contemporary world religion had surrendered its objective validity as a category of metaphysics or experience. Nevertheless, as we have seen in the early reading of Kierkegaard, he adhered to a paradoxical mode of reasoning that (in a 1934 letter to Benjamin) he had characterized as an "inverse theology." I will return to this theme in Chapter 5; for now it will suffice to note that much of the force of Adorno's critique of the jargon was due to the way it appealed negatively—and *only* negatively—to a theological truth the jargon had ostensibly debased. Throughout his life Adorno would permit himself to pay homage to this negative truth only on the rarest of occasions, and, in the text of the *Jargon* where the negative task of polemic remains dominant, we can catch a glimpse of it only in a very few passages. But its meaning is clear. In condemning the jargon as a species of idolatry, Adorno appealed counterfactually to the holiness it betrayed: "A profane language," he explained, "could only approach the sacred one by distancing itself from the sound of the holy, instead of by trying to imitate it. The jargon transgresses this rule blasphemously."[24]

Unanswered in Adorno's polemic was the question as to why even such a distant appeal to the sacred would retain any validity in a profane age. Further reflection on the theological implications of such an argument must await another occasion. Here it will suffice to note that Adorno's condemnation of the jargon as an *illicit* secularization of the religious aura does not logically require his prior commitment to the religion that has been debased. It only requires that he condemn the jargon for borrowing contents that might have once held a redemptive meaning. "Previously," Adorno observes, "the unbearable transience of a false and unsatisfied life was counteracted by theology, which gave hope to an eternal life. This hope disappears in the praise of the transient as absolute."[25]

The critique of existentialism's pseudoreligious veneration of the quotidian recalls an earlier moment in Weimar-era controversy surrounding the Buber-Rosenzweig translation of the Hebrew Bible into German, a project that both Walter Benjamin and Siegfried Kracauer regarded with some skepticism and which prompted Kracauer's deeply critical review in the pages of the left-liberal daily *Frankfurter Zeitung*. The Buber-Rosenzweig Bible, Kracauer claimed, represented an exercise in self-conscious archaism that "only pretends to be sacred and esoteric" even while aping the mannerisms of the George-Kreis (George Circle).[26] Kracauer himself later makes a cameo appearance in *Jargon of Authenticity* when Adorno (in the passage quoted above) mentions an unnamed friend, presumably Kracauer, who was not permitted to attend the quasi-religious meetings of "anti-intellectual intellectuals" in the 1920s: the initiates apparently felt that Kracauer had "hesitated before Kierkegaard's leap" and thereby betrayed the shameful truth that he was "not authentic enough."[27]

As Adorno explained, the object that the jargon wished to decorate with a sacred halo was nothing other than human existence itself. In taking Kierkegaard's philosophy of subjectivity and erasing its religious meaning, Heidegger and his epigones assured that nothing else would remain as a horizon of sanctification but the "mineness" that was ostensibly the only site from which to practice phenomenology. The methodological pediment for phenomenological description was thereby smuggled into an ostensibly nonmetaphysical philosophy, gracing the human being with the halo of a vanished metaphysics. "The angel's voices with which the jargon registers the word 'Man,' are derived by the jargon from the doctrine of man as the image of God," Adorno explained. "The word "Man" sounds all the more irrefutable and persuasive the more it seals itself off against its theological origin." This movement—from creator to creation—accounted for the strangely devotional attitude with which the jargon approached mere contingency. Whereas one could have imagined that the collapse of religious metaphysics would have plunged the entire world into sheer unholiness it was the cunning of the jargon to ward off this scenario: "The jargon," Adorno concluded, "sanctifies [the] everyday world."[28]

This thesis—which we might call an idea concerning "false" secularization of the sacred—also permitted Adorno to draw upon the memorable analysis of the aura by his late friend and mentor Walter Benjamin, who recognized that the aura's dissolution in a technological age brought not only emancipatory possibilities but also political risks. Communism, Benjamin explained, took advantage of desacralized art and deployed the wholly modern promise of technical reproduction to mobilize the masses, whereas fascism used the authoritarianism and atavistic qualities of the aura to *resacralize* its own modern political movement and it thereby reduce the masses to a condition of spectatorial passivity. Fascism was therefore an aestheticized politics. Adorno's own analysis of the jargon offers an elaboration and modification of Benjamin's claims, for the chief effect of the jargon is to impose a quasi-sacred aesthetic on social conditions that are in fact wholly disenchanted: "The fact that the words of the jargon sound as if they said something higher than what they mean suggests the term 'aura,'" Adorno wrote. "As words that are sacred without sacred content, as frozen emanations, the terms of the jargon of authenticity are *products of the disintegration of the aura*."[29] The jargon, in other words, only came on the scene once the gods had fled. But in its effort to obscure this condition the jargon required that its agents devote themselves to an unreflective repetition of its sublime phrases. "The perpetual charge against reification," Adorno explained, "is itself reified." In this way the atavistic struggle to reenchant the disenchanted world was itself just as mindless as the world it opposed. "Those who have run out of holy spirit," Adorno concluded, "speak with mechanical tongues."[30]

"The Wurlitzer Organ of the Spirit"

Benjamin's analysis of fascism as aestheticized politics served as an instructive model for Adorno's own theory of the jargon. For the basic conception of the jargon, as a *secular* pseudoreligion, also implied that the jargon was a purely *modern* phenomenon, notwithstanding the fact that it often traded in atavistic or antimodern imagery and conjured up romanticized notions of long-vanished forms of artisanal and pastoral life. Such imagery only confirmed for Adorno that the jargon was a reflex of nostalgia that bore witness through negation to the irresistible power of industrial society. The jargon, he observed, was "a waste product of the modern that it attacks."[31]

The argument for seeing the jargon as an altogether *modern* phenomenon occasioned some of Adorno's most withering and humorous comparisons—especially the comparison to advertising. It may be helpful to recall that *Jargon* was composed during the 1960s in the midst of the so-called economic miracle, the resurgence of production and consumerism financed by the Marshall Plan and buttressed by an ideology of Cold War competition that helped to transform postwar West Germany from a land of rubble into an industrial and commercial giant.[32] As a young man in the 1920s, Adorno had already witnessed the power of advertising techniques that left their imprint everywhere on forms of entertainment and on the cityscapes of both Frankfurt and Berlin. In some of his earliest criticism of commercial music, for example (its internal "fetishism" and the consequent "regression" of the subjects who consumed it), Adorno remarked on the way in which the "advertising function" had become the internal and formal characteristic of the culture industry, especially in popular music and commercial jazz.[33]

By the 1940s Adorno came to believe that fascism, too, owed much of its success to techniques first developed in advertising (such as the use of mass-produced logos and carefully crafted appeals to personal satisfaction) along with the "repetition of designated words" that magically invoked states of personal and collective bliss. "The blind and rapidly spreading repetition of designated words links advertising to the totalitarian slogan," Adorno observed. "The layer of experience which made words human like those who spoke them has been stripped away, and in its prompt appropriation language takes on the coldness which hitherto was peculiar to billboards and the advertising sections of newspapers."[34]

In Adorno's view, the jargon of authenticity functioned in a manner similar to popular music and fascist propaganda, stereotyping and hollowing out the subjectivity it claimed to preserve. Even when it assumed the rarefied status of an existential "ontology," the jargon betrayed the "musty instincts of petty-bourgeois kitsch." As illustrations Adorno named popular brands of alcohol. The jargon, he wrote, "becomes practicable along the whole scale, reaching from sermon to advertising. In the medium of the concept the jargon becomes surprisingly similar to the habitual practices of advertising. The words of the jargon and those like *Jägermeister, Alte Klosterfrau, Schänke,* are all of a piece. They exploit the happiness promised by that which had to pass on to the shadows. Blood is drawn from that which has its appearance of concreteness only after the fact, by virtue of its downfall."[35]

As a functional analogue to commercial music and fascist propaganda, the jargon thus served to degrade the human being even while making the deeply felt longing for authenticity the very cornerstone of its appeal. Just as commercial jazz promoted itself as a vehicle for spontaneous human expression while reinforcing the mere stereotyping of this expression, so too jargon served as a ready-made lexicon of magical terms for genuine existence, even while the repetition of those terms became standardized and hopelessly unreflective. This was the logic behind Adorno's truly wicked remark that the jargon was "the Wurlitzer organ of the spirit." Within the context of Adorno's broader argument the comparison made some sense: "For advertising purposes," Adorno explained, "the Wurlitzer organ humanizes the vibrato, once a carrier of subjective expression, by mechanically superimposing it on the mechanically produced sound. The jargon likewise supplies men with patterns for being human, patterns which have been driven out of them by unfree labor."[36]

The Miserable Consolation of Self-Identity

No doubt many readers would reject the comparison between the jargon of authenticity and modern advertising as not only excessively polemical but also philosophically adventitious. Adorno's self-acknowledged antipathy toward Heidegger and the broader fashion of postwar existentialism surely predisposed Adorno to see the jargon as a mere instrument of social rigidity rather than entertaining the question of its possible merit within the confines of formal philosophical systems. But as we will see in Chapter 4, Adorno's antipathies did not prevent him from reading Heidegger's philosophy for its inner argumentation as well. The purposes of the *Jargon* book, however, were chiefly sociological, as Adorno clearly admitted in the prefatory note. We might therefore consider Adorno's decision to publish the *Jargon* separately from *Negative Dialectics* as a sign of his enduring belief in the genre distinction between external (or sociocultural) critique and a mode of philosophical interpretation that entails a frontal engagement with arguments. Indeed, to collapse these two strategies of reading entirely would have left Adorno vulnerable to the charge of sociological reductionism, a method that would "extirpate, with the false, all that was true also."[37] Still, it would nevertheless be a methodological violation of Adorno's own theoretical stance to distinguish too sharply between philosophical and sociological criticism, as if mind could be dissociated utterly from the world. With this proviso we must explore the ways in which the social analysis served as an illustration for a genuinely philosophical critique.

Most important, the comparison to advertising helped to illustrate the socially affirmative status of the jargon, reinforcing Adorno's basic verdict that existentialism remains caught in a species of identity theory. Insofar as identity theory involves the ideological collapse of any distinction between subject and object, it forecloses upon the possibility of a critical stance toward existing conditions. Identity theory is therefore intrinsically *affirmative:* it effaces negativity and solidifies the prison walls of an integrated society.[38] Recalling a comparison he had introduced in his Frankfurt lectures on "The Actuality of Philosophy," Adorno proposed an analogy between the jargon and positivism, both of them philosophical-ideological formations that affirmed the world merely as it is: "The highest maxim of such an attitude results in saying that 'it is so,' that one has to obey—or, in positivistic terms, that one has to adapt oneself. This is that pathetic commandment that he must obey that which is. It is not even really obeying, for in any case Dasein does not have a choice."[39]

The hidden complicity between existentialism and positivism best reveals itself in their shared view of language as something "archaic" that contains remnants of its origins in myth. The difference is that positivism would prefer to expel this mythical remainder so as to forge a scientific and quasi-mathematical language in which the world would reveal itself with undistorted immediacy, whereas the jargon wishes to preserve this mythical remainder for the sake of a similar immediacy that they feel science has destroyed. The two philosophies converge, however, in their undialectical understanding of language because neither of them appreciates its *critical* and *demythologizing* relation to the world it grasps. Both see chiefly its mythical dimension only from opposing sides: "What the positivists bewail as retrogressive," Adorno explained, "the authentics eternalize as a blessing."[40]

In sacralizing the given state of affairs, the jargon therefore positivistically degenerates into sentences whose structure appears nearly tautological. Adorno did not mention the most famous cases from Heidegger—"the world worlds," and "the nothing nothings"—although such phrases (which also drew the ridicule of the logical positivist Rudolf Carnap) might have illustrated his point.[41] Instead Adorno fastened his attention on passages in which Heidegger seemed determined to affirm little more than the self-identity of the human being. Such was the case in a passage from Heidegger's 1936 essay, "Hölderlin and the Essence of Poetry" which informs us that "Man is he, who he is, precisely in testifying to his own *Dasein*."[42] These and similar cases illustrated the conceptual dilemma into which the jargon rushed headlong once it had disenchanted Kierkegaard's originally religious gesture of decision: "The distinction between authenticity and inauthenticity—the real Kierkegaardian one—depends on whether or not this element of being, Dasein, chooses itself, its mineness." Once again Adorno saw secularization as the birth process for the jargon of authenticity. With Heidegger the subject is detached from any relation to a being higher than itself—except, of course, for its relation with the being that belongs to its own manner of being. *Dasein* could no longer be distinguished from its surroundings on any basis other than the fact of its own subjective relation to itself: "The fact that Dasein belongs to itself, that it is "in each case mine," is picked out from individuation as the only general definition that is left over after the dismantling of the transcendental subject and its metaphysics."[43]

For Adorno, then, the methodological premise of Heideggerian phenomenology—that *Dasein* is in each case characterized by "mineness [*Jemeinigkeit*]"—only encouraged an affirmative and conformist stance on present conditions. Because *Dasein* was both facticity and a manner of being, both ontic and ontological, its relation to itself was subsumed under its own *Seinsverständnis:* it existed only in virtue of its understanding of being. But this meant that Heidegger's philosophy, notwithstanding the fact that it was meant to be a philosophy of this-worldly existence, ended in the cul-de-sac of self-affirmative idealism. For this reason Adorno saw Heidegger as a philosopher of identity whose appeals to the unity between *Dasein* and its world served merely as a ruse for elevating *Dasein* into the evacuated space of theological sovereignty. The world surrendered the last traces of its nonidentity and thereby became *Dasein*'s absolute dominion. "Identity thinking," wrote Adorno, "would have swallowed up the non-identical element, the existent, which the word Dasein intends. Thus Heidegger secretly reinstates the creator quality of the absolute subject, which was supposedly avoided, as it were, by starting with mineness in each case. The notion of the double character of Dasein, as ontic and ontological, expels Dasein from itself. This is Heidegger's disguised idealism."[44]

If one recalls Heidegger's explicit emphasis on the "ontological difference" (that is, the difference between Being and beings), the charge that Heidegger upholds identity over difference may seem counterintuitive. According to Adorno, however, the drive to proclaim Being as the underlying condition or *transcendens* for being (including *Dasein*) had the effect of reaffirming a principle of holism as the very logic of the ontological difference. Robbed of its worldly prestige, *Dasein* was thereby restored to the unifying horizon of the *Seinsverständnis.* The idealistic and self-identical character of *Dasein* culminated in what Adorno called the "miserable consolation" of self-affirmation. Isolated by the anticipatory phenomenon of being-toward-death, *Dasein* rediscovered itself as a unity dissociated from the social world. Lacking any external support, *Dasein* was expected to take comfort in the tautological affirmation of itself *as* the being it already is: "The societal relation, which seals itself off in the identity of the subject, is de-socialized into an in-itself. The individual, who himself can no longer rely on any firm possession, holds on to himself in his extreme abstractness as the last, the supposedly un-losable possession. Metaphysics ends in a miserable consolation: after all, one still remains what one is."[45]

For Heidegger, as for his epigones, the pseudodecision *to be what one already is* functioned as a conservative ideology: the normative affirmation of what is deemed factually inevitable. For Adorno, however, such an affirmation was vacuous, since it conferred an aura of ideological satisfaction on any condition without imposing any demand for change. "Since men do not remain what they are by any means, neither socially or biologically, they gratify themselves with the stale reminder of self-identity as something which gives distinction, both in regard to being and meaning." This was the gratification of a modern subjectivity that has grown so impoverished it can imagine no higher ambition than the Nietzschean injunction to "become what you are." From Adorno's perspective, this is hardly an ideal but in fact that very *absence* of an ideal. In the jargon of authenticity, "what man is anyway once more becomes his goal."[46] Regarding the question as to what *sort* of identity might deserve normative assent the jargon has no answer.[47] It remains at such a level of formalism that it can affirm any condition and any identity—even that of a torturer "to the extent that he was simply a true torturer."[48]

Grace and Dignity

As we have seen, Adorno's polemic regarding the jargon of authenticity begins with the premise that it originated as a modern and secularized variant of the Kierkegaardian subject, the "knight of faith" who decides upon the right life in the absence of any and all objective criteria.[49] The secularization of this ideal devolved into a thoughtless affirmation of what is given merely *as* it is given—a denouement in which Adorno saw the ironic convergence of existentialism with positivism. But there is one further dimension to the jargon that deserves mention: this is the theme of self-mastery and its relation to the domination of nature.

In *Dialectic of Enlightenment,* Adorno and Horkheimer had claimed that human emancipation from the terror and mindlessness of our enslavement to nature was achieved only at the cost of self-mutilation, and, eventually, self-negation. We gain our freedom from nature only by dominating our own natural being. Self-determination is therefore simultaneously self-domination; and the metaphysical apotheosis of the self ends in its dissolution. The rationality we use to wrest ourselves free of nature becomes the instrumental reason that organizes all of human society. This is the ironic denouement of the history of enlightenment, a pattern of thought traceable to the very origins of human consciousness and culture. Even our most primitive systems of magic and mythology, for example, were originally attempts to anthropomorphize and thereby gain some measure of control over our natural surroundings. But as it grew in power and sophistication the Enlightenment gradually dismantled these anthropomorphic projections as well, until nature was fully disenchanted. The fully enlightened world is therefore also a fully administered world: nature presents itself to the modern subject as little more than a meaningless and fungible substratum upon which reason can thoughtlessly exercise its authority. But the triumph of unreflective reason locks us into gestures of fatalistic repetition that ironically resemble the myths reason aimed to destroy. The Enlightenment that once promised freedom as its highest ideal has ended by creating a human world in which freedom is little more than a counterfactual hope.[50]

Although Adorno completed *The Jargon of Authenticity* no less than two decades after he and Horkheimer had composed the initial drafts of *Dialectic of Enlightenment,* the two works show a remarkable continuity in argumentation. According to Adorno, one of the major ironies of the jargon of authenticity is that it disguises its bourgeois-ideological strategies of social conformity as gestures of dissent: the pastoral imagery and nostalgic appeals to artisanal practice all conspire to affirm what Heidegger called "the splendor of the simple," as if such simplicity promised an authentic release from the rationalistic constraints of modernity.[51] The jargon's rueful remarks on "curiosity" and "homelessness" only solidify the impression that Heidegger is at heart a convinced antimodernist who admires the reticent farmers of the countryside and feels nothing but disdain for the "rootless intellectual" who wears the "yellow mark" signifying an antipathy to the established order.[52] But according to Adorno it would be a mistake to assume that this impression captures the objective social meaning of the jargon. For, in fact, antimodernism is little more than manufactured rhetoric that labors in service to the rationalized order. "The bourgeois form of rationality," Adorno explains, "has always needed irrational supplements, in order to maintain itself as what it is, continuing injustice through justice. Such irrationality in the midst of the rational is the working atmosphere of authenticity."[53] Heidegger's apparent antimodernism was therefore little more than a symptom of his own modernity.

The ideological function of the jargon becomes readily apparent once we consider its treatment of death. According to Adorno, the existential effort to discover a superior meaning in death is actually an attempt to "cleanse death of its misery and stench." In other words, it represents "the integration of death into hygiene." But this means that Heidegger is guilty of the same sin of which he accuses the inauthentic: "By means of authenticity of death as he flees from it."[54] The objective meaning of the jargon is therefore the *opposite* of its manifest pathos: the injunction that *Dasein* should confront death as its "ownmost possibility" is in fact an injunction to conform to the imperatives of social rationalization. "Death is sublimated because of a blinded drive for self-preservation; its terror is part of the sublimation."[55] What Adorno means to say here is that, in wresting a higher and ostensibly "philosophical" significance from the fact of our mortality, existential ontology is actually trying to achieve a kind of mastery over the unmasterable. Even Heidegger's famous analysis of *Angst* as *Dasein*'s anxiety when faced with the possibility of its own nothingness displays an erudite will to sublimate by converting fear into meaning. But any such sublimation is therefore one chapter in the history of bourgeois self-mastery. Heidegger's analysis of death, then, only serves to reinforce an ethic of antisensual renunciation. In the movement from death to authenticity, *Dasein* learns the punishing lesson that survival requires the sublimation of one's own nature: "self-control is hypostatized" as the very meaning of subjectivity.[56] But this means that the jargon does not offer a genuine release from modernity; it only works as a faithful servant to the dialectic of enlightenment.

In the closing pages of *Jargon,* Adorno drives home precisely this point with a brief commentary on the well-known 1793 essay by Friedrich Schiller, "Über Anmut und Würde" (On grace and dignity). Although Schiller drew inspiration from Kantian aesthetics and morality, he had objected to Kant's ideal of dignity, which seemed to require (in Adorno's phrase) a kind of "self-seclusion" or "self-securing [*in sich selbst Verschließen oder Festmachen*]"; instead Schiller proposed that the highest perfection of the human being would be one in which nature and morality would act in harmony. "True dignity," Schiller observed,

> is content to prevent the domination of the affections, to keep the instinct within just limits, but there only where it pretends to be master in the involuntary movements; false dignity regulates with an iron scepter even the voluntary movements, it oppresses the moral movements, which were sacred to true dignity, as well as the sensual movements, and destroys all the mimic play of the features by which the soul gleams forth upon the face. It arms itself not only against rebel nature, but against submissive nature, and ridiculously seeks its greatness in subjecting nature to its yoke, or if this does not succeed, in hiding it. As if it had vowed hatred to all that is called nature, it

swathes the body in long, heavy-plaited garments, which hide the human structure; it paralyses the limbs in surcharging them with vain ornaments, and goes even the length of cutting the hair to replace this gift of nature by an artificial production. True dignity does not blush for nature, but only for brute nature; it always has an open and frank air; feeling gleams in its look; calm and serenity of mind is legible upon the brow in eloquent traits. . . . True dignity wishes only to rule, not to conceal nature; in false dignity, on the contrary, nature rules the more powerfully within because it is controlled outwardly."[57]

Schiller's distinction between true and false dignity presumed that dignity did not require the *full* renunciation of natural instincts but rather permitted their expression within just and proper limits. Adorno, however, reads this essay against the grain, suggesting that Schiller failed to recognize the instability of this distinction: the idea that dignity requires a "rule" of the self over its own nature only prepared the ground for nature's thoroughgoing domination. "Dignity," in other words, "contains the form of its decadence within itself." This argument obviously serves as one instance of that pan-historical process that Adorno and Horkheimer diagnosed as the dialectic of enlightenment. Once we recognize this dialectic, Adorno concludes, we can discern the historical and logical complicity between the graceful ideal of late eighteenth-century morality and the late modern existentialist ideal of self-possession. The taming of instinct implies its renunciation, just as the ennoblement of death implies a more rationalized administration of life: "The Kantian dignity finally disintegrates into the jargon of authenticity."[58]

The basic thrust of this interpretation is to undo Schiller's apologetic distinction between true and false dignity, by showing that what passes for only a taming of instinct in eighteenth-century ideals of personal comportment only prepares the way for the thoroughgoing repression of nature that modern society demands. According to Adorno the jargon of authenticity is best understood as high-minded propaganda for this very same ethic of repression. Masquerading as a rebellion against the constraining forces of instrumental reason, existentialism is in truth its secret ally, controlling and ultimately conspiring to destroy the "mimetic play" of nature that Schiller had once extolled.

Endgame as Negative Ontology

Anticipating arguments in both *The Jargon of Authenticity* and *Negative Dialectics,* Adorno developed some of his strongest philosophical reflections on existentialism in his readings of Beckett, whose work he deeply admired and whose uncompromising aesthetic of catastrophe would furnish crucial illustrative material in *Aesthetic Theory.*[59] (We should recall that Adorno had actually planned to dedicate *Aesthetic Theory* to Beckett.[60]) It was partly through his interpretation of Beckett's work that Adorno came to formulate the basic axiom that "art can only be reconciled with its existence by exposing its own semblance, its internal emptiness." This axiom was grounded in Adorno's stringent antiutopianism, which saw the administered world as so powerful as to inhibit any critical perspective beyond its own bounds: "Art emigrates to a standpoint that is no longer a standpoint at all," Adorno observed, "because there are no longer standpoints from which the catastrophe could be named." The loss of any external perspective obviates the possibility of a "message" or "content" even when the message offers only the bleak message of existential meaninglessness. This principle reached its consummation in Beckett's *oeuvre*: "In all art that is still possible," Adorno explained, "social critique must be raised to the level of form, to the point that it wipes out all manifestly social content."[61]

Such arguments first came into view in early December 1960, when Adorno had finished a draft of the "Trying to Understand *Endgame,*" part of which he presented in February 1961 as an evening lecture for the Suhrkamp Verlag (and which was published later that year in the second volume of his *Notes to Literature*).[62] The essay merits our attention here because it offers a vigorous rejoinder to contemporary opinions in Adorno's day that ranked Beckett alongside Sartre and Ionesco as an "existential" playwright, notwithstanding the fact that Sartre himself had expressed serious reservations regarding the ostensibly "bourgeois" content of Beckett's work.[63] To Adorno, *Endgame* defeats any such attempts to assign it an existential meaning, for the crucial reason that it resists the very expectation of meaningful content.[64] "Objectively and without any polemical intent," Adorno explained, Beckett's play offers an answer to "existential philosophy, which under the name of "thrownness" and later of "absurdity" transforms senselessness [*Sinnlosigkeit*] itself into sense [*Sinn*], exploiting the equivocations inherent in the concept of sense. To this Beckett juxtaposes no world view, rather he takes it [senselessness] at its word." Eschewing the formality of philosophical argument, Beckett demonstrates the "calamity" of a world in which "sense" has actually become senseless. "Being, trumpeted by existential philosophy as the meaning of being [*Sinn von Sein*] becomes its antithesis. Panic fear of the reflex movements of living entities does not only drive untiringly toward the domination of nature: it also attaches itself to life as the ground of that calamity which life has become."[65]

As Lambert Zuidervaart has explained, Adorno discerned a truthful relation between the senselessness of Beckett's plays and the senseless irrationality of contemporary society.[66] Alongside this dialectical interrogation of meaninglessness, however, Beckett also offered an indirect critique of existentialism's ideological attempt to transform meaninglessness into meaning. As a last bid for subjective survival, existentialism placed special emphasis on the heroism and absurdity of the authentic individual. Echoing the argument from *Jargon* that existentialism breeds both conformism and the domination of nature, Adorno claimed that *Endgame*, with greater efficacy than any explicitly philosophical argument, achieves nothing less than the undoing of existentialism itself. This was an argument that would be developed at length only in *Negative Dialectics,* where Adorno would argue that existentialism, in both its Heideggerian and Sartrean forms, cleaves *malgré lui* to a species of subjective idealism: "sense" is given to the phenomenological ego within the privileged sphere of "mineness [*Jemeinigkeit*]" that distinguishes its experience of the world.

This claim is anticipated already in the essay on Beckett. For even as the phenomenological theme of sense is bowdlerized into existential "senselessness" it retains the aura of universal "meaning," and this last-ditch effort to recuperate meaning through meaninglessness explains existentialism's popularity as a skeleton key for aesthetic critics who still crave moralizing lessons in art. In Beckett's case, however, the drive to extract a universal content proves fruitless: "Absurdity in Beckett is no longer a state of human existence thinned out to a mere idea and then expressed in images." This is because Beckett does not make absurdity into an *idea.* "Absurdity is divested of that generality of doctrine which existentialism, that creed of the permanence of individual existence, nonetheless combines with Western pathos of the universal and the immutable." The assault on universal meaning in Beckett cannot be turned into yet another kind of universal meaning. But this objective feature of Beckett's aesthetic also militates against existentialism's subjective *ethic,* by which meaninglessness becomes a normative encouragement to pull oneself together for the sake of one's authentic or "ownmost [*eigenste*] life." Just as Beckett inhibits the alchemical process that would transform "meaninglessness" into meaning, so too does he withhold the existential consolation by which "authenticity" for the individual becomes the universal lesson for everyone. "Existential conformity—that one should be what one is—is thereby rejected along with the ease of its representation."[67]

Whereas existentialism retains an "idealist core," Beckett's play presses toward the negative; its "tribunal over individuality" does not affirm but rather "condemns idealism." The subject that was supposed to seize upon meaning in the midst of its own absurdity stands exposed as itself a philosophically absurd idea, since it no longer retains its character as the foundation for philosophical meaning: "For the norm of existential philosophy—people should be themselves because they can no longer become anything else—, *Endgame* posits the antithesis, that precisely this self is not a self but rather the aping imitation of something non-existent." Such an illusion of solid individuality is hardly the kind of selfhood upon which one can freely "decide" in an act of existential resolve, since Beckett destroys even the formalist humanism that would make this resolution into a philosophical category: "What would be called the *condition humaine* in existential jargon," Adorno writes, "is the image of the last human which is devouring the earlier ones—humanity. Existential ontology asserts the universally valid in the process of abstraction which is not conscious of itself." The effort of abstraction thereby lends philosophical prestige even to existential labor that disguises itself in the false pathos of the artisanal and the concrete: "Ontology appeals to those who are weary of philosophical formalism but who yet cling to what is only accessible formally."[68]

In this discussion of Beckett, Adorno does not mention Heidegger, whose interrogation of humanism might seem at least prima facie to immunize him against this critique. But Adorno does fault other exponents of "existentialism" for evading society's culpability in liquidating the humanist self: "The catastrophes that inspire *Endgame*," Adorno wrote, "have exploded the individual whose substantiality and absoluteness was the common element between Kierkegaard, Jaspers, and the Sartrean version of existentialism. Even to the concentration camp victims, existentialism had attributed the freedom either inwardly to accept or reject the inflicted martyrdom. *Endgame* destroys such illusions."[69] The self-taught man in Sartre's *Nausea* offers the existential credo that, although he cannot believe

The Jargon of Authenticity / 111

in God, since God's existence has been disproved by science, "in the internment camp, I learned to believe in men."[70] For Adorno, however, this humanist *profession de foi* holds no greater legitimacy than the faith it displaced. Indeed, even more than the internment camps of the First World War (the historical reference for Sartre's protagonist), the death camps of fascism vitiated the humanist faith that Sartre extolled in his 1946 "Existentialism is a Humanism." In the wake of modern catastrophe Beckett renders this latter-day humanism unthinkable.

No less noteworthy in the essay on *Endgame* is Adorno's return, after an interval of three decades, to the theme of bourgeois interiority that had served as the object of his aesthetic-materialist criticism in *Kierkegaard: Construction of the Aesthetic*. In the habilitation, Adorno had focused his attention on the *intérieur* as an object lesson in Kierkegaard's bourgeois solipsism. In Beckett's play, however, this *intérieur* makes its reappearance but it is now robbed of the comfortable trappings that once disguised it as a space of bourgeois sovereignty and self-satisfaction. Hamm, *Endgame*'s antihero, has himself wheeled about the room "like a tyrant in his last days," but in his limited mobility he mocks any oration on the dignity of man:

> The hubris of idealism, the enthroning of man as creator in the center of creation, has entrenched itself in that "interior without furnishings" [*Innenraum ohne Möbel*] like a tyrant in his last days. There man repeats with a reduced, tiny imagination what man was once supposed to be; man repeats what was taken from him by social strictures as well as by today's cosmology, which he cannot escape. Clov is his male nurse. Hamm has himself shoved about by Clov into the middle of that Interieur [*in die Mitte jenes Interieurs*] which the world has become but which is also the inner realm of his own subjectivity [*Innenraum seiner eigenen Subjektivität*].[71]

The sheer fact that the bourgeois *intérieur* makes its return in the *Endgame* essay should not strike us as remarkable, since the *intérieur* serves as an obvious and convenient symbol for bourgeois property. By philosophical inference, Adorno uses it to illustrate idealism's claim to proprietary control over the known contents of the world.

All of this, needless to say, recapitulates Adorno's critique of the philosophy of interiority. More striking, perhaps, is Adorno's concern to mark the historical distance separating Kierkegaard's well-ordered social milieu from Beckett's landscapes of absolute ruin: The former stands as an exponent for the truth of the nineteenth-century bourgeoisie at the height of its powers; the latter, in the figure of Hamm, for the withered and late modern cipher of "what man was once supposed to be." Between them lies the actual events of historical catastrophe—Auschwitz, Hiroshima, the gulag, and the persistent threat of nuclear war—which mark the culminating phase in the dialectic of enlightenment.

In the conclusion of the *Endgame* essay Adorno makes precisely this point so as to draw out the play's implicit critique of existentialism. The argument is unusually condensed, even for Adorno: instrumental reason, he claims, is responsible for creating a world that now seems to lack all "meaning"; but, much like the jargon of authenticity, it capitalizes on its own disenchantment and awakens a yearning for the meaning that has been lost: "*Ratio*, having been fully instrumentalized, and therefore devoid of self-reflection and of reflection on what it has excluded, must seek that meaning that it has itself extinguished."[72] Existentialism, as a symptom of reason's self-made historical condition, responds to this meaninglessness by enfolding it within the mystified and eternalized language of ontology; and yet, precisely because no meaning lies at hand, it can offer little more than the theme of nothingness, which it then elevates into the purported truth of the human condition: "But in the condition that necessarily gave rise to this question, no answer is possible other than nothingness, which the form of the answer already is. The historical inevitability of this absurdity allows it to seem ontological; that is the veil of delusion produced by history itself."[73] Existentialism, then, is nothing less than a mystified description of social meaninglessness; it is a historical truth beneath a philosophical veil. *Endgame,* by contrast, critically negates any illusions of ahistorical permanence and thereby demystifies existential philosophy.

Yet even here the notion of *Endgame* as a "negation" of existentialism courts misunderstanding. Adorno admonishes us to see that we would be mistaken to interpret the play as a mere *illustration* of a philosophical insight, for this would once again repeat existentialism's error of promoting generalized "lessons" for humanity: "The historical fiber of situation and language in Beckett does not concretize—*more philosophico*—something unhistorical: precisely this procedure, typical of existential dramatists, is both foreign to art and philosophically obsolete." Rather, Adorno saw *Endgame* as the accurate historical presentation of a historical condition that assumes, for historical reasons, the appearance of ahistorical calamity: "Beckett's once-and-for-all is rather infinite catastrophe." Whereas ontology obscures social reality beneath a veil of apparent meaning, "Beckett's drama rips through this veil. The immanent contradiction of the absurd, reason terminating in senselessness, emphatically reveals the possibility of a truth which can no longer even be thought; it undermines the absolute claim exercised by what merely is." Adorno condenses this argument into a singularly powerful formula: "Negative ontology is the negation of ontology [*Die negative Ontologie ist die Negation von Ontologie*]: history alone has brought to maturity what was appropriated by the mythic power of timelessness."[74] This formula recalls the well-known remark from the "Finale" of *Minima Moralia* that "consummate negativity, once squarely faced, delineates the mirror-image of its opposite." Here Adorno asserts the similar point that, in revealing senselessness of social reality, Beckett's *Endgame* "emphatically reveals the possibility of a truth which can no longer even be thought." A social reality that presents itself as seamless whole prohibits us from thinking of a truth that contradicts it. In *Minima Moralia,* Adorno had likewise explained that gaining such a critical perspective is "the utterly *impossible* thing," since it "*presupposes a standpoint removed,* even though by a hair's breadth, *from the scope of existence* [*dem Bannkreis des Daseins*]."[75] Because all thought is socially conditioned, one cannot hope to gain such a standpoint through the illusory route of intellectual transcendence. It is found instead only in the "mirror image" of its opposite. The *Endgame* essay offers a similar claim: "Art emigrates to a standpoint that is no longer a standpoint at all because *there are no longer standpoints from which the catastrophe could be named.*"[76] It is for this reason that Adorno can assign Beckett's play the critical role of a "negative ontology," which, precisely in its consummate negativity, appeals counterfactually to the unrealized possibility of a genuinely meaningful existence. Understood as "negative ontology" in this sense, *Endgame* serves as a refutation of ontology; *it negates existentialism.* Or, as Adorno summarizes the point elsewhere in the same essay, "Beckett turns existential philosophy from its head back on its feet."[77]

On Hölderlin and Parataxis

If *The Jargon of Authenticity* ranks as the most vigorous and sustained of Adorno's polemics against Heidegger, it is matched in critical verve by the essay first presented in 1963 as a keynote address for the Hölderlin Society in Berlin that appeared in print as "Parataxis: On Hölderlin's Late Poetry."[78] Alongside the essay on Beckett's *Endgame,* which offers a similar critique of existentialism via aesthetic categories, the essay on Hölderlin merits careful reading on several counts, not least for the theoretical defense of parataxis as a mode of both aesthetic and philosophical juxtaposition that escapes the existentialists' allure of false reconciliation. J. M. Bernstein provides an excellent definition of the key term: "Parataxis," he writes, "involves placing concepts or propositions or larger trains of thought one after the other without indicating relations of coordination or subordination between them. Paratactic orderings are subversive of the force of logical syntax: the lack of a guiding connective forces the reader to establish the linkage between propositions, or larger blocks of text, substantively rather than relying on the familiar connects to do the work for her."[79] In this respect the essay on parataxis serves as far more than a meditation on Hölderlin's poetry; it might also be read as a formal excursus on negative dialectics itself. As in Beethoven's late style, Adorno discerns also in Hölderlin's poetry the wounds and fissures of a broken syntax that express a principled resistance to mediation. The "middle element" that would stand "outside the moments it is to connect" is "eliminated as being external and inessential."[80]

In Heidegger's well-known commentaries on Hölderlin, however, this resistance dissolved into a neoromantic aesthetic of organic unity. Artificially and with willful misrecognition, Heidegger had imposed upon Hölderlin's poetry not only an aesthetic but also a philosophical meaning that lay at the farthest remove from its actual significance. The parataxis essay thus occasioned Adorno's bold rejoinder to Heidegger's act of philosophical misappropriation. "It is astonishing," wrote Adorno,

> that no one has been bothered by the unaesthetic quality of these commentaries, their lack of affinity with their object. Clichés from the jargon of authenticity, such as the notion that Hölderlin places one "in decision"—it is useless to ask in what decision, and it is presumably only the obligatory mechanical choice between *Sein* and *Seienden*—and immediately afterwards the ominous *Leitworte,* "das echte Sagen," clichés from minor local art like "pensive," high-faluting puns like "language is a good [*Gut*] in an original sense; it guarantees it [*gutsteht*],

that is: it provides a guarantee that man exists as a historical being," professorial turns of phrase like "one who has been thrown out," which remains a humorless unintended joke even if it can cite a reference from Hölderlin to support it: all that runs rampant in the commentaries.[81]

Adorno expressed hostility to such interpretations not simply because he felt that Heidegger had arbitrarily imposed his own aesthetic and political preferences onto Hölderlin's work. Far more worrisome, however, was Heidegger's specific attempt to claim Hölderlin's poetry as a wellspring of ontological insight, resulting in philosophical interpolations that radically distorted what they purported to understand. Especially vexing to Adorno was the attempt to read the poems as affirmations of "unity [*Einheit*]" and "total identity [*totale Identität*]."[82] Throughout his Hölderlin interpretations Heidegger asserted this conformist ideology and suppressed all countervailing evidence. One especially intriguing epigram poses the following question:

woher ist die Sucht denn
Unter den Menschen, dass nur Einer und Eines nur sei?

[whence comes the mania
Found among men that there is One Thing and only the One?][83]

Heidegger never cited this passage, however, since it would have contradicted his effort to turn Hölderlin into a prophet of ontological holism. Such interpretative distortions and evasions illustrated Heidegger's enduring but disavowed bond with idealism, which conceived of Being as a "substantive." This permitted Heidegger to elevate Being idealistically above merely natural existence: "Being and the One have been coupled since Parmenides," Adorno observed. "Heidegger forces Being on Hölderlin, who avoids making the concept a substantive. For the Heidegger of the commentaries, the concept is reduced to a simple antithesis: 'Being is never a being.' Being thereby becomes something freely posited, as in the idealism which is taboo for Heidegger and to which he secretly belongs. This permits an ontological hypostasis of the poet's foundational activity."[84]

For Adorno, the misguided attempt to read Hölderlin as an ontologist missed the deeper significance of parataxis as the "antiprinciple" that permeated all of his later lyric poetry. Announcing his own premise for interpretation, Adorno warned that any appeal to wholesale "synthesis or identity" would only abet the "domination of nature." Hence we can grasp the importance of parataxis as the stylistic figure of antisynthesis, an implicit protest against the totalizing ambitions of modern subjectivity. "While all poetry protests the domination of nature with its own devices," Adorno explained, "in Hölderlin the protest awakens to self-consciousness." Such a protest became most evident in poems such as "Nature and Art," where Hölderlin aligns himself with "fallen nature" against the dominant powers of "Logos." Adorno was careful to note that even in this alliance Hölderlin remained immune from irrationalist nostalgia: On the one hand, he resisted "in Enlightenment fashion" any regression into "matriarchal romanticism." But on the other hand the poet acknowledged "what has been overthrown" and dialectically grasped "the domination of nature as itself a part of nature, with its gaze focused on humanness, which wrested itself from the amorphous and "barbaric" only through violence."[85] Thus Hölderlin recognized the basic contours of the dialectic of enlightenment and sustained the memory of suppressed nature without succumbing to infantile fantasies of a primal return: "Philosophically, the anamnesis of suppressed nature, in which Hölderlin tries to separate the wild from the peaceful, is the consciousness of non-identity, which transcends the compulsory identity of the Logos."[86]

Most of all, however, Adorno faulted Heidegger for sacrificing the concreteness of Hölderlin's poetry to the gods of ontological abstraction. In Heidegger's interpretations, spare and protomodernist imagery metamorphosed into kitsch homages to natural simplicity, imposing on Hölderlin a mindless nostalgia for lost unity to which the poet was typically immune:

> The meager, reduced elements of empirical reality in Hölderlin's late work, the frugal customs on the poverty-stricken island of Patmos, are not glorified as they are in Heidegger's statement: "The gentle spell of familiar things and their simple relationships is close at hand." For the philosopher of Being, these are the "old and true," as though agriculture, historically acquired under circumstances of immeasurable hardship and effort, were an aspect of Being in itself; for Hölderlin, they are . . . a reflection of something irretrievable. Hölderlin's asceticism, his renunciation of the false romantic riches of available culture, refuses to participate through the color of colorlessness in propaganda for the restorationist "splendor of the simple."[87]

It is hardly accidental that Adorno fastens his attention here on "Patmos," the late Hölderlin hymn with the opening lines regarding the common origin of "danger" and "the saving power" that Heidegger used in his 1953 essay, "The Question concerning Technology."[88] The relevant fragment from the later version of "Patmos," in Michael Hamburger's translation, reads as follows:

> Most kind is; but no one by himself
> Can grasp God.
> But where danger threatens
> That which saves from it also grows.

> Voll Güt ist, keiner aber fasset
> Allein Gott.
> Wo aber Gefahr ist, wächst
> Das Rettende auch.[89]

For Adorno, what remains truly astonishing in Heidegger's appropriation of Hölderlin's poetry is the philosopher's readiness to transform everything that is concrete and historically specific into the quasi-divine pronouncements of universal appeal. This is especially the case for Heidegger's much-cited use of the "danger/saving-power" motif, which would inspire ongoing reflections on the place of technology in modern life. As a reader of poetry, then, Heidegger revealed his own "technological" genius by transforming the irreducible elements of poetic language into mere raw material for philosophical edification.

It takes little effort to see that in his criticism of Heidegger's Hölderlin interpretations Adorno recapitulates his basic critique of existential ontology. Heidegger had wished to impose on Hölderlin's poetry a species of crypto-idealism, in which "identity" and "unity" remained dominant as organizing philosophical norms. For Adorno, however, Hölderlin's poetry manifestly *resists* precisely these norms. Parataxis, then, was more than a formal or merely stylistic device; it was sign of Hölderlin's resistance to ontological holism, and it bespoke the poet's "consciousness of non-identity." Within the confines of the Hölderlin essay Adorno did not have the space to develop this theme of nonidentity with the philosophical rigor it would truly demand. The full assessment of nonidentity, together with the definitive argument against existential ontology, would appear only in *Negative Dialectics*.

4

Negative Dialectics

The dirge over the forgetfulness of being
is the sabotage of reconciliation

—THEODOR W. ADORNO, *Negative Dialectics*

Adorno's "Fat Child"

In the autumn of 1965, during the final stages of preparation for
his book on negative dialectics, Adorno offered a series of lectures
on the same topic. In the lecture of November 30, he recalled the
critical arguments from *The Jargon of Authenticity*, and he confessed
to his auditors that criticism of that sort would not suffice. The sociological polemic of the earlier book had served the necessary purpose of disenchantment, breaking the aura of sanctity surrounding
the philosophy of existence. "But of course," Adorno hastened to
explain, "in such situations it is never enough just to make a critical
case; the task of philosophy—what distinguishes philosophy from
mere cultural chatter—is to analyze rigorously what has been criticized."[1] The remark suggests at least a hint of contrition. Interlaced
with claims that Adorno himself characterized as "sociological,"
Jargon was no doubt a critical work and at some points, one might
say, *excessively* so, since it did not always develop its claims in the
manner of wholly *immanent criticism* and with the philosophical
rigor its author recommended. But this distinguished it from *Negative*

Dialectics, a masterpiece of immanent criticism and the culminating philosophical work of Adorno's career. After seven years of great effort, he put the final touches on the manuscript in late July 1966 and then traveled to Sils Maria (once Nietzsche's residence) for a much-needed six-week vacation. In a letter to Helene Berg he referred to *Negative Dialectics* as "my chief philosophical work." Elsewhere in more colorful language he called it his "fat child."[2]

Negative Dialectics is indeed a work of formidable ambition, bringing to completion many of the impulses that had animated its author since he was a young man. In the book's preface Adorno recalls an early remark by his late friend Walter Benjamin, who in 1937 said of Adorno's early work on Husserl, *Zur Metakritik der Erkenntnistheorie,* that it had been necessary to "cross the frozen waters of abstraction to arrive at concise, concrete philosophizing." Finishing Benjamin's metaphor after nearly three decades, Adorno added that "*Negative Dialectics* now charts such a crossing in retrospect."[3] The metaphor is remarkably apt. As we will recall from Chapter 2, Adorno had condemned Husserlian phenomenology for its abstraction and its failure to break free of subjectivism to make contact with the worldly object.

Lorenz Jäger has claimed that in matters of philosophy, "Adorno's main concern during the 1960s was his critical engagement with Heidegger and above all with the language of Heidegger." But this is an obvious exaggeration; it neglects Adorno's no less important work throughout the 1960s on Hegel's philosophy, which serves as a major foil for the arguments in *Negative Dialectics*. Nor is Jäger any more accurate when he claims that "Adorno signally failed to understand Heidegger's philosophy."[4] The fact is that Adorno's engagement with Heidegger's philosophy was extensive and bespeaks a powerful if admittedly controversial interpretation of its implications. It is true, however, that Adorno's engagement with Heidegger gained special intensity during the 1960s. For the winter semester 1960–1961, Adorno offered a lecture course at the

Goethe University Frankfurt, "Ontology and Dialectics," and then, in March 1961, he was invited to the Collége de France, where he presented three lectures in rapid succession (Wednesday, March 15; Saturday, March 18; and Tuesday, March 21) with the titles, respectively, "Le besoin d'une ontologie," "Être et Existence," and "Vers une dialectique négative." His French contemporaries, especially those phenomenologists who had drawn instruction from Heidegger, did not respond with favor. In a summary of the lectures, Jean Beaufret wrote, "Merleau-Ponty had a heartfelt wish to stop what he took to be a scandal" at the Collège de France "where Heidegger had just been publically vituperated."[5] Scandalous or not, Adorno's lectures of the early 1960s in both Frankfurt and Paris help us to recall the enormous significance of Heidegger's philosophy as a testing ground for arguments that would come to fruition only in *Negative Dialectics*.[6]

It would be misleading, however, to suggest that this single book could stand as the summation of Adorno's philosophical career. For many philosophers the very idea of a magnum opus would suggest a system or final synthesis that unifies all prior insights and arguments into a single whole. Logical completion would correlate with biographical fulfillment, as if work and life could be seen as a harmonistic totality. But for the interpretation of Adorno the very idea of a *summa* is clearly unsuitable. In the preface to the book he draws a comparison between his own resistance to the idea of a philosophical system and contemporary aesthetics: "As the latest aesthetic discussions feature the 'anti-drama' and the 'anti-hero,' this *Negative Dialectics* in which all aesthetic topics are shunned might be called an 'anti-system.' " The stated aim of Adorno's book (which I quoted in part in Chapter 2) appears in the preface: "It attempts by means of logical consistency to substitute for the unity principle, and for the total domination of the supra-ordinated concept, the idea of what would be outside the sway of such unity. To use the strength of the subject to break through the fallacy of constitutive subjectivity—this is what the author felt to be his task ever since he came to trust in his own mental impulses; he did not wish to put it off any longer."[7] This antipathy to the idea of the unified system reflected Adorno's conviction—as signaled already in the title—that at the late and most catastrophic stage of history, when philosophy's original promise of a seamless reunion between subject and object had been missed, it was necessary to wrest the principle of negation from the affirmative ideal of reconciliation, or *Versöhnung*. The dream of a harmonious end (realized via Hegel's "negation of negation") was to be shattered, giving independent life to a genuinely critical style of philosophy that would hold open what philosophical affirmation wished to close. Hence the principle of a *negative* dialectic.[8]

Much of the difficulty of the book stems from the fact that it eschews the systematic exposition of philosophical content as a matter of philosophical principle. Yet this also marks it as a very *personal* and even idiosyncratic work, in which on each and every page it was Adorno himself who appeared as the antihero. One might say that the "strength of the subject" was Adorno's own strength as a stylist and philosophical author, even while this strength was deployed so as to shatter the illusion of a philosophical system. If a system, however, draws its transcendental justification from what Adorno called "the fallacy of constitutive subjectivity," then we might think that it was Adorno *himself* who best embodied this aesthetic paradox. As Axel Honneth notes, Adorno's "stylistic ideal" involved a synthesis of "expression and stringency."[9] Difficulty and rigor emerged through a highly distinctive voice, what we might call Adorno's literary persona. Needless to say, this appeal to persona within a philosophical text was not new; it may recall one of Hegel's first critics, the ironist who found in subjectivity a point of critical leverage against the harmonistic ambitions of reason. The drama of a subject who wishes to shatter the system is a theme that consumed Adorno's attention

already at the beginning of his career when he devoted his dissertation to that earlier nemesis of Hegelian systematicity—Kierkegaard.

Needless to say, neither Kierkegaard nor any other philosopher
could serve as a skeleton key for unlocking the entirety of *Negative
Dialectics;* its targets and interlocutors are manifold, and the very
asystematicity of the book surely forbids a totalizing explanation.
But Adorno's own characterization of the book suggests that we
should take seriously its dialectical relation to its various objects of
criticism (Hegel, Heidegger, Husserl, Kierkegaard, and so forth)
since the author develops his own insights chiefly through an immanent critique of prior philosophies. This is especially the case for
those existential thinkers and themes that are foregrounded in the
present study. My claim here is that Adorno's characterization of
his philosophical task alerts us to the intriguing irony that *Negative
Dialectics* contains *both* a critique of existentialism *and* a reprisal
of gestures associated with the philosophy of existence itself. This
does not mean, however, that the book founders in self-contradiction.
On the contrary, it remains faithful to its own principle of a negative
dialectic precisely because it does not attempt to rise above the
sphere of immanent critique. To dismantle existentialism merely as
"untruth" would be to deny the partial truth that it contains. The
plateau of an untroubled reconciliation beyond this negative labor is
for Adorno merely a mirage. Indeed, the singular power of the book
derives from the way it resists reconciliation and implicates itself in
the objects of its own criticism.

Rage against Nature

Of the disparate themes in *Negative Dialectics,* among the best
known is the indictment of idealism as a rage against nature.[10] To
explain this idea Adorno extends the genealogical analysis of reason
that was already adumbrated in *Dialectic of Enlightenment.* According to Adorno, idealism represents an intellectualized and for-

malized variant of the archaic impulse that first revealed itself in the behavior of human predators when attacking their prey. The hunger and difficulty of such an attack only intensifies the feeling of rage at the victim, a rage that further terrifies the prey and makes its death all the more likely. The subject not only aims to destroy the object but also projects upon it the evil and danger of own actions: "The life-form to be devoured must be evil." Over the course of human history, Adorno claims, this originally predatory stance did not disappear but only underwent a trial of rationalization, eventually manifesting itself even in formal philosophical doctrines: "This anthropological schemata has been sublimated all the way into epistemology. In idealism—most obviously in Fichte—the ideology unconsciously rules that the non-Ego, *l'autrui,* finally everything reminiscent of nature, is inferior, so that the unity of the thought bent on preserving itself may devour it, thus consoled." According to Adorno, this basic pattern of "rationalized rage at the nonidentical" reappears throughout the history of Western philosophy. But even while rage is "the signature of each and every idealism," the effort to destroy the independence of the object reaches its apogee in the systems of German idealism. For the "system," Adorno explains, is "the belly turned mind [*der Geist gewordene Bauch*]."[11]

This critique of idealism as the mind's self-preservation in the face of the object ranks among the major themes of negative dialectics.[12] But Adorno does not wish to suggest that idealism is a unified or self-identical doctrine. On the contrary, anticipating his dialectical remarks on Heidegger, Adorno claims that Hegel's philosophy already bears within itself a momentary recognition of its own undoing. The young Hegel longed for "positivity" and "self-preserving solidity" and yet in the preface to the *Phenomenology of Spirit* he also portrayed the negative principle of thought itself as "archenemy" of positivity.[13] The tension that runs through Hegel's early philosophy between self-preservation and negativity thus signifies the struggle between object and subject, where "negation" stands for *both* the subject's domination *and* the object's resistance. The systematic longing for a dialectical completion, where the object would serve to embody the ambitions of the subject, betrays precisely this ambivalence: it represents *both* the subject's ambition finally to make contact with the nonsubjective world *and* its will to master and finally abolish the world's objectivity. The dialectic is supposed to satisfy both ambitions at once: abolishing while preserving the otherness of the object. Yet Adorno faults Hegel for promoting the reconciliation between subject and object *only in one direction,* to the advantage of an inflationary subjectivity that no longer acknowledges the object in its otherness. Ultimately, "all his statements to the contrary notwithstanding, Hegel left the subject's primacy over the object unchallenged."[14] On Adorno's reading, the Hegelian *Aufhebung* does not preserve, but only negates, the object's otherness.

Adorno's critique of Hegel is not a major focus of the present study, but it is instructive for our purposes here insofar as it illustrates the larger critique of idealism that runs through the entire length of *Negative Dialectics.* According to Adorno, bourgeois philosophy in all its forms recapitulates the characteristic struggle of the subject to preserve its "primacy" or preponderance over the object, but in doing so it sabotages its own longing to achieve solidity and worldly objectivity. The subject therefore *both* succeeds *and* fails. It succeeds in remaining merely a subject precisely because it fails to break free of its own constitutive subjectivity. As we have seen in previous chapters, Adorno discerned this very same theme of ambivalent victory not only in Hegel but also in Heidegger and Husserl; indeed, the more general theme of the subject's self-enclosure appears in the early critique of Kierkegaard as well. In this respect, all four thinkers subscribe to what I have called the philosophy of interiority. Indeed, the consuming task of *Negative Dialectics* is to sketch an alternative route *beyond* the power of constitutive subjectivity so as to reach, at last, the object that has eluded bourgeois philosophy in all its forms. My chief claim in this chapter will be twofold: first, that Adorno sees in existentialism a failed attempt to break free of idealism; and second, that Adorno conceives of his own philosophical effort as the successful realization of the very same task.

Toward a Primacy of the Object

According to Adorno, the philosophies of bourgeois interiority (as typified by Kierkegaard, Husserl, and Heidegger, alongside Hegel) exhibit a similar ambition to preserve the subject's dominance over the object, a dominance that defeats itself when the subject fails to establish enduring contact with the exterior world. A truly *critical* philosophy, Adorno claims, would overcome the ambivalence of this idealistic legacy by insisting on what he calls "the primacy of the object [*Vorrang des Objekts*]."[15] The reasoning that motivates this idea closely resembles a transcendental argument (as Brian O'Connor has proposed in his lucid reconstruction).[16] Briefly, Adorno establishes the notion of the object's primacy by examining the interrelation between subject and object. It turns out that this relation is not reciprocal; that is, "the subject falls to the object totally differently than the latter to the former." On the one hand, it is clear that even to *think* the object requires a subject: there can be no thought without a subjectivity that thinks. But the object that is grasped in thought nonetheless (in Adorno's phrase) "preserves itself." Stated differently, the object retains a moment of objective identity even outside the event of its conceptualization. Yet on the other hand, it is no less clear that each and every subject is *already also* an object. This is so because, notwithstanding the subject's capacity to conceptualize the world, the subject is *also* a worldly being and therefore at the mercy of its own material conditions (its corporeality, its sensual relation to its surroundings, its dependency on the human collective, and so forth). But this means that the relation between subject and object can never exhibit a thoroughgoing reciprocity: "In the meaning of subjectivity is also the reckoning of being an object; but not so in the meaning of objectivity, to be a subject."[17] Every object is an object even when it is not an object-for-a-subject, but *every* subject is necessarily *also* an object. Affirming the basic insight of materialism, the very category of objecthood therefore enjoys a certain primacy, or preponderance *(Vorrang)*.

According to Adorno, then, we can only escape the authoritarian and affirmative implications of identity theory if we start out from the other direction by acknowledging the primacy of the object. This primacy points away from idealism and toward a broadly construed "materialism" that will grasp reality as a historically and socially changing landscape whose very richness and temporal movement must forever overwhelm the subject's ambitions of conceptual totalization. But Adorno also claims that the primacy of the object is not only a social or materialist phenomenon; this primacy is in fact *logically presupposed* in the very concept of experience. This is something that Kant himself had already grasped: in transcendental idealism, the memory of the primacy of the object persists in the idea of the *thing-in-itself*. Perhaps more than the extravagant idealists who followed after him, who claimed to consummate the ambitions of his system only by abolishing the metaphysical residuum of the nonconceptual object, Kant had recognized that idealism would only sustain its meaning as a theory of worldly experience if it allowed for an "insufficiency" in the subject. The otherness *(Andersheit)* of the object to subjective conceptualization was precisely the mark of this subjective insufficiency. Without this otherness, Adorno observes, "knowledge [*Erkenntnis*] would degenerate into tautology; what is known would be knowledge itself [*das Erkannte wäre sie selbst*]."[18] It would be the defining task of a negative dialectic to acknowledge the primacy of the object; it would not claim to subsume reality into a cognized whole but would instead admit and even thematize the object's resistance to any final or complete conceptualization. A negative dialectic, in other words, is the conceptual homage the subject pays to the object's resistance.

Pseudo-Concreteness

Adorno's global indictment of idealism for its failure to acknowledge the primacy of the object can serve as a helpful overture as we begin to reconstruct Adorno's specific critique of existentialism in *Negative Dialectics*. This critique begins with the counterintuitive claim (already glimpsed in the metacritique of Husserlian phenomenology) that existential ontology itself remains a version of idealism. As we have seen, Adorno had already developed this line of criticism in his *Habilitationsschrift,* where Kierkegaard himself appeared as an idealist, trapped within the confines of the bourgeois *intérieur.* During that same decade Adorno was already also turning his attention to Heidegger as well, as we have seen in the lectures of the early 1930s examined in Chapter 2. In "The Idea of Natural History," Adorno characterized what he calls "neo-ontology" (i.e., the philosophies of both Heidegger and Scheler) as a philosophical doctrine that had never managed to overcome its idealist point of departure. As we have seen, its idealism consists in two interrelated doctrines: first, neo-ontology subscribes to an especially strong species of holism according to which all of reality coheres into a "structural unity or totality"; but this alerts us to the second doctrine: neo-ontology also affirms a strong *identity* or even "tautology" according to which subject and object are one. Adorno discerned this identitarian tendency most of all in Heidegger's readiness to subsume all of historical being under the "subjective category of historicity." Insofar as historicity is a categorial mode that belongs to *Dasein*'s own manner of being-in-the-world, it falls onto the side of human subjectivity. But it follows that, for Heidegger, all of history itself is subordinated to this subjective modality. Heidegger therefore belongs, despite his self-conception, to the older idealist tradition that denies the otherness of the object and instead forces Being "to conform to the categories with which historicity stamps it." Adorno considered this conclusion a tautology: it is merely "a new camouflage of the old classical thesis of the identity of subject and object." But this identity is in truth only an inflationary species of subjectivism.[19]

The early lecture on natural history precedes the publication of *Negative Dialectics* by more than thirty years, and, during the interim, Adorno's assessment of Heidegger had deepened philosophically, but as we have seen it had also acquired a sharply polemical edge. This was due primarily to the scandal of Heidegger's support for National Socialism, growing knowledge of which would slowly transform the way many saw Heidegger's philosophy. In this regard it is crucial to note that Adorno developed his mature critique of Heidegger only in the aftermath of formidable criticism by two other authors, Karl Löwith and Günther Anders. First published in 1953, Löwith's *Heidegger: Denker in dürftiger Zeit* (Heidegger: Thinker in a destitute time) was a book of modest size—it was only 109 pages in length—but great ambition.[20] A portion of the text had already been published in 1946 in *Les Temps Modernes* under the title "The Political Implications of Heidegger's Philosophy of Existence," and it would be fair to describe this essay as the opening salvo in the *Affaire Heidegger* that for many years to come would preoccupy intellectual debate concerning Heidegger's philosophy in France. In the preface to the second edition of his book in 1960, Löwith said it "helped to break a spell of awkward silence and sterile repetition that had encumbered a group of adherents."[21] But when we examine Adorno's assessment of existentialism, it would appear that Löwith's book made a far weaker impression. Although Adorno cites it in *Negative Dialectics*, Löwith was chiefly concerned with Heidegger's view of history; for Adorno this theme remained of secondary importance.

More significant for Adorno's interpretation was a 1948 essay by Günther Anders that bore the acerbic title "On the Pseudo-

Concreteness of Heidegger's Philosophy."[22] Like Löwith, Anders had studied with both Heidegger and Husserl in Freiburg and then in Marburg: he received his PhD under the guidance of Husserl in 1923. Also like Löwith, Anders (born Günther Stern) was of German Jewish descent; as it happens, he was a cousin to Walter Benjamin, and also the first husband of Hannah Arendt, from their marriage in 1929 to their separation a little more than eight years later.[23] Like so many of the German Jewish students who trained in phenomenology, Anders grew disenchanted with Heideggerian teachings and after the war published a series of critical essays that furnish ample evidence of his discontent.[24]

Adorno refers to both Löwith and Anders in the first portion of *Negative Dialectics*, but his critique bears a far stronger affinity to the essay by Anders that expressly indicts Heidegger's philosophy for its "pseudo-concreteness." According to Anders, existential ontology remained trapped in a species of idealism that forgets both the actual body and actual society. Although *Dasein* presented itself as a philosophical corrective to the erroneous metaphysics of transcendental consciousness, it was not so much a worldly corrective to idealism as a mystified expression of the very same idealism. According to Anders, everything once assigned to transcendental consciousness—most of all, its constitutive power to confer order and meaning upon reality—returned in the guise of *Dasein* as the coordinating power of all worldly beings. Heidegger had "blown up the concept of 'consciousness' with his pragmatic cartridges" only to "make the result of his explosion a kind of 'consciousness'" once again. Heidegger's reputation as a thinker of "concrete" existence was therefore undeserved, because in fact human existence remained throughout Heidegger's work a mere placeholder for an abstraction—an understanding of Being—that vitiated the so-called "worldliness" of *Dasein*. "Although avoiding all things supranatural," Anders wrote, Heidegger's philosophy "never reaches nature. . . . As a matter of fact, his Dasein does not know of any *concupiscentia*, of any instinct, of any toothache." The paradoxical consequence was that Heidegger only philosophized *about* the worldly embeddedness of human existence without breaking free of idealism: "*his philosophy,*" Anders concluded, "*is the first and unique sample of the species 'philosophy of life hostile to life.'*"[25]

Anders could be unsparing and occasionally harsh in his criticism, but much like Adorno he also permitted himself moments of humor. In one especially cutting observation, he wrote that the key claim in *Being and Time,* that "Dasein ist ein Sein, dem es um es selbst geht [*Dasein* is a being, for whom its being is at issue]," resorts to an expression from everyday German parlance, "Es geht um." This expression, Anders observed, conveyed all the existential virtues in that it was "deliberately blunt, extra-academic, 'concrete.' " It conflated sheer reports of fact with moral ultimata in a manner that invited ridicule, moving from the commonplace expressions such as "Es geht um Leben und Tod [It's a matter of life and death]" to "Es geht um die Wurst [It's time for the sausage]." More sobering, however, was Anders's suggestion that Heidegger's philosophy should be understood as an illicit and belated attempt to revive the prestige of atheism: Heidegger, Anders claimed, "found himself in the peculiar situation of *still being a heretic—in a period in which the secularization* of both the inner and the outer life *had been a matter of course for many generations.*"[26] This was due to the fact that Heidegger borrowed from the heritage of Christianity but then felt it necessary to deny God even in an age when atheism had grown altogether commonplace. Only this anachronistic gesture of heresy could explain why existential ontology presented such a curious combination of theistic and atheistic motifs. Thus, for example, Anders noted that the "negative idea of *Geworfenheit*" (typically translated as "thrownness," but rendered in Ander's English-language text as "being cast into") somehow avoided any mention of a *Werfende*—a divine being who could perform the original throw.[27]

In *Negative Dialectics,* Adorno borrowed from (and expressly credited) Anders's diagnosis of existential pseudo-concreteness. But he added a further twist of the dialectical screw, noting that Heidegger had grafted the pathos of the concrete onto an idealistic formalism inherited from Husserlian phenomenology. "Fundamental ontology," Adorno wrote, "eludes itself not the least because it holds up an ideal of "purity" which stemmed from the methodologization of philosophy—the latest link of the chain was Husserl—as the contrast of being to the existent, nevertheless philosophizing as if over something substantive. This habitus was to be reconciled with that purity only in a realm where all determinable distinctions, indeed all content blurred together."[28]

Adorno concludes that Heidegger's formalism thus vitiated its celebrated claims to worldliness. "Haunted by Scheler's weaknesses," Adorno writes, "Heidegger does not permit *prima philosophia* to be crassly compromised by the contingency of the material, the transience of the momentary eternities." All the same, Heidegger was loath to surrender "the concretion originally heralded by the word existence." This ambivalence placed Heidegger in a deeply ironic position: On the one hand, he inveighed against the distinction between mere concept and material world as "the original sin" of modern philosophy, yet on the other hand, he resurrected this distinction in his own classificatory ranking of the ontological over the ontic. The preferential treatment of the ontological permitted Heidegger to confer a "higher dignity" on mere existence even while he retained a nostalgic memory trace of that very existence as a realm anterior to all "differentiation and antagonism." For this reason Adorno claimed that the ambivalent yet alluring aesthetic of "concreteness" functions less as a concept than a mark of virtue without philosophical consequence. "Being tempts alluringly," he writes; it is "eloquent as wind-blown leaves in bad poetry. But what it praises harmlessly slips out of its grasp, while it is insisted upon philosophically like something it owns, over which the thought, which thinks it, has no control."[29]

Developing Anders's insight, Adorno further pursues the claim that Heidegger was an idealist *malgré lui*. The specific accusation of an idealistic species of pseudo-concreteness refers back to his *History and Freedom* lectures (delivered in 1964–1965, just before the publication of *Negative Dialectics*), in which Adorno had already leveled the accusation of "pseudo-concreteness" at Hegel—namely, at Hegel's controversial investment in the idea of the nation. "The category of national spirits as collective individuals," Adorno then wrote, "fits in very conveniently with Hegel's desire to give concrete shape to the relations between universal and particular, but it is essentially a pseudo-concreteness. The universal character of a people, a nation is regarded as an individual and hypostatized; it is even treated as something possessing an essence of its own." In Hegel's case concrete reality was supposed to instantiate the universal, but in fact the nation simply assumed a false universality, resulting in a repressive subordination of the particular individual to the group. Adorno's hostility to this gesture of "pseudo-concreteness," however, did not prevent him from embracing concreteness for the task of a truly materialist philosophy. With reference to the example of Benjamin's *Trauerspiel* book, Adorno noted in the 1964–1965 lectures that "the transition to concreteness [. . . is] something that philosophy must implement in all seriousness." The concreteness of a materialist philosophy, he explained, "differs from the usual philosophizing about the concrete, in that the concrete references here [with Benjamin] are apprehended allegorically in their specific meaning, instead of serving as examples or paradigms for more general concepts whose validity they are supposed to demonstrate." Thus Hegel's concept of the nation falsely elevated the particular into concrete universal rather than permitting the concrete to stand forth in all its concrete specificity. For a materialist philosophy, Adorno suggested, "Eternity no longer appears as such, but only as refracted through the most ephemeral of things." The Hegelian idea of the concrete thus contained within itself a disavowed materialism, notwithstanding the "official tenor" of Hegel's idealism.[30]

In Heidegger's work, meanwhile, Adorno also detected a fetishized longing for the concrete, though Heidegger did not succeed any more than the idealists before him in unifying the universal with material reality.[31] Adorno readily admitted the irony of this charge, since existential ontology had explicitly presented itself as a dramatic overturning of the ancient prejudice that grants thought a metaphysical priority over being. But according to Adorno this rebellion had failed, and existential ontology had lapsed back into idealism—a failure due in part to Heidegger's own insistence on distinguishing merely ontic existence from an essential stratum of being. In Heidegger's philosophy, Adorno wrote, being appeared with an "iridescent shimmer" and—notwithstanding Heidegger's own much-celebrated critique of the intellectualist bias in philosophy—being retained the old prestige of conceptual essence over worldly appearance. Thus, for example, when *Being and Time* assigned itself the task of rescuing Being from oblivion, it construed this as a struggle to recall the proper "meaning" or "sense" (*Sinn*) of Being. (Indeed, though Adorno did not bother to mention it, he might have supported his charge of intellectualism by citing the very first page of Heidegger's magnum opus, which quotes the exchange from Plato's *Sophist* about "what you mean by being [*was ihr eigentlich meint*]" and thus prompts Heidegger's call for renewing "the question into the sense of being [*die Frage nach dem Sinn des Seins*].")[32] Despite Heidegger's intentions, this intellectualistic isolation of Being from the existent with its sublime retreat into the higher realms of "meaning" thus recapitulated a species of Platonism. "If true being is conceived of as radically *chôris* [Greek: separately] from the existent," Adorno reasoned, "then it is identical with its meaning." Heidegger's ontological ambitions overwhelmed any concern for the existent as such since "one need only cite the meaning of what is

essential [*Wesenheit*] to being and one has the meaning of being itself." The unembarrassed preoccupation with an ostensibly forgotten
meaning showed quite clearly that "the breakout attempt from idealism" had collapsed in failure: "the doctrine of being regresses into
one of a thinking which removes everything from being, which
would be different from pure thought."[33]

Aura and Mimesis

Adorno's critique of pseudo-concreteness lends greater strength to
the earlier charge (first articulated in *Against Epistemology*) that
Heidegger followed after Husserl's example in disdaining all "ontic"
questions as merely matters of empirical fact. Like Husserl, Heidegger marginalized or bracketed from consideration "everything
which would not, in the words of the former, be eidetic phenomenology, onto the unphilosophical particular sciences." Heidegger,
notwithstanding his reputation as the more this-worldly phenomenologist, only extended the "prohibition [*Bann*]" on predication
further than Husserl such that it eliminated nearly everything that
could be said, "even to the Husserlian *eidê*, to the highest, fact-free,
conceptual unity of the factual, in which traces of substantiality are
intermixed." The paradoxical result was a species of phenomenology
that submits to a ban on phenomenological description: "Ontology,"
explained Adorno, "ends up due to its own consistency in a no-
man's land. It must eliminate the *a posterioris*, nor is it supposed to
even be logic, as a doctrine of thinking and a particular discipline;
every thinking step would take it over the point, at which it hoped
to satisfy itself alone. In the end it scarcely dares to predicate anything, even of being."[34]

The absence of predicates elevated being into a quasi-sacred object: "That being would be neither a factum nor a concept exempts
it from critique." Every attempt to render it in conceptual form was
condemned as blasphemy: "Whatever could be picked on is dis-

missed as a misunderstanding." The nonconceptual character of being thereby "hypostasizes itself as something higher than the reflective understanding which slices the existent and concept from each other with the dissecting-knife." The incapacity of the mind to grasp being as a proper object of criticism became the mark of its grandeur, "as if the emptiness of the concept of being were the fruit of the monastic chastity of that which was original, unconditioned by the aporias of thought. Adorno continues, "Even the meagerness of what all this leaves Heidegger in hand, he coins into an advantage: it is one of the pervasive invariants of his philosophy, although never named as such, to revalue every lack of content, every non-possession of a cognition into an index of profundity. Involuntary abstractness presents itself as voluntary vow."[35]

Being thus acquired what Adorno (borrowing once again, as in *Jargon,* from Benjamin) called "the aura of the more than factual being [*die Aura des mehr denn faktisch Seins*]." The aura for Benjamin was that quality that distinguishes the artwork as something singular, a quality of uniqueness that originally distinguished the artwork as a creation embedded within a traditional context of religious ritual.[36] In such a context the auratic work of art can be venerated only at a distance, with the sobriety that is due to any cultic object: "The artwork's auratic mode of existence is never entirely severed from its ritual function," Benjamin explained, and this quality never entirely disappears, even in the "secular worship of beauty."[37] Drawing upon this analysis, Adorno suggests that in modern existentialism the auratic aspect of being conspires to *resacralize* the everyday, hallowing all that is given and just *as it is given:* "nothing remains but the naked affirmation of what is anyway."[38] Once endowed with an aura, the factual becomes the dwelling of the holy: "Heidegger squeezes a blessing from everything he owes."[39]

Such a worshipful affirmation of the given means that existential ontology answers to the subject's archaic desire to gain absolute control over nature by mirroring its power. The nonconceptual authority of the natural is projected into philosophy as a doctrine that denies the authority of the concept. Mind adapts to fact, and thought mirrors thoughtlessness. If this seemingly paradoxical and self-subverting doctrine seems to offer a kind of consolation, it is only because it bespeaks the "falsely resurrected faith that one might break the spell of nature by soothingly copying it." Recalling a theme that was central to *Dialectic of Enlightenment,* Adorno characterizes this strategy as a mimetic bid for self-preservation. The subject tries to sustain itself by surrendering itself, identifying with the nature it fears. Ironically, however, mimesis ends by confirming the naturalistic rule of power as the sole criterion of justice. "Existential thinking," writes Adorno, "crawls into the cave of a long-past mimesis. In the process it is nonetheless accommodating the most fatal prejudice from the philosophical history which it has laid off like a superfluous employee: the Platonic prejudice that the imperishable must be the good—which is to say no more than that in permanent warfare the stronger is always right."[40]

Unlike Platonism, however, existential ontology allows what is impermanent to usurp the role of the permanent, arrogating to itself the reified prestige of a primordial or "ontological" temporality: "Time itself, and thus transiency, is both absolutized and transfigured as eternal."[41] This is a strategy of self-preservation; by making "the concept of existence" into the "essentiality of transience [*Wesenhaftigkeit von Vergängnis*]" it thereby "keeps existence away by naming it."[42] A further distinction between Platonism and existential ontology is that even while Plato extolled "martial virtues" he enlisted them into the service of justice as the "highest idea," whereas "in the darkened sky of the teaching of existence [*Existenzlehre*] there no longer shines a star." Like Lévinas (whose mature critique of Heidegger appeared in *Totality and Infinity* in 1961, just five years before *Negative Dialectics*), Adorno saw in existential ontology an attempt to enclose the whole of being with a sacralizing aura that drew illicitly on the pathos of theism even while disavowing God. In Heidegger's philosophy, Adorno concludes, "Existence is sanctified without the sanctifying factor [*Existenz wird geweiht ohne das Weihende*]."[43]

French Existentialism

Similar problems afflicted Sartrean existentialism, which Adorno described as "the most recent attempt to break out of conceptual fetishism."[44] But in his view, existentialism in its French form proved no more successful than Heidegger's fundamental ontology in liberating itself from its "idealistic bonds," despite the fact that Sartre and his colleagues plunged into this-worldly political adventures.[45] Ironically, even their conception of political commitment betrayed their fidelity to an unconditioned subjectivity and hence to bourgeois idealism. Recognizing the dangers of communistic bureaucracy, Sartre placed the greatest emphasis on "spontaneity" in the moment of radical decision: "Despite his extreme nominalism, Sartre's philosophy in its most effective phase was organized according to the old idealistic category of the free act of the subject." The theme of decision, Adorno noted, was derived from Kierkegaard, though in the hands of the French existentialists it swelled in importance even while the "objective chances" for decisions of genuine political consequence atrophied: "Kierkegaard drew the meaning of the category [of decision] from Christology, its *terminus ad quem*; Sartre made it the absolute it was to serve."[46]

Adorno's strongest critique of French existentialism did not appear in *Negative Dialectics* but rather in the essay "Engagement," originally a lecture for Radio Bremen and first published in *Die Neue Rundschau* in 1962.[47] Responding to Sartre's famous meditation on literature and political commitment, *Qu'est-ce que la littérature?*, Adorno fastens his critical attention on Sartre's view that committed art must reflect "the free choice of the agent," a choice that Adorno finds vacuous insofar as Sartre ignores the conditioning and constraints that are imposed on such ostensibly free choice.

Adorno traces this problem back to the secularization of Kierkeg-aard's idea of decision: "In Sartre," he writes, "the notion of choice—originally a Kierkegaardian category—is heir to the Christian doctrine 'He who is not with me is against me,' though this dualistic slogan is now evacuated of any concrete theological content. What remains is merely the abstract authority of a choice enjoined, with no regard for the fact that the very possibility of choosing depends on what can be chosen." Indeed, it turns out that Sartre's own plays were "bad models" for Sartre's own existentialism, since in their respect for truth they accurately represent the administered universe that his philosophy ignores: "the lesson we learn from them is one of unfreedom." Ironically, then, Sartre proves more effective as a social critic within the bounds of his aesthetic work than he was when he burdened aesthetics with the unmediated task of social criticism.[48] Free from the ideal of *littérature engagée,* his theatrical works portray unfreedom with greater reality than the philosophy that celebrated unconditional freedom. "Sartre's theater of ideas," Adorno concludes, "sabotages the very thing for which he thought up the [existential] categories."[49] The undifferentiated character of absolute freedom in Sartrean existentialism disallows any concrete acknowledgment of the unfree conditions under which real choices can be made.

No less abstract was the portrait of the human condition developed by Karl Jaspers in his 1946 meditations, *The Question of German Guilt.*[50] According to Adorno, Jaspers shares with Sartre the basic assumption that "even in the so-called extreme situations, indeed in them most of all, humanity flourishes." In Jaspers's philosophy, however, this idea takes the form of "a dismal metaphysic which does its best to work up atrocities into limiting situation [*Grenzsituation*] which it then accepts to the extent that they reveal authenticity [*Eigentlichkeit*] in men." Just as Sartre imposed on the victim an extravagant responsibility for action that obscured the difference between that victim's suffering and the person who actually bears responsibility for inflicting harm, so too does Jaspers's notion of metaphysical guilt elevate questions of historical complicity onto the empyrean plane of a generic and indistinct human condition. "In such a homely existential atmosphere [*anheimelnden existentiellen Klima*]," writes Adorno, "the distinction between executioners and victims becomes blurred; both, after all, are equally suspended above the possibility of nothingness, which of course is generally not quite so uncomfortable for the executioners."[51]

The French existentialists, then, notwithstanding their strong ethic of political action, are no less bourgeois and quietist than their German analogues. Freedom of action itself becomes a license for persistent idealism: "Out of fear of reification they shrink back from what has substantive content." All that remains is the celebration of "irrational decisions" and "contingent borrowings, especially from psychology." Hence the popular appeal of "humanity" and the tautological injunction to "choose oneself" that dominated existentialism in the humanist mode. Such an ethic did little more than insist on "the pure form of the invariant as the only possible answer." In celebrating the absurdity of freedom, freedom was degraded into an absurd decision for existence even if its contours remained essentially unchanged: "What human beings are supposed to be, is always only, what they were: they are chained to the cliff of their past. They are not only what they were and are, but just as much what they could be. . . . They illustrate existence [*Existenz*] in the existing [*Existierenden*]."[52]

For Adorno, then, French existentialism was no more "activist" and no more successful in its rebellion against bourgeois convention than the Heideggerian project of fundamental ontology that, in the famous "Letter on 'Humanism'" supplanted Sartrean actionism with the contemplative mantra, "thinking acts in that it thinks." Needless to say, Adorno's indictment of French existentialism goes against the grain of conventional wisdom. Even those who are sharply critical of Sartrean existentialism today will tend to agree that Sartre's philosophy provides a far stronger justification for political agency in the usual sense.[53] But Adorno's verdict fully accords with the broader claim in *Negative Dialectics* that the philosophies of existence in all their forms, whether French or German, offered little more than variations on an idealist theme.[54]

Kierkegaard's Nominalism

The constant reprisal in *Negative Dialectics* of the charge that existential ontology reverts to idealism will hardly surprise the reader who has followed the narrative thus far, in which we have traced Adorno's critique, from the 1930s onward, of both transcendental and existential phenomenology. More surprising, perhaps, are those moments in *Negative Dialectics* when Adorno turns back explicitly to Kierkegaard, so as to demonstrate with greater precision the striking historical-philosophical irony that the theistic Kierkegaard could inspire the atheistic philosophers of existence. This unlikely connection hinges upon what Adorno called Kierkegaard's "nominalism," a term originally used in medieval Scholasticism (associated chiefly with Ockham) to express the view that universals enjoy no extramental existence and that only particulars qualify as metaphysically real. In Adorno's eyes, Kierkegaard, too, was a nominalist—at least in the sense that he rejected the Hegelian universal and insists on the priority of the solitary and finite individual who cleaves to God. Thus Kierkegaard, in Adorno's words, "nominalistically plays off existence against essence as the weapon of theology against metaphysics." Kierkegaard developed this quasi-nominalistic disdain for the general to such a degree that only the individual, created in the image of God, remains a site of "meaningfulness."[55]

The argument would seem to suggest that Kierkegaard's nominalism locks the individual subject into a kind of pious solipsism where the rest of the world loses all meaning and reality: the existent individual "sucks [ontology] dry" of nearly all its attributes.

The knight of faith is plunged once again into a sphere of idealism where only the subject is said to exist. But Adorno hastens to explain that when it is severed from its surroundings the nominalistic subject cannot retain its realist density. The subject for Kierkegaard achieves a "transparency" in relation to itself and this prepares the way for Heidegger's own notion of transparency as the quality of authentic *Dasein*. Hence Heidegger's claim (in Adorno's quotation from *Being and Time*) that "*Dasein* is on the grounds of its existential determination 'ontological' in itself." Like Robin Hood, the nominalist robs all universals of their right to ontological dignity only to award the isolated subject their stolen prestige. Yet the "concept of subjectivity iridescently shimmers no less than that of Being," and in the end the subject retains no other distinction than its ontological "attunement."[56] The nominalist rebellion against abstraction thereby adverts to a higher abstraction.

In Adorno's view, nominalism remains of paramount importance if one wishes to understand the philosophical connection between Kierkegaard and Heidegger. This is true not least because nominalism anticipated the existential disdain for universal concepts, and the hostility to abstract or disembedded cognition that informs Heidegger's analytic of being-in-the-world. "Nominalism, one of the roots of existential philosophy of the Protestant Kierkegaard, endows Heideggerian ontology with the attractive power of what is not speculative." Yet Adorno saw a contradiction in Heidegger's antispeculative nominalism, since even while it celebrated existence and sought to "extirpate" the non-conceptual, the existential analytic could not help but transform existence itself back into a concept. But nominalism has the further and even more ironic consequence of capitalizing on the prestige of realism (which it has robbed from universal concepts) and assigning it to the individual subject whose will becomes the sole remaining arbiter of the real. In medieval nominalism this subject was divine; but in modern nominalism, where divinity either turns into a *deus absconditus* or vanishes altogether, reality thereby becomes the exclusive property of the *Dasein,* "which is in each case mine [*jemeinig*]."[57] Adorno objected to this model of the individual as the product of social illusion. The very idea of the self as a *solus ipse* was merely a conceptual abstraction, a fact that was betrayed in the very instant of its utterance since the self-as-idea is barely formulated before it is deployed to exemplify a general condition. Nor could Adorno accept why a methodological point of departure also enjoys metaphysical priority: "Why the individual consciousness of every speaking person, which already presupposes a linguistic generality in the particle 'my,' which it denies through the primacy of its particularity, is supposed to be prior to anything else, is unfathomable." Kierkegaard's lonely but pious self-before-God anticipated and even helped to inspire the isolated but authenticated self of Heidegger's *Sein-zum-Tode.* Both transform the methodological self of philosophical description ("the sheer contingency [that] impels [them] to commence with the consciousness") into a license for disdaining the social world and making the individualistic methodological point of departure into an ontological necessity.[58]

According to Adorno, the modern philosophers of existence and existential ontology (Jaspers and Heidegger) had inherited Kierkegaard's subjectivist doctrine of truth. Even when, as in Heidegger's case, the advocates of existential ontology meant to disavow all subjectivism, their understanding of objectivity nonetheless bore the imprint of a constitutive subjectivity (an inheritance ultimately traceable to the Kantian doctrine of the transcendental unity of apperception). The original pattern of Kant's idealism (as announced in the famous dictum from the *Critique of Pure Reason*) that the singular and unifying power of the "I think" must accompany all my representations thus found an unlikely repetition even in the modern philosophies that claimed to have overcome idealism.[59] Heidegger joined to this epistemological inflation of subjective truth an existential or distinctively Kiergegaardian ethic of truthful individualism, a normative theme which, in Adorno's view, might help to explain the enormous success of *Being and Time:* "What contributed to its German popularity," he wrote, "was the fact that the radical pose and the sacred tone could be recombined into the newly-minted ideology of a person who was authentic and rock-solid [*Kernigen*], qualities which individuals in the spirit [*Geist*] of privilege reserve for themselves with sly dim-wittedness."[60] The existential motifs associated with both Kierkegaard and Heidegger therefore betrayed a certain "provincialism," not only in the sociological sense that "the cult of existence blossoms in the provinces of all countries" but also in the philosophical sense that they confined truth to the "narrowness" of the individual subject.

The bravura of this argument notwithstanding, Adorno's verdict on the subjectivism that disabled existential philosophy from Kierkegaard through Heidegger and Jaspers merits our attention chiefly because it served as an overture to Adorno's own philosophical alternative. "The utopian potential of thought," he explains, would be "that thought, mediated through the reason incorporated in individual subjects, would break through the narrowness of the thinker." Once again we can see how Adorno proposes negative dialectics not merely as an alternative for existential ontology but as its *realization*. It achieves the *breakthrough* to the object—and that is its "utopian" promise—whereas existential philosophy only collapses back in failure upon its own subjective-idealist beginnings. *Negative dialectics is the overcoming of existentialism but also its fulfillment.* Needless to say such a dialectical overcoming of existentialism breaks from its earlier errors in profound ways. Crucial here is Adorno's enduring faith in *reason* as the mediating element by which thought can break free of the subject's narrowness. Insisting on the rational moment in all individual cognition, Adorno argues that thought must not foreswear its "best power," the only medium by which thought can "surpass the weak and fallible thinker."[61] This is not only a general comment on the utopian potential of reason but also a specific comment on Adorno's own strategy of immanent critique. Once again we can see how Adorno arrives at his own insights only by *passing through and beyond* the established confines of modern philosophy. In this journey even a "fallible thinker" such as Heidegger can bear within his work a latent but utopian possibility. Before we can turn to this utopian alternative, however, we must trace out the last stages of Adorno's critique.

Heidegger's Critique of Reification

In one of the most sustained and formidable arguments of *Negative Dialectics*, Adorno finally takes up the systematic question as to how Heideggerian thought sabotages its own task and fails to realize its utopian potential. In answering this question Adorno must take seriously Heidegger's own critique of reification *(Verdinglichung)* which first appears in *Being and Time*, with reference to Lukács, as a central problem for existential ontology. According to Heidegger, every traditional and ontologically unexamined idea of a subject takes as its starting point a fallacious model of the subject, since it presupposes the *subjektum* as a *hypokeimenon*. This is so even for those who would spend great effort in "ontical protestations against the 'soul substance' or the 'reification of consciousness.' " In an obvious allusion to Lukács, Heidegger suggests that any critique of reification cannot leave unexamined the deeper ontological status of the subject in question: "Thinghood itself, which such reification implies, must have its ontological origin demonstrated if we are to be in a position to ask what we are to understand *positively* when we think of the nonreified *Being* of the subject, the soul, the consciousness, the spirit, the person." This nod to Lukács's critique of reification is hardly incidental to Heidegger's argument. After all, existential ontology presents itself as a remedy to "ontological forgetting," the pathological condition of a modernity in which both consciousness and world have solidified into thing-like opposition. Near the conclusion of his magnum opus Heidegger returns to this idea and offers a direct rejoinder to Lukács, who is charged with having misunderstood reification merely as a problem of objectification rather than recognizing its more profound and ontological connection to world temporality: "If world-time thus belongs to the temporalizing of temporality," Heidegger writes, "then it can neither be violated 'subjectivistically' nor 'reified' by a vicious 'objectification.' "[62]

Adorno enters into this familiar debate between Lukács and Heidegger chiefly because he thinks it reveals Heidegger's unfortunate habit of shifting philosophical problems onto the (ostensibly) higher stratum of ontological understanding, where any dialectical relation to the contingencies of society and history remains obscure. For Adorno this betrays the enduring bond of existential ontology with idealism: "Heidegger's critique of reification summarily loads up the reflecting and realizing intellect with what has its origin in reality, which is itself reified [verdinglicht] along with its world of experience." Such critique only blames the victim, since the intellect is not in fact the ultimate source of metaphysical error as Heidegger supposes but is merely one moment within a constellation of social forces. "What the Spirit does, is not the fault of its irreverent presumptuousness, but it gives back, what it is compelled to by the context of reality, in which it itself forms only a moment." In blaming an intellectualist (ontological) misunderstanding for a contingent sociohistorical unfreedom Heidegger commits an ideological sleight of hand: "To slide back reification into being and the history of being, thereby mourning as fate and consecrating what self-reflection and the praxis it can spark would perhaps like to change," Adorno writes, "is solely untruth."[63]

This critique takes up the disenchanting attitude toward existential ontology that Adorno had already presented in *The Jargon of Authenticity*, where the jargon appeared as a socially affirmative ideology. But in *Negative Dialectics* Adorno develops the philosophically more instructive claim—namely, that Heideggerian thinking also inherits from Kant and Hegel a salutary critique of reification even while it disables it from achieving any proper solution. The German idealists recognized the dialectical interrelation of objectivity with constitutive subjectivity, and Heidegger's attempting dismantling of the metaphysical subject retains at least a memory-trace of this salutary idealist heritage. As Adorno observes, "the doctrine of being hands down, legitimately against positivism, what the entire history which it slanders grounded, notably Kant and Hegel: that the dualism of the inner and outer, of subject and object, of essence and appearance, of concept and fact are not absolute." Heidegger's philosophy *rightly* expresses a complaint against positivism for seeing the relation between subject and object in merely dualistic terms: "Their reconciliation however is projected onto the irretrievable origin and thereby the dualism itself, against which the whole was conceived, is hardened against the reconciling impulse [*den versöhnenden Impuls*]. The dirge over the forgetfulness of being is the sabotage of reconciliation [*Sabotage an der Versöhnung*]."[64]

Adorno's critique thereby underscores the point that Heideggerian thinking cannot be summarily dismissed as outright falsehood. Rather, its enduring if paradoxical force is due to the fact that it both awakens *and* defeats the longing for reconciliation. Existential ontology, after all, would not be nearly so effective if it merely *annulled* the complaint against reification. On the contrary, its efficacy derives from the fact that it redirects the longing for reconciliation into "the mythic impenetrable history of being" where "hope still clings [*an welche Hoffnung sich klammert*]" but where the hope for any genuine reconciliation is also disabled. Such a critique suggests once again that Adorno does not feel he can casually dismiss the history of being as mere jargon. The path beyond its "fatality" cannot be evaded; it must be "broken through [*durchbrechen*]."[65] Such passages help us to see that Heidegger's critique of reification as a species of ontological forgetting, or *Seinsvergessenheit*, bears more than a superficial resemblance to the critique of reification in *Dialectic of Enlightenment*, where Adorno and Horkheimer observed, "All reification is forgetting [*Alle Verdinglichung ist ein Vergessen*]."[66]

Ontology as Wish Fulfillment

In *Negative Dialectics*, Adorno conjoins a *philosophical* critique of Heidegger's failure to break free of consciousness with an *ideological* critique of the way that Heidegger's philosophy serves the contemporary needs of mass society. Seen as an ideological palliative, existential ontology serves as a complement to the "primitive wish-fulfillments [that] that culture-industry feeds the masses." Much like the wish fulfillments of the culture industry, however, the solace existentialism provides is merely an ersatz for a genuine fulfillment that would actually respond to present desires. "The most urgent of [society's] needs today," Adorno observes, "seems to be that for something solid." And rightly so, since the development of an increasingly administered society leaves the individual helpless, longing for "security" but fearing to be "buried by a historical dynamic against which one feels powerless." These cultural observations prompt Adorno to entertain the thought that existential ontology is nothing less than a philosophical apology for social invariance. But it misrepresents this invariance as if it gives solace to the bourgeois self that is actually threatened with extinction: "That which is immovable would like to conserve that which is condemned as old. The more hopelessly the existing social forms block this longing, the more irresistibly does despairing self-preservation strike a philosophy, which is supposed to be both in one, despairing and self-preservation. The invariant structures are created in the spitting image of omnipresent terror, the vertigo of a society threatened by total destruction."[67]

To treat a philosophical system as a "wish fulfillment," however, implies the counterfactual possibility—namely, the possibility that with the removal of this threat, the actual philosophy (as the threat's "positive inversion") would also thereby dissolve.[68] Here, then, Adorno's enticing investment in the "wish" of existentialism comes into view. His interpretation implies that existentialism is analogous to a Freudian dreamwork—that is, an attempt within consciousness to fulfill a need whose actual fulfillment beyond consciousness remains socially blocked. What Adorno does not clearly spell out is the correlative implication, that any such dreamwork bespeaks genuine longings that would find their true satisfaction not in fantasy but in social reality. The critique of existentialism as a fantasy of real need thus implies the nonfantastical possibility of meeting this need with a real solution. Existential ontology thus represents a failure to realize an objective that will remain the preeminent task for negative dialectics itself.

Into the Looking Glass

It should not surprise us that this critique of Heidegger recapitulates a key verdict from *The Jargon of Authenticity*, where Adorno had accused modern existentialism of complicity with the alienated world of capitalism. In that work Adorno claimed that existentialism bought off a legitimate human longing for redemption from commodified existence with a language that was no less commodified. The critique of reification was itself reified; the polemic against idle-chatter was itself idle chatter.

We may therefore appreciate why Adorno devoted an entire essay, "Parataxis: On Hölderlin's Late Poetry," to combatting Heidegger's interpretation of Hölderlin's poetry. Whereas Heidegger detected in Hölderlin the exponent of an otherwise forgotten holism, Adorno extolled the poet for his "consciousness of non-identity."[69] Heidegger's readings of Hölderlin are not merely falsifications, Adorno suggests; they are also wish fulfillments that buy off the longing for the nonidentical with rhapsodies to a holism society has rendered impossible. In *Negative Dialectics* Adorno develops a similar insight, though in a less polemical fashion, alerting us to the irony that existentialism terminates in the idealism it wished to destroy. "Modern ontology," he writes, "is an ersatz in itself: what promises to be beyond the approach of idealism remains latent idealism and prevents its incisive critique."[70]

Existential ontology, then, *holds out and then betrays* its promise of release; it articulates in rarefied form the same dream of solidity that the culture industry extends to the masses in commodified form. Existential ontology speaks the very same language of concreteness, but it then deceives the consumer by landing itself back in the same abstraction of subjective meaning from which it promised escape. "Not only the primitive wish-fulfillments, which the culture-industry feeds the masses without the latter ever quite believing in them, are generally ersatz. Deception has no borders there, where the official cultural canon places its goods, in the presumed sublime of philosophy. The most urgent of its needs today seems to be that for something solid. It inspires the ontologies; it is what they take the measure of. It has its right in this, that one wishes to have security, to not be buried by a historical dynamic against which one feels powerless."[71]

Heidegger's philosophy, in other words, is a subjectivism yearning for the solidity of the object. It offers the salvation of reconciliation in its attempt to recollect a mode of being beyond the supremacy of the modern subject; but it remains trapped within the same "immanence of consciousness" as the Husserlian (transcendental) phenomenology against which it rebelled. Heidegger, however, deserves at least some credit for aiming at the proper target even if he fails in the attempt. Such considerations inspire one of the more intriguing passages in *Negative Dialectics*:

> More determinedly than the phenomenology which stops at the halfway mark, Heidegger would like to break out of the immanence

of consciousness. *His breakout however is one into a mirror,* blind towards the moment of the synthesis in the substrate. He fails to note that the Spirit, which in the Eleatic philosophy of being worshipped by Heidegger professed to be identical with being, is already contained as an implication of meaning in what it presents as that pure selfness, which faced opposite it. Heidegger's critique of the tradition of philosophy becomes objectively contrary to what it promises.[72]

The argument in the passage above merits close attention, especially if we attend to Adorno's distinction between Heidegger's philosophical ambition and his actual achievement. Clearly, it is Heidegger's ambition to recollect a mode of being beyond subjectivity, but in actuality Heidegger achieves nothing more impressive than a breakout "into a mirror." For Adorno, Heidegger thus bears a curious resemblance to Alice, the heroine in Lewis Carroll's story who believes she glimpses an entirely new reality on the other side of the looking glass but actually remains a captive to her own fantasies. This is the very same metaphor that Adorno used in his habilitation to illustrate the problem of interiority in Kierkegaard, in whose writings the mirror reflected back and even magnified the primacy of the individual. The repetition of this metaphor would seem to confirm Adorno's view that all three philosophers (Heidegger, Husserl, and Kierkegaard) remain caught despite their best intentions within an idealist hall of mirrors, where the only reality they can see is the bourgeois subjectivity that is endlessly reflected back at them. Confirming only the constitutive power of the subject, they fail to reach the object toward which they strive.[73]

More intriguing still, Adorno claims that precisely this *failure* in the history of existentialism illumines the path toward the successful *realization* of negative dialectics. For our purposes, the following is among the single most instructive passages in the entirety of *Negative Dialectics,* since it helps us to appreciate the positive stakes of Adorno's immanent critique of existential ontology: "*Heidegger reaches the very borders of the dialectical insight into the non-identity in identity. But he does not carry through the contradiction in the concept of being. He suppresses it. Whatever could be thought under being, mocks the identity of the concept with that which it means;* but Heidegger maltreats it as identity, as itself pure being, excluding all its otherness. He hushes up the non-identity in absolute identity like a family scandal."[74] The challenge here is one that, in an earlier discussion of this passage, Iain Macdonald has addressed with great lucidity. Although his conclusions are rather different than my own, Macdonald is right to fasten upon this claim as a key to the philosophical encounter between Adorno and Heidegger. Specifically, we must understand what Adorno means when he suggests that Heidegger reached "the borders" of the dialectical insight into the "non-identity in identity."[75] How does that which is "thought under being" contradict (or even "mock") Heidegger's assertion of an identity between the concept and what the concept means? This charge presupposes that Heidegger *actually does assert such an identity.* We may wonder, however, if this charge is fair. For we know of course that Heidegger insisted on the "ontological difference" between Being and beings (that is, between the mere entities that exist, or *Seiende,* and our understanding of their ontological manner, or *Seinsweise*). Did Adorno thereby condemn Heidegger for a crime he did not commit? And, if so, does the entirety of Adorno's immanent critique of existential ontology rest on a mistake? Or, if not, then just what did Adorno have in mind when he found Heidegger guilty of asserting an "identity" between the concept and its meaning?

To answer this question we must begin with the charitable assumption that Adorno did not simply misunderstand the ontological difference. Rather, let us consider the possible merits of his basic charge. On Adorno's view, the inquiry into the *Seinsfrage* commits Heidegger to a species of idealism *precisely because* it locates the Being of entities on the near side of the subject-object divide. In posing the question as to the *meaning* of Being (a question that interrogates the human being as the privileged site of ontological understanding), Heidegger does not break free of traditional subjectivity however much this may have been his stated purpose. On the contrary, he confirms the dominance of the subject over the object to such a degree as to make the subject's own *understanding* of Being the very condition for the disclosure of the world at all. That the world is "there" at all remains dependent upon the disclosure occasioned through the being who understands it. The suspicion that the world "in itself" may be "there" in the absence of *Dasein* is a remnant of the Kantian dogma of the world-in-itself, but this is a dogma that Heidegger wishes to disavow by condemning it as the spurious scenario of counterfactual reason.[76] Where he did comment on this question he placed intelligibility wholly on the side of *Dasein*'s worldhood and even claimed that the deworlded realm of nature is "the unintelligible [*unverständlich*] pure and simple."[77] Worldliness thus resides always and only *within Dasein*'s understanding of Being (or *Seinsverständnis*) and it is just this understanding that belongs uniquely to the human being as part of its own existential endowment. Borrowing from Heidegger's own words in his 1927 lectures on *The Basic Problems of Phenomenology*, it follows that "the world is something 'subjective.' "[78]

Disenchanting the Concept

If this interpretation is correct, we may find it easier to accept Adorno's rather startling and controversial claim that Heidegger asserts an *identity* between the concept and the concept's meaning. For Adorno, then, existential phenomenology would rank alongside Husserlian phenomenology as yet another specimen of the philosophy of identity. As we have seen, in *Negative Dialectics* Adorno assigns himself the task of *breaking through* the philosophy of identity to achieve what he called "the disenchantment of the concept."[79] A key to this task is the recognition that what a concept *means* is not internal to conceptuality but lies *beyond* the concept in the nonconceptual realm of the object. It is this *nonidentity* of the concept with its object that Adorno likens to a "family scandal" in philosophy.[80] Whereas Husserl suppressed this scandal by means of the phenomenological *époché,* Heidegger silenced it with the suggestion that the subject's own thought of Being is the condition for world disclosure. But in Adorno's view, what is disclosed in virtue of Being "mocks the identity" between *Dasein* and world no less than it mocks the identity between subject and object. The actual task for philosophy would be to recognize their nonidentity and thereby to annul what Adorno calls "the autarky of the concept."[81]

The task of "disenchanting the concept" in this manner would dissolve the quasi-archaic aura of posttheistic existentialism. And it would thereby contribute to a genuine *secularization of philosophy.* The ultimate effect would be to dismantle the idealist paradigm, awakening philosophy to the materialist truth that the conceptual is always "enmeshed in a non-conceptual whole." Here we must recall that for Adorno the concept can never achieve self-sufficiency, since it is always mediated through the nonconceptual. Indeed, Adorno believes that the very "signification" of a concept would not be possible at all were it not for this nonconceptual status.[82] In this sense the nonconceptual must always play a "constitutive" role in the concept. Awakening to this constitutive role is central to Adorno's own project: "To change this direction of conceptuality, to turn it towards the non-identical," Adorno explains, "is the hinge of negative dialectics."[83]

At first glance it may seem that this task is simply a matter of philosophical *insight.* At one point early in the book, Adorno even entertains the tempting idea that insight alone might effect the necessary transformation: "Before the insight [*Vor der Einsicht*] into the constitutive character of the non-conceptual in the concept, the compulsion of identity, which carries along the concept without the delay of such a reflection, dissolves [*zerginge*]." But it is crucial to note that this task would involve a truly profound transformation that would lift it well beyond the exercises in philosophical criticism. Indeed, whatever sort of transformation is implied, it would seem to demand more than yet another turn of the discursive wheel in philosophical argument, since Adorno actually calls it the "antidote to philosophy."[84] It signifies, in other words, not just a shift in philosophical understanding but also a breakthrough in the larger understanding of reification. "The philosophy which recognizes this, which cancels out the autarky of the concept, strikes the blinders from the eyes. That the concept is a concept even when it deals with the existent, hardly changes the fact that it is for its part enmeshed in a non-conceptual whole against which it seals itself off solely through its reification, which indeed created it as a concept."[85]

The argument above suggests that a full and satisfactory dismantling of reification would first require a philosophical recognition that the conceptual is not self-sufficient—that is, it would require a philosophical realization of the "primacy" of the object. As we have seen, the argumentative work of *Negative Dialectics* is confined chiefly to immanent critique: the path toward materialism is developed via the internal and dialectical reading of prior idealist philosophy than through independent argument. But the task of immanent criticism is more than this; it is simultaneously a form of ideology critique, since in Adorno's view the primacy of the concept corresponds to a mode of life that actively *denies* the primacy of the nonconceptual; indeed, this denial *is the very meaning of ideology*. The shift toward the primacy of the object would therefore entail a dismantling of this ideology and a consequent turn toward materialism.[86]

We have come to the conclusion of Chapter 4 of this book, and yet a great many questions about Adorno's interpretation of the philosophy of existence remain unanswered. Chief among these is the curious matter of his enduring attachment to Kierkegaard, whose philosophy Adorno had earlier in his life excoriated and caricatured as the very paradigm of bourgeois interiority. It is a remarkable fact about Adorno's career that at the end of his life he returned once more to Kierkegaard and found resources in the Dane's philosophy that would help him to grasp the unexpected relation between religion and materialism, between modern theology and "the disenchantment of the concept." The relation, needless to say, is as unlikely as it is instructive. I will explore this question in the fifth and final chapter, and we will see once again how negative dialectics was not merely the negation of existentialism but also its fulfillment.

5

Kierkegaard's Return

... eternity does away with all worldly authority
—SØREN KIERKEGAARD, *The Present Age*

Salvaging Metaphysics

On March 14, 1967, Adorno wrote a letter to Gershom Scholem, the great historian of Jewish mysticism, in which he sought to explain the idea of a negative dialectic. "In the immanent epistemological debate," Adorno wrote, "once one has escaped from the clutches of idealism, what I call the primacy of the object . . . seems to me an attempt to do justice to the concept of materialism. The telling arguments that I believe I have advanced against idealism present themselves as materialist. But the materialism involved here is no conclusive, fixed thing, it is not a worldview. This path to materialism is totally different from dogma, and it is this fact that seems to me to guarantee an affinity with metaphysics, I might almost have said, theology."[1]

The letter is remarkable on several counts. First, we should note the care Adorno takes in holding orthodox or "dogmatic" Marxism at a safe distance even while he aligns himself with philosophical materialism. The critique of idealism that (as we have seen already) plays such a prominent role in *Negative Dialectics* helps to prepare the way for what Adorno calls "the primacy of the object." Indeed, the idea of the object's ontological primacy is surely among the foremost principles of any recognizably materialist philosophy. However, for this very reason we should find it all the more intriguing to see that Adorno grants a possible identity (or coexistence) between this kind of materialism and what he calls "metaphysics." Indeed, it is truly striking to witness his gesture of terminological self-amendment: *"metaphysics, I might almost have said, theology."*

As a beginning to this final chapter, we should pause to consider the significance of these unusual lines. Let us begin by noting their indecision. Adorno tells Scholem that his materialist orientation guarantees "an affinity" with metaphysics, but he adopts the casual gesture of a confession that this is something he *almost wrote, but did not*. Metaphysics *might have been* theology, though Adorno does not *in fact call it theology*. It is as if he turns back at the last moment, confessing only to a temptation with which he wrestled but ultimately managed to resist. Especially in the form of a personal letter such a confession of what he might have written may strike us as too casual to warrant philosophical analysis. Nor can we exclude the writer's anticipation of Scholem's likely response: Adorno might possibly have sensed that his correspondent would respond favorably to the suggestion that *Negative Dialectics* bespoke theological rather than materialist commitments. Adorno's momentary "confession" (if that it is what it is) may call to mind the well-known 1931 letter in which Scholem chastised his friend Walter Benjamin for the latter's "self-deception" in aligning himself with materialism, an alignment Scholem saw as a confused amalgam between politics and religion.[2] The comparison is especially instructive since Adorno does not confess to any such "error" nor does he openly *assert* a syncretistic and unworkable fusion of materialism with theology of the kind that Scholem found objectionable in Benjamin's work. Elsewhere in the same letter Adorno confirms, "The wish to salvage metaphysics is in fact central to *Negative Dialectics*."[3]

We might therefore conclude that "metaphysics" serves as the acknowledged horizon for analysis, or, as a kind of *tertium comparationis*. A similar line can be found in *Negative Dialectics* itself, where Adorno claims, "At its most materialist, materialism comes to agree with theology."[4] We are therefore left with the formidable question: How did Adorno conceive of the relation between theology and materialism?

We have come now to the fifth and final chapter in my discussion of Adorno and existence. In this chapter we must finally confront the question that has repeatedly recurred to us throughout the previous chapters without coming fully into view—namely, whether Adorno sustained an enduring, if dialectically mediated, allegiance to the philosophy of existence. We have seen already how Adorno returned throughout his life to Kierkegaard and how, eventually, he came to modify the rather stringent verdict of his earliest study, in which he had scrutinized the Dane's philosophy with the instruments of a so-called materialist criticism. We have also seen that for Adorno the historical path that traverses a century from Kierkegaard to Heidegger describes an arc of increasing disenchantment. The theology Kierkegaard openly professed began slowly to dissolve, until with Heidegger the language of existence seems to surrender its appeal to metaphysical transcendence. And yet for Adorno this arc is not quite as unidirectional as it may seem, since it bends back upon itself in a covert regression to its religious point of departure. Indeed, it is the paradox of existential ontology that it simultaneously exploits the sacred aura it claims to rescind.

According to Adorno, this story of simultaneous disenchantment and illicit *re*enchantment belongs to the larger dialectical narrative of bourgeois modernity. Since philosophy is its age comprehended in thought, bourgeois philosophy expresses both the ambition and the self-destruction of the bourgeoisie itself. In an earlier phase in the history of the bourgeois self, Kierkegaard could still draw nourishment from an idea of an incommensurable transcendence that was already out of phase with the logic of universal exchange: he cleaved to the absolute in an age when all absolutes were beginning to yield to the marketplace logic of equivalency. In this sense Kierkegaard—despite his political conservatism—made the philosophy of interiority into the last refuge for a critique of incipient reification. In the modern phase of capitalism, however, the very ideal of a strong subject can no longer appeal to a transcendent support, and the language of bourgeois heroism becomes no less mythical than the instrumental rationality that has already dissolved all other myths. It is to this predicament that Heideggerian philosophy offers an illusory solution, giving to reified consciousness the stereotyped promise of a life beyond reification. In Heidegger, the jargon of authenticity only commodifies the promise of transcendence. With its yearning for "solidity," it represents the last phase in the capitalist process by which all that is solid melts into air.

To be sure, in this verdict one would be hard-pressed to find anything like a strong admiration for existentialism. Partisans of the existential tradition might feel moved to object that Adorno was not the most careful of readers. From a strictly philosophical point of view, his narrative of disenchantment may seem to place far too much emphasis on the social significance of ideas rather than what one might call their "inner truth." Those who wish to defend Kierkegaard or Heidegger (or others in the traditions of existence and phenomenology) may hasten to object that the actual argumentation in this tradition is one thing and its instrumentalization is another thing altogether. As a proponent of critical theory, however, Adorno would insist that any attempt to hold these two moments as entirely distinct is no less ideological than their specious conflation. For it is a cardinal principle of negative dialectics that we must reject *both* thoroughgoing dissociation *and* thoroughgoing identification—both idealism and sociologism. Even readers who are not already convinced of the merits of critical theory, however, may nonetheless worry that Adorno has not furnished a truly philosophical justification for his claims. It is therefore important to see that Adorno's philosophical writings on both Kierkegaard and Heidegger were chiefly instances of *immanent* critique, in that he felt they had both articulated genuinely philosophical problems in the history of metaphysics even if they had not arrived at wholly satisfactory conclusions. In fact, for Adorno it was their very *failure* to achieve this solution that proves instructive, since a critical reading of their difficulties helps to clear the way toward negative dialectics itself.

In this chapter, I want to address this claim directly, and I will suggest that the "primacy of the object" serves as Adorno's name for the metaphysical insight that both Kierkegaard and Heidegger were striving toward, but without success. Now, we can best appreciate the nature of this metaphysical insight if we grasp the essential point that, for Adorno, *theology and materialism are in a certain sense aligned*. This, I would argue, is the insight that animates his quasi-confessional letter to Scholem. In this chapter, it is my task to expand upon what this alignment might entail. I will therefore begin, in the first half, with Adorno's reading of Heidegger, and I will then turn, in the second half, to Adorno's last reflections on Kierkegaard. We will therefore end by describing a full circle, returning with Adorno at the end of his life to the topic of his *Habilitation*.

Materialism as Demystified Idealism

To any reader of *Negative Dialectics,* it should be apparent that Adorno wished to affirm a materialist perspective insofar as the primacy of the object is the name for a doctrine that exceeds the bounds of idealism. At the very least, he wished to affirm the "primacy of the object," a phrase that signals his desire to burst free from idealism's constraints. But the materialism that emerges from this philosophical project does not represent a merely abstract negation or a straightforward alternative to idealism. We should recall that for Adorno the tradition of German idealism—from Kant to Hegel—retained a certain paradigmatic status, insofar as it realizes the greatest possibilities of bourgeois philosophy from which Adorno himself continued to draw instruction. As Brian O'Connor has observed, "the concepts that support the negative dialectic have conspicuous Kantian and Hegelian colors."[5] Moreover, it is a characteristic theme in all of Adorno's philosophical work that idealism is *both* false *and* true. Idealism is false because it asserts the subject's primacy and is thereby motivated to forget the very nature of human nature. Indeed, the self-assertion of the idealist subject is a species of repression; it responds with shame and denial to the very fact of human embodiment, and its strategy of repression is carried forward into the modern philosophies of existence that only acknowledge death under the sanitized name of *Dasein*'s "possibility." Despite this falsehood, however, idealism also articulates a species of truth, since it bespeaks an emancipatory consciousness that resists any complacent subordination to the merely given. The theme of constitutive subjectivity that animates transcendental idealism is in this respect not only a discrete philosophical doctrine, it is also a formalized expression of a basic anthropological need: the shaping action of the subject who transforms an otherwise terrifying nature into humanized nature and thereby strives to reduce the terror of its own animal existence. The Kantian categories, for example, are analogous to the tools by which primitive humanity carved out a place with nature for its own domestic existence and made space and time themselves into hospitable forms.

Moreover, idealism also retains a moment of truth insofar as it *qualifies* the metaphysical reach of this shaping activity. As Adorno reminds us in his late essay "Subject and Object," the Kantian doctrine of the thing-in-itself is a remnant within idealism of a reality "free from the subjective spell."[6] So, too, in Hegel's philosophy the principle of negativity can be turned against the sovereignty of *Geist*. In the first of his *Three Studies on Hegel*, Adorno reminds us that Hegel's aim was never merely an affirmation of the subject's domination, since "the dialectic demonstrates the impossibility of reducing the world to a fixed subjective pole." Even Hegel's emphasis on negativity, however, could not break free of its idealist ambitions: "Like Fichte," Adorno writes, "Hegel attempted to outdo Kant in idealism by dissolving anything not proper to consciousness—in other words, the given moment of reality—into a positing by the infinite subject."[7] Nevertheless, this should not deter us from recognizing that Adorno's own model of negative dialectics was conceived, in some sense, as a radicalization and transformation of Hegel. In his *Lectures on Negative Dialectics* he actually goes so far as to declare that "of the ideas that I am presenting to you, *there is not a single one that is not contained, in tendency at least, in Hegel's philosophy.*"[8] Notwithstanding this powerful inheritance, however, Adorno felt that he could remain faithful to the critical promise of negation only if he resisted the principle of final reconciliation that served as the *ens realissimum* for Hegel's mature system. Although the younger Hegel understood the dangers of what he called positivity, the later Hegel (in Adorno's words) believed that "the affirmative could be discovered at the end of all negations." Adorno therefore proposes *negative* dialectics precisely *against* Hegel's principle of an affirmative totalization.[9]

All of this suggests that for Adorno we can discern the truth of idealism only if we also discern the falsehood this truth promotes, for idealism ultimately subverts its own truth insofar as its concept of freedom breaks away from the objective world in which that freedom would have real meaning. In *Negative Dialectics*, Adorno discerns this self-undermining of idealism in *both* the Kantian antinomies *and* in Hegel's dialectic itself: "The antinomies of freedom in Kant, just like the dialectics of freedom in Hegel, form an essential philosophical moment; after them academic philosophy, at least, swore by the idol of a higher realm beyond empiricism. The intelligible freedom of individuals is praised, so that one can hold the empirical ones even more ruthlessly accountable, to better curb them by the prospect of a metaphysically justified punishment. The alliance of the doctrine of freedom and repressive praxis distances philosophy ever further from genuine insight into the freedom and unfreedom of living beings."[10] For Adorno, then, the idealist break between subjective freedom and external necessity ultimately betrays the emancipatory promise that inspired the idealist tradition. But this break has the further consequence of setting up the conditions for bourgeois domination: although the subject cannot locate its freedom *within* nature, it nevertheless orients itself *toward* nature as the object to be dominated. Idealism is in this sense expresses a "rage against nature." And because it turns reason into an instrument of domination it serves as the metaphysical and ideological warrant for the dialectic of enlightenment.

Given this global critique of the idealist tradition, the basic question for Adorno is clear: How can we can ever hope to break free of idealism without lapsing into an uncritical affirmation of givenness or sheer positivity? In the letter to Scholem he explains that the proper escape from "the clutches of idealism" points toward "the primacy of the object" and that such primacy will "do justice to the concept of materialism." Now, it is vital to Adorno's conception of materialism that we do not misunderstand the notion of the *object's* primacy as merely an *inversion* of idealism. According to Adorno, idealism understands the primacy of the subject in the *extravagant* sense of an identity between being and thought. In other words, it sees the totality of what there is as the successful realization of self-positing subjectivity. Materialism, however, is not extravagant in this sense: it does not represent merely an *inversion* of idealism, because it does not recapitulate the idealist gesture of reconciliation by asserting the mere identity between the totality and "objectivity." The mere inversion of idealism would be positivism—and Adorno does everything he can to ward off positivism as the very negation of critical philosophy. Rather, materialism properly conceived actually *incorporates the truth of idealism,* and this means that, *precisely from the perspective of the subject,* it must radicalize the notion of the object's *resistance to subjectivity.* As was discussed above, both Kant and Hegel already glimpsed this phenomenon of resistance and in this sense we might plausibly say that their idealism contained a moment of self-negation. Adorno's conception of materialism, with all its allusions to the body and the remembrance of forgotten nature, might therefore be described as first and foremost an articulation of *just this resistance.*[11]

In the early pages of *Negative Dialectics,* Adorno elaborates on this idea when he says that he wishes to deepen our insight into the constitutive character of *"the non-conceptual in the concept."*[12] The critical phrase here is *"in the concept,"* since this phrase alerts us to the fact that negative dialectics emerges precisely as a *radicalization* of the resistance that is *internal to idealism* itself. To radicalize this resistance would not entail stepping fully "outside" the concept, since philosophical reflection necessarily requires an acknowledgment of conceptuality. Philosophy, after all, cannot wholly disavow its own discursivity in some misguided nostalgia for primitive immediacy. Rather, Adorno wishes to develop *within* conceptuality a recognition of the nonconceptual; idealism must *reflect upon its own meaning* and awaken to the exterior beyond its domain.[13] This defining task finds its most programmatic statement at the very beginning of *Negative Dialectics:* "To change this direction of conceptuality, to give it a turn toward nonidentity, is the hinge of negative dialectics. Insight into the constitutive character of the nonconceptual in the concept would end the compulsive identity which the concept brings unless halted by such reflection. Reflection upon its own meaning is the way out of the concept's seeming being-in-itself as a unit of meaning."[14] A materialist philosophy would permit us to escape the concept's "being-in-itself," and it would therefore demystify idealism.[15] Such a materialist perspective serves a critical function in that it dismantles what Adorno calls the "autarky of the concept." Such autarky is never in fact a real possibility and it therefore ranks as a form of self-deception. Indeed, it would not be an exaggeration to say that the idealistic dream of conceptual autarky represents in philosophical form the self-deception of bourgeois society itself, a society in which the overpowering fact of material determination and the stark reality of domination can never be fully acknowledged without calling into question the modern illusion of subjective freedom. Materialism, however, "strips the blindfold from our eyes" by alerting philosophy to objective conditions that resist the subject's epistemological ambitions and therefore its domination as well. In this sense Adorno clearly thinks that materialism demystifies the very metaphysics that serve as the foundations for bourgeois ideology. "Disenchantment of the concept," he concludes, "is the antidote of philosophy."[16] In his *Lectures on Negative Dialectics* Adorno characterizes the movement toward nonidentity as nothing less than "the *utopia of cognition.*"[17]

The Family Scandal

It is crucial to note that, for Adorno, Heideggerian ontology represents the self-deception of idealism but it does so *in an unusually conflicted way.* As we have already seen in the previous chapters, Adorno is convinced that existentialism remains caught in a species of idealism despite its own anti-idealist ambitions. But these ambitions are nonetheless significant, since they awaken a philosophical longing for a realization of a still-unrealized promise. Such a realization, however, would require a species of dialectical self-overcoming— that is, it would demand *both* a negation *and* a fulfillment of the promise that existentialism bears within itself. In a highly revealing passage, Adorno had suggested that Heidegger comes up against the very limits of a genuinely dialectical insight but then fails to realize this insight with a determination that would suffice to leave idealism behind. "*Heidegger reaches the very borders of the dialectical insight into the non-identity in identity. But he does not carry through the contradiction in the concept of being.* He suppresses it [Heidegger gelangt bis an die Grenze der dialektischen Einsicht in die Nichtidentität in der Identität. Aber den Widerspruch im Seinsbegriff trägt er nicht aus. Er unterdrückt ihn]. Whatever could be thought under being, mocks the identity of the concept with that which it means; but Heidegger maltreats it as identity, as itself pure being, excluding all its otherness. He hushes up the non-identity in absolute identity like a family scandal [*Familienschande*]."[18]

In the passage above, Adorno identifies a "contradiction" in the concept of being because the concept refers to a phenomenon that is exterior to the concept. "Being," according to Adorno, has the status of a concept that names a nonconceptual phenomenon. But to grasp this nonconceptual condition by means of a concept therefore misses precisely the nonconceptual status to which the concept refers. The concept and the phenomenon are nonidentical. The reader will note that this argument recapitulates a critique remarkably similar to the one laid out in Adorno's 1924 dissertation on the transcendence of the thing and noema in Husserlian phenomenology. Applied to Heidegger, however, the critique may strike us as rather more controversial.

Indeed, one might quarrel with Adorno on this point insofar as the kind of nonidentity he mentions is a trivial and obvious feature of all reference: all concepts inhere in thought, whereas (in many cases) the objects to which concepts refer are worldly things and do not *themselves* inhere in thought. But Adorno seems to think that that Heideggerian concept of Being is afflicted by a special kind of nonidentity that Heidegger refused to acknowledge. This is precisely because Heidegger's own idealism stands in conflict with its own anti-idealist pretentions. On the one hand, Adorno (following Anders, Ryle, and others) sees Heidegger as an idealist in the technical sense that "Being" is just a mode of *understanding* or a condition of disclosure that *belongs to Dasein*. It is thanks to this special endowment that Heidegger emphasizes the ontic and ontological "priority" of *Dasein* for the project of existential ontology. This priority does not indicate merely the methodological contrivance of beginning with the being that has an understanding of being, or for whom being is "at issue." In *Sein und Zeit*, Heidegger himself admits the relative advantage of idealism over realism, insofar as it recognizes that being is "in the consciousness" and is "transcendental" for every entity.[19] And in *Basic Problems of Phenomenology* (which Adorno did not read), Heidegger notes, "The world is not the sum total of extant entities. It is quite generally, not extant at all. It is a determination of being-in-the-world, *a moment in the structure of Dasein's mode of being*. The world is, so to speak, *Dasein-like [Daseingemäßiges]*."[20]

Elsewhere Adorno repeats the charge of existentialism's "scandalous" or disavowed commitment to identity theory. For example, in his 1964 essay on Hölderlin, "Parataxis," he condemns Heidegger as not just an opportunistic reader of poetry but—more important—as a thinker who "betrays utopia to imprisonment in selfhood." For Adorno, existential ontology also betrays its claustrophobic and self-affirming character when Heidegger fails to comprehend those dissonant motifs in Hölderlin's poetry that allude to what is foreign, including a foreign woman who is (in Heidegger's words) "the one who at the same time makes us think about our native land." For Adorno, such a defensive and nationalistic reading is clearly a distortion, a symptom of the "endogamous ideal" that governs existential ontology itself. In his zeal to make Hölderlin an amanuensis for his own philosophy, Heidegger forced Hölderlin's concept of love into a species of nationalism; as Adorno notes, "Hölderlin is driven up hill and down dale in the service of a conception of love that circles around inside what one is anyway, fixated narcissistically on one's own people."[21] Heidegger revealed himself once again as a zealous partisan of identity theory and proved unable to honor the parataxis that—in both Hölderlin's poetry and the late style of Beethoven—signified an escape, from *both* the self-identity of an endogamous and narcissistic ethic *and* from the luxurious *intérieur* of bourgeois life.[22]

In *Negative Dialectics* Adorno pursues this criticism of Heidegger with unflagging zeal. The idealistic strain in Heidegger's existential ontology runs into fatal difficulties, he argues, when the idealist affirmation of *Dasein*'s primacy is pressed upon the reader in combination with an *anti-idealist* pathos of "solidity" or "worldliness." For as Adorno reminds us, the ambition to break free from the abstractions of conceptual philosophy was one of the major selling points of the existential rebellion; indeed, it is this promise of concreteness that helps to explain the postwar vogue in existential jargon. The paradox of Heideggerian existentialism, however, is that it combines its promise of existential worldliness with a doctrine of transcendental idealism that rescinds this very promise. By interrogating the question of being as a special endowment of *Dasein,* it places the being of the world itself back inside the cabinet of consciousness from which it was supposed to escape. Now, it is precisely *this* paradox that Adorno thinks existential ontology cannot acknowledge without conceding the nonidentity between concept and world. This nonidentity is what Adorno seems to have in mind when he claims that what could be "thought under being [i.e., the concept of being] *mocks the identity* of the concept *with that which it means.*" If Heidegger were to acknowledge this nonidentity, he would suffer a fatal embarrassment: the unwanted and much-maligned Cartesian distinction between subject and object would reveal itself at the core of his own philosophy. Hence the "family scandal."[23]

Adorno's critique of Heideggerian existentialism, then, is that it is a philosophy that strives for the object but remains caught in the idealistic trap of subjectivity. The same point is made elsewhere in *Negative Dialectics,* where Adorno observes, "Nonidentity is the secret telos of identification; it is the part that can be salvaged [*Rettende*]; the mistake in traditional thinking is that identity is taken for the goal."[24] Once we have grasped this crucial point we may better understand why Adorno felt such an urgent need to develop an immanent and genuinely dialectical critique of Heidegger's philosophy. Adorno conceives of his own project of negative dialectics as *a realization of the promise existentialism betrayed*. But, much as Heidegger himself pursued a "destructive" reading of the philosophical canon so as to reveal the "unthought" in its thought, so too Adorno believed that the promise remains in a very important sense the unrealized truth of existentialism itself. And it is this latent meaning that is disclosed by means of immanent critique. As J. M. Bernstein explains, "For the thought of the nonidentical to become significant some phenomenon of it must be found in existing conceptual practices."[25] For Adorno, the canons of existentialism remain a crucial resource in precisely this respect.

But even this explanation courts grave misunderstanding if we do not take care to distinguish between promise and goal. For the "promise" that Adorno sees as the latent *truth* of existential ontology is surely not its self-declared *aim*. The aim of existential ontology as Heidegger himself conceives it is to overcome the metaphysical chasm between subject and object by a process of redemptive recollection that restores *Dasein* to its own postlapsarian status. Heidegger would like to expel the subject out of itself and into the world, but he also insists that this expulsion has always already occurred. *Geworfenheit* is nothing less than the *peccatum originale* for a being that was never innocent and never *otherwise than* being-in-the-world. This is a crucial distinction—and perhaps it is even *the* crucial distinction—between Adorno and Heidegger: existentialism longs for the solidity of the object in a manner that is supposed to evacuate the very meaning of traditional subjectivity altogether. Negative dialectics, by contrast, sustains the solidity of the object, but it does so in the name of a persistent difference rather than an extorted and premature reconciliation. The subject that confronts the object loses its sovereignty over the world but nonetheless *resists* its wholesale absorption by the object it confronts. In one of the *Lectures on Negative Dialectics,* Adorno specifically warns his auditors that "the *elimination* of the subjective qualities always implies a reduction of the object."[26] The materialist primacy of the object is therefore not to be confused with a positivistic evacuation of conceptuality. This distinction between Adorno and Heidegger helps us to see why "materialism" in Adorno's lexicon can never serve as merely another name for mindless positivism, as if the primacy of the object meant little more than surrender to sheer facticity. In the very last of the *Lectures on Negative Dialectics,* Adorno makes just this point: "Existentialism, as the name already indicates, *duplicates* the bare existence of mankind. It becomes its mentality as if there were any option other than existence—meaning, by virtue of its absence, becomes a tautology."[27]

For Adorno the affirmative character of existential ontology reveals itself most of all in its false belief that it can "break the spell of nature by soothingly copying it."[28] In this respect existentialism bespeaks an atavistic desire to regress: it yearns for the prerational state in which human being felt it could survive only by thoughtlessly repeating the patterns of the nature that threatened it. But this mimetic strategy is fatalistic, and it represents a positivistic self-abandonment to power:

> Existential thinking crawls into the cave of a long-past mimesis. In the process it is nonetheless accommodating the most fatal prejudice from the philosophical history which it has laid off like a superfluous employee: the Platonic prejudice that the imperishable must be the good—which is to say no more than that in permanent warfare the stronger is always right. Yet if Plato's pedagogy cultivated martial virtues, the Gorgias dialogue still made these virtues answerable to the highest idea, to the idea of justice. In the darkened sky of the existence-teaching, however, no star is shining any more. *Existence is sanctified without the sanctifying factor [Existenz wird geweiht ohne das Weihende].* Of the eternal idea in which the entity was to share, or by which

it was to be conditioned, nothing remains but the naked affirmation of what is anyway—the affirmation of power.[29]

What Adorno calls the primacy of the object, then, must not be confused with a positivistic affirmation of the given. Existential ontology sanctifies whatever happens to be the case and subordinates the subject to the object, as if the subject were a slave to social reality. Negative dialectics, by contrast, sustains the subject even while affirming materialism. The primacy of the object, then, also entails the *persistence* of the subject who confronts it. This subject, in fact, remains the only source of critical resistance against positivism. Existence can be affirmed only if it can also be judged deficient, but any such judgment must appeal to some standard external to existence itself. It can only be "sanctified [*geweiht*]" if the "sanctifying factor [*das Weihende*]" remains nonidentical to existence, just as critique can only reveal the brokenness of the world by a light that is not identical to the world itself. And this originally theological idea of a criterion *external to existence* alerts us to Adorno's belief (mentioned earlier in the letter to Scholem) that there is a hidden affinity between materialism and theology. To be sure, Adorno's conception of theology had to be precisely that: a *conception,* internal to philosophy, and altogether distinct from any affirmation of religious dogma or feeling. Just what might satisfy this stringent criterion, however, remains to be seen.

Odradek as Damaged Life

In his December 17, 1934, letter to Walter Benjamin, Adorno referred to Benjamin's essay on Kafka and he compared it to his own interpretation ("my own earliest attempt to interpret Kafka") which he had apparently written nine years earlier. We lack further information about such an early interpretation—Adorno's "Notes on Kafka" was published much later, in 1953—except that in his letter

Adorno makes the further observation that Kafka "represents a photograph of our earthly life from the perspective of a redeemed life [*er sei eine Photographie des irdischen Lebens aus der Perspektive des erlösten*]."[30] Adorno goes on to elucidate this rather striking claim with an unusual metaphor: whatever it is that Kafka may consider "redeemed life," it is something that does not show itself directly and with positive content. It is revealed instead as nothing more than "the edge of a black cloth" (most likely a reference to the covering which hides the photographer) while "the terrifying distanced optics of the photographic image [*die grauenvoll verschobene Optik*] is none other than that of the obliquely angled camera itself."[31] This interpretation of Kafka bears a certain resemblance to Adorno's closing remark in *Minima Moralia* that critique reveals the world to be "as indigent and distorted [*bedürftig und entstellt*] as it will appear one day in the messianic light."[32] But what most deserves our attention here is the further suggestion, that in their Kafka interpretations, both Adorno and Benjamin subscribe to a certain philosophical stance that Adorno calls an "'inverse' theology." (In the original German, Adorno placed the term in quotation marks: "'inverse' Theologie."[33]) Adorno further specifies that such an inverse theology is "directed against natural and supernatural interpretation alike," and that his own study of Kierkegaard was "concerned with nothing else [*ja meinem Kierkegaard war es um nichts anderes zu tun als darum*]."[34]

This should strike us as a remarkable claim, especially if we recall that in his *Kierkegaard: Construction of the Aesthetic* (published just a year before the exchange with Benjamin quoted above), Adorno had virtually nothing to say about theology. Indeed, it is hardly an exaggeration to suggest that the entire task of the Kierkegaard book was to examine the Danish philosopher from the disenchanted perspective of a "materialism" that took aesthetics more seriously than the purported theology for which Kierkegaard was most celebrated. Furthermore, we should not ignore the fact that Adorno expressly rejected interpretations that claimed to find theological and existential motifs in Kafka's work. In his postwar essay, "Notes on Kafka," Adorno complains that of what has been written on Kafka, "little counts; most is existentialism." Here, too, he explicitly dismisses the relevance of Kierkegaard: "Kafka used motifs from Kierkegaard's *Fear and Trembling*," Adorno avers, though "not as heir but as critic." He harbors a special hostility toward dialectical theologians who wished to appropriate Kafka's texts for religious ends: "Dialectical theology fails in its attempt to appropriate him [Kafka] not merely because of the mythical character of the powers at work, an aspect that Benjamin rightly emphasized, but also because in Kafka, unlike *Fear and Trembling*, ambiguity and obscurity are attributed not exclusively to the Other as such but to human beings and to the conditions in which they live. Precisely that 'infinitely qualitative distinction' taught by Kierkegaard and Barth is leveled off."[35] Such principled antipathy to theological readings of Kafka's work forbids us from adopting any facile interpretation of Adorno's "inverse theology" that would construe it as a species of theology in the conventional sense. Yet the near total disregard for anything that would count prima facie as "theology" in the 1933 book makes Adorno's remarks in the letter to Benjamin all the more puzzling. One possible solution suggests itself: What if the "materialist" perspective that Adorno wished to exemplify in the Kierkegaard book were somehow an expression of the "inverse theology" to which he refers? Is it possible that what Adorno calls materialism bears some intrinsic relation to inverse theology?

We can best explore this possibility if we consider the strange story by Kafka that Adorno goes on to mention in his letter to Benjamin. The story is titled "Die Sorge des Hausvaters" (The cares of a family man), and it seems fair to say that its enigmatic imagery ranks it among the most unsettling of the short stories left to us by Kafka.[36] At the center of the story is a creature called Odradek:

At first glance it looks like a flat star-shaped spool for thread, and indeed it does seem to have thread wound upon it; to be sure, they are only old, broken-off bits of thread, knotted and tangled together, of the most varied sorts and colors. But it is not only a spool, for a small wooden crossbar sticks out of the middle of the star, and another small rod is joined to that at a right angle. By means of this latter rod on one side and one of the points of the star on the other, the whole thing can stand upright as if on two legs. One is tempted to believe that the creature once had some sort of intelligible shape and is now only a broken-down remnant. Yet this does not seem to be the case; at least there is no sign of it; nowhere is there an unfinished or unbroken surface to suggest anything of the kind; the whole thing looks senseless enough, but in its own way perfectly finished. In any case, closer scrutiny is impossible, since Odradek is extraordinarily nimble and can never be laid hold of.

He lurks by turns in the garret, the stairway, the lobbies, the entrance hall. Often for months on end he is not to be seen; then he has presumably moved into other houses; but he always comes faithfully back to our house again. Many a time when you go out of the door and he happens just to be leaning directly beneath you against the banisters you feel inclined to speak to him. Of course, you put no difficult questions to him, you treat him—he is so diminutive that you cannot help it—rather like a child. "Well, what's your name?" you ask him. "Odradek," he says. "And where do you live?" "No fixed abode," he says and laughs; but it is only the kind of laughter that has no lungs behind it. It sounds rather like the rustling of fallen leaves. And that is usually the end of the conversation. Even these answers are not always forthcoming; often he stays mute for a long time, as wooden as his appearance.

I ask myself, to no purpose, what is likely to happen to him? Can he possibly die? Anything that dies has had some kind of aim in life, some kind of activity, which has worn out; but that does not apply to Odradek. Am I to suppose, then, that he will always be rolling down the stairs, with ends of thread trailing after him, right before the feet of my children, and my children's children? He does no harm to anyone that one can see; but the idea that he is likely to survive me I find almost painful.[37]

Let us begin by noting that this is a tale rich with the same tonalities of enchantment that are familiar to us from other stories by Kafka such as *Blumfeld an Elderly Bachelor* (in which the protagonist is tormented by two lifelike toy balls that bounce around his flat) and, of course, the better-known *Metamorphosis* (in which the protagonist Gregor Samsa awakes one morning to find he has been transfigured into an unspecified kind of insect). A cousin to both Gregor and to the children's balls that lurk in Blumfeld's apartment, the creature known as Odradek exists at the uncanny crossing point between inanimate things and organic life. In "Notes on Kafka," Adorno observes that in Kafka's stories the "boundary between what is human and the world of things becomes blurred. . . . The zone in which it is impossible to die is also the no-man's land between man and thing: within it [is] Odradek, which Benjamin viewed as an angel in Klee's style."[38] That Odradek is not truly a mortal being is registered in the complaint of the father (the narrator in the story) who notes that, although everything that dies must eventually wear out, this is not true of Odradek, who "will always be rolling down the stairs, with ends of thread trailing after him."[39]

In the 1934 letter to Benjamin, Adorno grapples with the philosophical significance of this creature:

If his origin lies with the father of the house, does he not then precisely represent the anxious *concern* and danger for the latter, does he not anticipate precisely the overcoming of the creaturely state of guilt, and is not this concern—truly a case of Heidegger put right side up—the secret key, indeed the most indubitable promise of *hope*, precisely through the overcoming of the house itself? Certainly, as the other face of the world of things, Odradek is a sign of distortion—but precisely as such he is also a motif of transcendence, namely of the ultimate limit and of the reconciliation of the organic and the inorganic, or of the overcoming of death: Odradek "lives on." Expressed in another way, *it is only to a life that is perverted in thingly form that an escape from the overall context of nature is promised [bloß dem dinghaft verkehrten Leben ist das Entrinnen aus dem Naturzusammenhang versprochen].*"[40]

The final lines from this passage are highly instructive, and in what follows I will suggest that they underline Adorno's unusual idea of a convergence between materialism and inverse theology. First of all, it should be entirely clear that Adorno does *not* endorse any kind of conventional theology for which transcendence would be a metaphysical possibility. An actual "escape" from our creaturely existence is held out as a hope only for a life that is so painful that such an escape promises the only respite. Transcendence, for Adorno, is *not* the ideal but rather the *reflex* of an existence that suffers from reification, a longing that emerges from damaged conditions—that is, from "a life that is perverted in thingly form [*dem dinghaft verkehrten Leben*]." But this seems to imply the counterfactual possibility, that an undistorted life would not require any such promise. Conventional theology is therefore a reflection of material conditions. We come here into the neighborhood of classical Marxism for which religion signifies "sigh of the oppressed creature" and the "haven in a heartless world." Clearly, then, Adorno remains in an important sense a materialist, and he shares the materialist's view of religion as an index of social suffering.

But we must press this analysis further if we wish fully to grasp the implications of Adorno's "inverse" theology. A crucial step would be to appreciate Adorno's reading of Kafka's tale as a philosophical allegory that offers a rejoinder to Heidegger and, implicitly, the broader tradition of existentialism. Whereas Heidegger would affirm existence as it is given and the constitutive "guilt" of *Dasein*'s being-in-the-world, the strange figure of Odradek embodies an enduring hope for an "overcoming of the creaturely state of guilt." Crucial to Adorno's interpretation is the need to sustain a certain modicum of this worldly hope even in the face of existential hopelessness. Yet such a hope must be "inverted." In an instructive passage from the "Notes on Kafka," Adorno captures the logic of this inversion, which makes explicit the unrealized or "unconscious" condemnation of existence that has remained a latent theme in existentialism itself. In Kafka's stories, Adorno explains, "absolute estrangement, abandoned to the existence from which it has withdrawn, is examined and revealed as the hell which it inherently was already in Kierkegaard, although unconsciously." Through such an inversion, Kafka portrays "hell seen from the perspective of salvation."[41] Whereas existentialism eternalizes hopelessness but lacks a metaphysical vantage from which to criticize our fallen condition, an inverse theology invokes the bare idea of such a vantage, but only to gain critical leverage against our actual despair.

Through this logic of inversion, then, a view of the consummate negativity of social suffering serves as an index to utopia. Kierkegaard, according to Adorno, precedes Kafka in this logic, but he leaves unconscious what Kafka renders explicit. The "secret key" of the Odradek tale is its "promise of hope." Only this can explain Adorno's suggestion that he shares with Benjamin an "inverse theology" that was thematized already in the study of Kierkegaard. If Odradek embodies a kind of *hope*, this is because Odradek is *himself* a sign of distortion and, precisely in his distortion, *he therefore bears witness as a photographic negative to a happiness we have been denied.* Odradek, we might say, is nothing but the debased image of God as he appears in a messianic light. Embedded in Kafka's allegory, we might say, is a gesture that partakes of a logic familiar to us from Christology: it is a species of *materialist* religion, but without the ideal of a higher subjectivity that remains free from the pain of incarnation. To affirm such a divine ideal beyond the world would be to indulge an ideological fantasy, and so the ideal of a transcendent divinity collapses *into the wounded object itself*. Following this logic, Odradek would be not only an inversion of incarnation but also its most sincere expression. But such an incarnation, in its suffering and distortion, belies any trust in a perfection beyond itself. It should not surprise us that in *Minima Moralia* Adorno entertains the thought that "Kafka's Odradek might almost be an angel" but actually represents "the offal of the phenomenal world."[42]

Here the idea of "inversion" plays a crucial role. In "Notes on Kafka," Adorno warns against reading Kafka's tales as elaborating themes associated with Kierkegaard or dialectical theology. This is because in Kafka's tales "what for dialectical theology is light and shadow is *reversed*."[43] This point should not be minimized; it stands at the very center of Adorno's thinking not just about Kafka but also about Kierkegaard and the entire tradition of theism he represents. "In the middle ages," Adorno notes, Jews were tortured and executed "perversely" ["*verkehrt*"; quotation marks in the original German], which is to say that for critics such as Tacitus their religion was branded as inverted or perverse and accordingly they were to be hung upside down.[44] Adorno sees in Kafka's writing a critical homage to just this inversion. The "perspective of redemption" presents itself to Kafka as "unmitigated torture" precisely because redemption is excluded completely from his world. Such relentless criticism of this-worldly happiness finds its anticipation in Kierkegaard. "The absolute," Adorno writes, "does not turn its absurd side to the finite creature—a doctrine which already in Kierkegaard leads to things much more vexing than mere paradox and which in Kafka would have amounted to the enthroning of madness." Whereas Kierkegaard and the partisans of dialectical theology cleave to the absolute as a perfection *beyond* the debased world, Kafka sustains no such hope in a worldly beyond but only makes use of its shadow, as a critical perspective by which to illumine this-worldly suffering: "The light-source which shows the world's crevices to be infernal is the optimal one."[45] This is what is meant by "inversion" (a term that Adorno used in English in the letter to Benjamin, "*inverse*," but writes in German in the essay on Kafka as "*verkehrte*"). Adorno, in other words, understands the resolute presentation of *unhappiness* as the only possible means by which we can keep happiness in view.[46] Hence his rejoinder to the dialectical theologians: to present our happiness directly would only reify perfection, as if it were truly a "beyond" that is indifferent to our current suffering.[47]

In "Notes on Kafka," Adorno specifies the distinctively historical and twentieth-century meaning of this inversion, insofar as Kafka portrays life not unlike "Bettelheim, Kogon, and Rousset." (In a similar manner, Adorno adds, "the bird's eye photos of bombed out cities redeemed, as it were, Cubism.") Theology in a post-Auschwitz world can survive, Adorno suggests, but it will persist only in its *inverted* form insofar as one takes an unflinching and unapologetic view of social suffering: "If there is hope in Kafka's work, it is in those extremes rather than the milder phases: in the capacity to stand up to the worst by making it into language."[48] We are not far here, I would suggest, from the 1984 Tübingen address by Hans Jonas on *Der Gottesbegriff nach Auschwitz,* the concept of God after Auschwitz.[49] It is as if the divine itself could not remain undamaged in a damaged world: *Es gibt kein richtiges Leben im falschen.*

We can therefore conclude that "inverse theology," as Adorno understands it, focuses our critical attention on *material* suffering but does so precisely in the name of its determinate negation. It demands that suffering be remedied and society redeemed. This negation was anticipated, Adorno thought, in Kierkegaard's theological resistance to the fallen society around him, though Kierkegaard lapsed into ideological complacency by misdirecting his resistance into theistic transcendence rather than focusing his criticism without restraint on society itself. The task for Adorno was to inherit this critical resistance

while redirecting it toward its proper object, inverting Kierkegaard's theological disdain for the unredeemed world into a practice
of this-worldly criticism that, much like its theistic counterpart, refuses all worldly consolation.

The Mirror Image

In 1963, just six years before his death, Adorno gave a lecture before
the philosophical faculty at the University of Frankfurt that addressed,
for the very last time, the topic of Kierkegaard. First published later
that same year in the *Neue deutsche Hefte* with the title "Kierkegaard noch einmal" (Kierkegaard once again), it was reprinted in
1966 as a supplement to the dissertation but this time with an
added dedication: "To the memory of Paul Tillich."[50] Tillich, the
director of Adorno's habilitation back in the 1920s, had died in Chicago only the year before. We must now reexamine this late address,
in which the philosopher, now sixty years old, revisited the thinker
who had served for so long as his *Doppelgänger* and had once
helped him to inaugurate his philosophical career.

In its very form, the late lecture on Kierkegaard is very much a
work of Adorno's maturity, comparable in both theme and mood to
the "late style" Adorno heard in Beethoven's final compositions.[51]
Written in the midst of his work on *Negative Dialectics* and during
the same year as *The Jargon of Authenticity*, it represents what
Adorno elsewhere called an "open" style of philosophical argumentation. Inviting a comparison with Kierkegaard's own literary sensibility, an open style cultivates paradox and tarries with the negative,
forgoing any premature bid for resolution.[52] Such a style, with all
of its readiness to deploy irony and wit against the authoritarianism
and bombast of the philosophical system, also confirms Adorno's
emerging belief that one must take care to distinguish Kierkegaard
from all of the so-called existentialists who appeared in the twentieth century. But this distinction was too often obscured: Karl Jaspers,

for example, had praised Kierkegaard in the abstract for "great-ness" of "world-historical rank" even while he rejected the Dane's particular categories such as "Religiousness B" (the absurdity of faith), which Jaspers called "the end of historical Christianity and also the end of the philosophical life as such." Adorno condemns such praise as the empty reverence one might bestow upon a monu-ment to Bismarck. Nor did he miss the irony of celebrating Kierke-gaard as a "world-historical" hero when Kierkegaard himself dis-dained the very idea of world history as vacuous display. Indeed, Adorno now saw the history of existentialism in the twentieth century as the history of Kierkegaard's betrayal rather than his ful-fillment, a betrayal that had reached its tragic denouement when the Kierkegaard scholar Emanuel Hirsch embraced the heresy of German Christianity: "From that individual there has arisen that mendacious idle chatter [*Gerede*] that boasts of itself that the others are inauthentic and have fallen into idle chatter. His fate was sealed when, in Germany before 1933 the National Socialist Emanuel Hirsch took him into the general pact." By uniting Kierkegaard with a mass political movement, Hirsch not only forced a reconciliation between subject and object, he betrayed the philosopher from whom he claimed to draw inspiration. This not only dishonored Kierkeg-aard, it abolished his philosophical purposes. In Adorno's pungent phrase, the political appropriation of Kierkegaard was "victory as defeat."[53]

The deepest tragedy of this reception from Adorno's perspective was that it utterly obscured the truth content of Kierkegaard's work. "Against the objectification and socialization of all relations among humanity in the hundred years since his death, the position of the individual, to which [Kierkegaard] ascribed the highest value, has proven itself a refuge from the ruling firms that are hostile to indi-vidual determination and degrade everyone to his role." Seen from this perspective, Kierkegaard represented not bourgeois conformity but rather an early protest against the incipient reification and effacement of all difference that would eventually characterize mass society in the mid-twentieth century. But Adorno also hastened to note that the individual Kierkegaard sought to defend was as much semblance as reality. The Kierkegaardian individual gained its reality only by means of a metaphysically impossible dissociation from all social being, an attempt that had the ironic effect of leaving the current order undisturbed: "He who punishes every intervention in external reality as a falling away from the purely inward-turning essence," Adorno observed, "must authorize and affirm given relations as they are." Still more ironic, however, was the consequence that in solidifying the merely existent individual against social contamination, Kierkegaard unwittingly transformed subjectivity into an invariant and metaphysical essence no less absolute than the Hegelian Absolute it opposed. Kierkegaard's doctrine of the individual was in this sense "a recollection of the human being as in the image of God."[54]

For Adorno, Kierkegaard's philosophy was therefore *both* a species of ideology *and* a protest against ideology. This suitably paradoxical circumstance reflected Kierkegaard's own deeply conflicted relation to Hegel, whose philosophy Kierkegaard on the one hand misunderstood and unknowingly recapitulated, but on the other hand understood all too well and therefore resisted for the sake of a subjectivity beyond the forces of administrative reason. Both sides of this paradox merit closer inspection.

It was an unfortunate truth, in Adorno's view, that Kierkegaard never properly grasped the meaning of mediation *(Vermittlung)* in Hegel's system, a logical instrument that Kierkegaard understood only as a "moderating compromise" rather than as the mediation between extremes. For Hegel, mediation served as the vehicle by which the concept itself swings over into its own contradiction—a movement that Kierkegaard considered utterly foreign to Hegel and against which he asserted the independent immediacy *(Unmittelbarkeit)* of the individual. Kierkegaard imagined that such an individual could occupy a space of innocence beyond the dialectic's reach, whereas in fact Hegel himself already anticipated the false and "abstract" immediacy of the isolated subject in the *Phenomenology of Spirit* in the guise of the "unhappy consciousness." Hegel's diagnosis, Adorno believed, was inescapable: isolated from the world and falsely assured of its immediacy in relation to itself, the Kierkegaardian individual was according to Adorno "just as little the True as the Hegelian Whole." Indeed, Kierkegaard's theory of subjective immediacy was no less idealist than the idealism it wished to overcome. "The opponent of Hegel remained in his spell."[55]

Most of all, however, Kierkegaard's ambivalent relation to Hegel revealed itself when it came to the question of identity theory. For Adorno, as for his colleague Max Horkheimer, a major distinction between nineteenth-century Hegelian dialectics and the late modern mode of dialectical reasoning known as critical theory was that the latter resisted Hegel's original ideal of a thoroughgoing reconciliation between subject and object, universal and particular.[56] Against the dialectical overcoming of difference as theorized by Hegel, Adorno believed that under present-day conditions of totalizing social domination, in which the subject's freedom threatened to vanish entirely, critical theory was charged with the task of sustaining difference and negativity rather than seeking their premature reconciliation. In Kierkegaard's struggle against the Hegelian absolute, Adorno thus discerned an anticipation of the Frankfurt school's own critique of identity theory. The struggle was all the more successful insofar as it exploited Hegel's own concepts: "Kierkegaard broke the parentheses of identity philosophy in an exemplary way," Adorno explained, "because the breach was immanent rather than the arbitrary positing of an oppositional stance against Hegel from without. When Hegel metastasized subjectivity into *Geist,* he not only inflated the subject into an instrument of totalizing domination, he also effaced the finite self as the only point of resistance against that totality. In the Kierkegaardian concept of the subject, as in that of existence, there breaks through that nonidentical real [*jenes nichtidentische Reale*], which the conception of the pure subject as spirit in idealism conjures away."[57]

For understanding Adorno's late rapprochement with Kierkegaard, this point is crucial: negative dialectics turns toward materialism only by passing *through* the subject and *not* by simply annulling its power. Needless to say, any such passage requires critical sensitivity to the inner life of the subject, whose nonidentical experience stands as a possible preserve for emancipation in the midst of an otherwise wholly reified objectivity. As Axel Honneth has observed, "the procedure of negative dialectics always also includes a layer of argumentation on which the phenomenon to be dealt with is presented in light of its effects on the subjective sensitivity of the individual researcher. *Only through this thematization of subjective experiences, Adorno is convinced, is the object presented in its factual objectivity.*"[58] The significance of subjective experience in Adorno's own interpretive work, as analyzed in Martin Jay's *Songs of Experience,* helps to explain why Kierkegaard could reappear no longer as a mere ideologue for bourgeois society but as a paradigmatic theorist of the *nonidentity* between subject and object. Even while resisting the consoling thought of subjective experience as an undamaged immediacy, Adorno nonetheless sustained the "normative" idea of the subject's experience of happiness, though—and this is crucial—only as a memory rather than a present reality.[59]

But we must also attend to the second perspective. Adorno, alive as ever to the latent tensions in bourgeois philosophy, also discerned in Kierkegaard's philosophy a retreat into asocial interiority and, more surprising still, an affirmation of identity theory. As idealism had subordinated the existent to totality, so too had Kierkegaard only succeeded in subordinating totality to the existent. In this respect Kierkegaard recapitulated the idealistic strategy of inflating and spiritualizing subjectivity: "The attempt to break free of idealism failed." The realm of interiority as a space commensurable with nothing outside itself thereby gained priority over the external and social world. For Adorno this was the ultimate irony of Kierkegaard's anti-idealist rebellion: "Thought itself, even as it hoped to escape the totality of the concept, is damned to a hopeless turning within itself and to the incantation of an unknown and incommensurable meaning which remains alien." The extravagant image of the absolute thereby assumed a mythical quality, "as threatening and hopeless as the gods of fate." Even here, however, Adorno detected a critical moment in Kierkegaard, whose protest against the absolute recalled the resistance of a mythic nature-religion against the unifying drive of rationalizing monotheism. One could even detect in Kierkegaard the traces of Nordic mythology (which, in a moment of uncharacteristic generosity, Adorno did not condemn as a sign of mythic irrationalism). Pitting the mythological gods against the sovereign God, Kierkegaard permitted the voices of nature to be heard in their protest against the authoritarianism of the monotheistic subject. Notwithstanding his effort to defend an authentic Christianity against its debased social forms, Kierkegaard himself was in this respect a theorist of the negative, speaking for the resistance of nature's "many" against the unity of the logos.[60]

Hope against Hope

Adorno ended his final reflections on Kierkegaard with a bold encomium that affirmed the philosophical intimacy that he had felt for the Danish thinker since the beginning of his career. The bond was due chiefly to Adorno's belief that in the era of late capitalism the promise of dialectical reconciliation of the subject with society remained not just unrealized but quite possibly unrealizable. It was thus all the more urgent for the subject to resist its own compulsory reconciliation with the false totality of the merely given world. Kierkegaard, Marx's contemporary in the era of high capitalism, stood alongside Marx as an early partisan of this resistance: "The absolute being-for-oneself of the Kierkegaardian individual is devised against the absolute being-for-another of the world of goods." Even if Kierkegaard conceived of his opposition as a distinctively theological complaint against world's failure to realize its own professed Christianity, he rightly conceived the relation between subject and object as one of insuperable negativity. For this reason Adorno discerned in Kierkegaard's "outré conservatism" a surprising consequence, that precisely the Dane's *antipathy* to progress also nourished "a greater sympathy with the condemned than with the victors, the stronger battalions of world history." This sympathy helped to explain why Kierkegaard could never fashion more than a paradoxical "hope against hope" that corresponded to an image of revolution as a rupture with the logical course of things. "The Kierkegaardian tendency," Adorno wrote, "is the inversion of the Brechtian yes-man, to whom the collective wants to pretend that before all else it is important to learn agreement. After Kierkegaard there is no longer any friendship with the world, because such friendship, in affirming the world as it is, eternalizes the bad and prevents the world from becoming what would admit of being loved."[61] A similar verdict would reappear in *Negative Dialectics,* where Adorno observed that "Kierkegaard's protest against philosophy was also one against the reified consciousness in which, as he put it, subjectivity has been extinguished: he opposed philosophy for philosophy's own sake [*er nahm gegen die Philosophie auch deren Interesse wahr*]."[62]

Aesthetics and Interiority

It was a remarkable transformation: Kierkegaard now stood as the rebel against the "official" ambition of bourgeois philosophy to reconcile subject and object, interiority and exteriority, self and world. But Adorno now saw in this rebellion not a betrayal of philosophy's higher purposes but rather philosophy's only possible salvation. Just as Adorno came to appreciate an affinity between the "late style" of Beethoven and the style of his own philosophical modernism, so too one might say that in his late writings Adorno awakened to a new appreciation for Kierkegaard's redemptive significance, and he came to see in Kierkegaard an early harbinger of the negative dialectic.[63] This new admiration for Kierkegaard's anticipatory reflections on aesthetic themes is most noticeable in the posthumously published *Aesthetic Theory*, where Kierkegaard makes a belated appearance in the context of meditations over the fate of "inwardness" in modern art. "With the growing powerlessness of the autonomous subject," Adorno wrote, "inwardness [*Innerlichkeit*] became completely ideological, the mirage of an inner kingdom where the silent majority are indemnified for what is denied them socially." The retreat of the modern subject into the illusory comfort of solipsism immediately contradicts itself insofar as it lacks the objectivity it would require for satisfaction. Inwardness thus becomes "shadowy and empty, indeed contentless in itself."[64] Modern art, insofar as it refuses to indulge this ideological illusion, resists the idea of inwardness as a spiritual refuge from the world.

At first glance, this argument bears at least a superficial resemblance to Adorno's early interpretation of the mirror as a symbol of bourgeois solipsism in the Kierkegaard book. But *Aesthetic Theory* offers a more nuanced interpretation. No sooner had Adorno repeated the verdict against solipsism than he qualified it with the claim that "art is scarcely imaginable without the element of inwardness." With this qualification the disagreement between Adorno and Benjamin came into view: "Benjamin," Adorno recalled, "once said that in his opinion inwardness could go fly a kite. This was directed against Kierkegaard and the 'philosophy of inwardness' that claims him as their founder, even though that term would have been as antipathetic to the theologian as the word ontology. Benjamin had in mind abstract subjectivity that powerlessly sets itself up as substance. But his comment is no more the whole truth than abstract subjectivity is. Spirit—certainly Benjamin's own—must enter itself if it is to be able to negate what is opaque."[65]

This argument is especially instructive insofar as it rescues the truth content of Kierkegaardian subjectivity even while contesting its adequacy. Adorno pursued this argument via a confrontation with Benjamin, who had rejected "the philosophy of inwardness" only because he conceived of it as an "abstract subjectivity" that arrogates all objective reality to its own inner sphere. For Adorno, however, such a conception missed the deeper significance of inward subjectivity as the necessary precondition for any dialectical relationship with the object. One could not overcome solipsism through an abstract negation of the subject since this would only lead to a one-sided and positivistic affirmation of the object as the given. Adorno thus resisted Benjamin's undialectical dismissal of inwardness (qua abstract subjectivity) just as he resisted Benjamin's demand that the aura of individually created art should dissolve so that the collective (qua abstract objectivity) might absorb a newly technologically reproduced mode art in a "state of distraction." But Adorno also faulted Kierkegaard's undialectical affirmation of interiority as bourgeois ideology, a false attempt to secure the autonomy of the isolated subject in an era when the actual subject was already threatening to dissolve. Kierkegaard, he complained, offered little more than the "mirage of an inner kingdom." Clearly, then, the ideological and distorted appeal to inwardness could not impugn the concept's critical importance. "Even inwardness participates in dialectics," Adorno explained, "though not as Kierkegaard thought."[66]

With these remarks on Kierkegaard in *Aesthetic Theory*, his final work, Adorno closed the circle, returning to considerations on the relationship between aesthetics and society that appeared in his very first published book, the inquiry into the aesthetic dimension of

Kierkegaard's philosophy. But he returned in the end with a new and deepened appreciation for Kierkegaard that summarized nearly four decades of intellectual transformation. If Adorno had once felt inclined to dismiss the Dane as little more than an ideologue for bourgeois interiority and saw in Kierkegaard's disdain for the aesthetic a materialist sign of a disavowed social truth, he now discerned a genuinely dialectical tension in Kierkegaard's work between affirmative and critical insight. This was especially true for Adorno's late appreciation of Kierkegaard's views on aesthetics and, in particular, Kierkegaard's contribution to the theory of the sublime. In *Aesthetic Theory*, Adorno explained (following Kant) that nature appears to us as sublime when spirit experiences its "empirical powerlessness vis-à-vis nature." The experience of impotence in the face of nature therefore awakens the subject to the primacy of the object and, by extension, opens up the possibility of the subject's reconciliation with nature: "Nature, no longer oppressed by spirit, frees itself from the miserable nexus of rank second nature and subjective sovereignty. Such emancipation would be the return of nature, and it—the counterimage of mere existence—is the sublime."[67]

For Adorno this meant that the sublime held a critical and emancipatory significance: "In the traits of dominance [*In den Zügen des Herrschaftlichen*] evident in its dimensions of power and magnitude, the sublime speaks against domination [*spricht es gegen die Herrschaft*]." A genuine reconciliation with the natural world would appear only if humanity were to abandon its claims to world mastery, an insight Adorno found in Schiller's dictum that "the human being is only fully human when at play." The human being could reach a "consummation of his sovereignty" only when "he leaves behind the spell of sovereignty's aim." But under current conditions any such realization of human nature was blocked, an impossibility registered in the aesthetic realm as a turn to the sublime. "The more empirical reality hermetically excludes this event [of the subject's

reconciliation with nature]," Adorno claimed, "the more art con-
tracts into the element of the sublime; in a subtle way, after the fall
of formal beauty, the sublime was the only aesthetic idea left to
modernism." As a marker of subjective impotence the sublime thus
stood as the truth of a society for which the subject's claim to sovereignty had become sheer falsehood. Ironically, however, the pre-
cedence of the sublime thereby ratified the view of the aesthetic as a
sacred space in which all notions of mere play would be sacrilege.
With the sublime Adorno therefore endorsed the "aesthetic seriousness" associated with Kierkegaard (even though Kierkegaard in his
typical subjectivism distorted this value into a quality of the individual): "Even the hubris of art as a religion, the self-exaltation of
art as the absolute, has its truth content in the allergy against what
is not sublime in art, against that play that is satisfied with the sovereignty of spirit. What Kierkegaard subjectivistically terms 'aesthetic seriousness,' the heritage of the sublime, is the reversal of
works into what is true by virtue of their content."[68] For Adorno,
then, the Kierkegaardian sublime anticipated the intensified and
contracted formalism of late modernist art, in which the earlier, now
defunct ideal of beauty as play yielded to aesthetic seriousness as
the last remnant of critical negativity. In the sublime, the subject is
compelled to recognize its own powerlessness before the autonomous work of art just as the subject cannot claim mastery over the
social whole. The sublime thus became an aesthetic mark of social
truth, the sign within aesthetics of a social condition that no longer
offered any consolation of subjective freedom.[69]

This late shift in judgment help us to see how Adorno could never
escape the habit of seeing in Kierkegaard a kind of mirror image.
When as a young man Adorno had read the Dane, he initially re-
sponded with skepticism, and all too often with the polemical spirit
of a critic who professed to feel little sympathy with his subject. But
over the course of his life Adorno continued to scrutinize the face in
the mirror and, eventually, came to glimpse an intellectual kinship

that, although it did not rule out the awareness of difference, none-theless made this difference a spur to greater self-understanding. The philosophy of bourgeois interiority, disdained and perhaps occasionally misunderstood, returned in the end as an unlikely ally in the task of redemptive criticism.

CONCLUSION

Adorno's Inverse Theology

> . . . metaphysics must know how to wish.
>
> —THEODOR W. ADORNO, *Negative Dialectics*

In the autumn of 1957 Adorno engaged in a discussion with Eugen Kogon that was broadcast by the Westdeutscher Rundfunk. The topic of their conversation was "Revelation or Autonomous Reason," and it should not surprise us that this theme prompted Adorno to speak of Kierkegaard.[1] Adorno's remarks reconfirm what we have learned over the course of this book: what he called Kierkegaard's "sacrifice of the intellect" deserved a certain admiration because it had once signified an act of "progressive consciousness." At a historical moment that bourgeois society had not yet secured its thoroughgoing domination over the totality of existence, Kierkegaard's religious sacrifice had required nothing less than the sacrifice of "one's entire life." But with the passage of time the objective significance of this sacrifice had transformed almost beyond recognition; it was now generalized into a sacrifice of critical consciousness reinforced by the affirmative society itself: "Whoever makes this sacrifice no longer feels any burden of fear or trembling," Adorno observed. "No one would have reacted to it with more indignation than Kierkegaard himself."[2]

Late modernity, in other words, had transformed not only the meaning of Kierkegaard's rebellion; it had also transformed the meaning of theology. It is therefore crucial to note that Adorno's affiliation with Kierkegaard did not imply anything like a genuine affirmation of religion. While resisting Kierkegaard's leap of faith, Adorno nonetheless saw in this faith a species of negativity, although this theological negativity could never be transformed into a positive religion. One must keep firmly in view the complaint against false transcendence that is articulated perhaps most clearly in the "Parataxis" essay, where Adorno warned against all efforts at healing the breach between subject and object by means of a tertiary principle. "Reconciliation," writes Adorno, "in which enthrallment to nature comes to an end, is *not above nature as something Other pure and simple,* which could only be domination of nature once again by virtue of its differentness and would share in its curse through suppression. What puts an end to the state of nature is mediated with it, not through a third element between them but within nature itself."[3]

This qualification is crucial, as it positions Adorno at the farthest remove from any dogmatic religious identification. Any attempt to assign him an honorary seat in the pantheon of modern theology must eventually fail, not only because by the very principles of negative dialectics the affirmation of this pantheon would imply holism of identity but also, and more important, because the direct affirmation of a transcendent other *beyond* nature would contravene the imperative of *this-worldly* redemption.

Needless to say this stricture against an unqualified affirmation of metaphysical alterity sharply distinguishes Adorno from Lévinas, with whom he is sometimes compared.[4] But one might still argue that this very prohibition pays homage to the thought of an "inverse theology" such as Adorno had mentioned in his early letter to Benjamin (see Chapter 5). Although Adorno did not go to the extreme of actually *denying* theology, he insisted that it could only retain its redemptive function if it remained—free of all romantic generalities—merely as a limiting concept that resisted all theological dogma. Adorno could therefore affirm "no other possibility than an extreme *ascesis* toward any type of revealed faith, an extreme loyalty to the prohibition of images, far beyond what this once originally meant."[5] In this regard, Kafka's strange creature known as Odradek became the materialist and critical negative to a revelation Adorno could not affirm. And yet Odradek would persist, and in his very materiality he signified the primacy of that transcendent object beyond all subjectivism that Kierkegaard had once called God. The reconciliation that is denied to humanity could show itself only through its negation, as a creature whose distortion serves as a reflection of a distorted world. In his "musical physiognomy" of Mahler, Adorno observes that "For him, as in Kafka's fables, the animal realm is the human world as it would appear from the standpoint of redemption."[6] The creature Odradek, we might say, was therefore an apparition of the nature within human nature, bearing all the wounds of our unredeemed condition.

In the foregoing chapters I have insisted that Adorno should be read as a materialist. I have further suggested that this materialist disposition helps to explain his particular fascination with existential ontology, chiefly because on his interpretation it failed to achieve its promised breakthrough to nonsubjective reality. A major burden of this book has been to explore how it was Adorno's very materialism that drew him back on innumerable occasions to this philosophical tradition, so as to develop through immanent critique the insights that might permit him to succeed where existential ontology had failed. The "preponderance of the object" was the title Adorno used to designate his own achievement.

My further suggestion is that the very stringency of Adorno's materialism also required a no less stringent withdrawal from positive theology, even while Adorno construed this resistance as the only means by which to honor, via negation, the conceptual truth of a theology he could not affirm. This resistance, moreover, helps to explain Adorno's seemingly paradoxical commitment to an "utterly impossible thing"—namely, "a standpoint removed, even though by a hair's breadth, from the scope of existence." Adorno understood that an uncritical or reductive materialism could not appeal to such a standpoint and would condemn it as "utterly impossible." But it is a requirement of Adorno's materialism that we sustain an absolutely critical posture toward the material world so as to imagine its absolute transformation. It is in this sense, and *only* in this sense, that "consummate negativity, once squarely faced, delineates the mirror image of its opposite."[7] The counterfactual appeal to a standpoint removed from existence does not contradict Adorno's materialism; it completes it.

We are therefore left with the intriguing thought that Adorno's *ascesis* may represent the final stage in the demythologization of faith. Such an asceticism would be the very practice of that "inverse theology" Adorno had once discerned in Kierkegaard. This would be surprising, of course, since bourgeois asceticism also belongs to the history of repression as diagnosed in the *Dialectic of Enlightenment*. The practice of rational *ascesis* against the consolations of revelation remains in tension with the no less pronounced critique of the asceticism that, in Protestantism as in philosophical rationalism, vanquished "all natural traces" of the embodied and sensual self.[8] For Adorno, then, Kierkegaard held a double meaning: Even as Kierkegaard stood as the very paradigm of bourgeois subjectivity, he also came to signify the possibility of *resistance against* the degeneration of that subjectivity. Kierkegaard's own *ascesis* in the face of public religion thus stood for Adorno as the last remaining form of bourgeois heroism in a society that had made *true* subjectivity a virtual impossibility. Indeed, this is the meaning of

Adorno's closing thought in *Negative Dialectics,* that one must sustain solidarity with metaphysics at the moment of its fall.

Theodor Wiesengrund-Adorno died in the late summer of 1969. In an eloquent elegy for his departed teacher, Jürgen Habermas records the graveside remarks of another student in attendance (actually Hans-Jürgen Kahl, though in Habermas's elegy he remains unnamed): Adorno, the student said, "practiced an irresistible critique of the bourgeois individual, and yet he was himself caught within its ruins."[9] Though intended as a rebuke, the remark might be construed differently as philosophical insight. Throughout his life, Adorno practiced a style of immanent critique, focused with special intensity on the philosophies of bourgeois interiority. These studies were not mere polemics; they were exercises in redemptive criticism, performed with a dialectician's eye toward not only the failures but also the unrealized promises of the modern philosophical tradition. The theorist who cleaved with what we might call religious conviction to the primacy of the object could only grant that primacy from within the housing of a critical subjectivity on the verge of collapse. Since almost the beginning, this had been Adorno's task: a redemption not from existence but of existence, in and through its critique.

NOTES

INDEX

Notes

Abbreviations

This book makes use of the edited German-language edition of Adorno's collected works, abbreviated as follows:

GS Theodor W. Adorno, *Gesammelte Schriften*, 20 vols., ed. Rolf Tiedemann (Frankfurt am Main: Suhrkamp Verlag, 1970–1986).

I have also consulted several English-language translations of Adorno's work, along with a variety of important monographs and edited collections by other scholars. I am especially grateful to Dennis Redmond for his new English-language translation of *Negative Dialectics* (2001), which is available online at http://members.efn.org/~dredmond/ndtrans.html. The following abbreviations are used in the notes:

AE Theodor W. Adorno, *Against Epistemology: A Metacritique,* trans. Willis Domingo (Oxford: Blackwell, 1982).

AH Iain Macdonald and Krzysztof Ziarek, eds., *Adorno and Heidegger: Philosophical Questions* (Stanford, CA: Stanford University Press, 2008).

AP Theodor W. Adorno, "The Actuality of Philosophy," in *AR*.

AR   Theodor W. Adorno, *The Adorno Reader*, ed. Brian O' Connor (Oxford: Blackwell, 2000).

AT   Theodor W. Adorno, *Aesthetic Theory*, ed. Gretel Adorno and Rolf Tiedemann, trans. Robert Hullot-Kentor (Minneapolis: University of Minnesota Press, 1997).

BC   Brian O'Connor, *Adorno's Negative Dialectic: Philosophy and the Possibility of Critical Rationality* (Cambridge, MA: MIT Press, 2004).

BT   Martin Heidegger, *Being and Time*, trans. John MacQuarrie and Edward Robinson (San Francisco: Harper & Row, 1962).

CC   Tom Huhn, ed., *The Cambridge Companion to Adorno* (Cambridge: Cambridge University Press, 2004).

DC   Detlev Claussen, *Theodor W. Adorno: One Last Genius*, trans. Rodney Livingstone (Cambridge, MA: Harvard University Press, 2008).

DE   Max Horkheimer and Theodor W. Adorno, *Dialectic of Enlightenment: Philosophical Fragments*, ed. Gunzelin Schmid Noerr, trans. Edmund Jephcott (Stanford, CA: Stanford University Press, 2002).

DI   Martin Jay, *The Dialectical Imagination*, 2nd ed. (Berkeley: University of California Press, 1996).

EH   Espen Hammer, *Adorno's Modernism: Art, Experience, and Catastrophe* (New York: Cambridge University Press, 2015).

HF   Theodor W. Adorno, *History and Freedom: Lectures 1964–1965*, ed. Rolf Tiedemann (Cambridge: Polity Press, 2006).

HS   Theodor W. Adorno, *Hegel: Three Studies* (1963), trans. Shierry Weber Nicholsen (Cambridge, MA: MIT Press, 1993).

JA   Theodor W. Adorno, *The Jargon of Authenticity*, trans. Knut Tarnowski and Frederic Will (Evanston, IL: Northwestern University Press, 1973). Originally published as Theodor W. Adorno, *Jargon der Eigentlichkeit* (Frankfurt am Main: Suhrkamp, 1964).

JB   J. M. Bernstein, *Adorno: Disenchantment and Ethics* (Cambridge: Cambridge University Press, 2001).

KC   Theodor W. Adorno, *Kierkegaard: Construction of the Aesthetic* (1933), trans. Robert Hullot-Kentor (Minneapolis: University of Minnesota Press, 1989).

KL   Theodor W. Adorno, "On Kierkegaard's Doctrine of Love," *Zeitschrift für Sozialforschung* 8 (1939–1940): 413–429.

KN   Theodor W. Adorno, "Kierkegaard noch einmal," in *GS*, vol 2.

LD   Theodor W. Adorno, *Lectures on Negative Dialectics,* ed. Rolf Tiedemann, trans. Rodney Livingstone (Malden, MA: Polity, 2012).

MD   Stefan Müller-Doohm, *Adorno: A Biography,* trans. Rodney Livingstone (Cambridge: Polity, 2005).

MJ   Martin Jay, *Adorno* (Cambridge, Mass.: Harvard University Press, 1984).

MM   Theodor W. Adorno, *Minima Moralia: Reflections from Damaged Life,* trans. E. F. N. Jephcott. (London: NLB, 1974).

ND   Theodor W. Adorno, *Negative Dialectics,* trans. Dennis Redmond (2001), http://members.efn.org/~dredmond/ndtrans.html. Citations are from this edition unless noted otherwise.

NH   Theodor W. Adorno, "The Idea of Natural History," trans. Robert Hullot-Kentor, *Telos* 57 (1985): 111–124.

NL   Theodor W. Adorno, *Notes to Literature* (1958, 1961, 1965, 1974), 2 vols., ed. and trans. Shierry Weber Nicholsen (New York: Columbia University Press, 1991–1992).

Introduction

1. The point has been made gracefully by Iain Macdonald, who writes of the "left-handed" nature of Adorno's manner of reading Heidegger; see Macdonald, "Ethics and Authenticity: Conscience and Non-Identity in Heidegger and Adorno, with a Glance at Hegel," in *AH*, 6–21.

2. Theodor W. Adorno, *Mahler: A Musical Physiognomy,* trans. Edmund Jephcott (Chicago: University of Chicago Press, 1996); originally in German as *Mahler: Eine Musikalische Physiognomik* (Frankfurt am Main: Suhrkamp, 1971).

3. G. W. F. Hegel, *Elements of the Philosophy of Right,* ed. Allen W. Wood, trans. H. B. Nisbet (Cambridge: Cambridge University Press, 1991), 21.

4. Theodor W. Adorno, "Cultural Criticism and Society," in *Prisms,* trans. Samuel and Shierry Weber (Cambridge, MA: MIT Press, 1981), 17–34; quote from 21.

5. "Copula," in *ND*, 107–111, German at *GS* 6:107–111.

6. "Das ontologische Bedürfnis," in *ND*, 67; German at *GS*, 6:67.

7. Macdonald, "Ethics and Authenticity."

8. Michael Gubser, *The Far Reaches: Phenomenology, Ethics, and Social Renewal in Central Europe* (Stanford, CA: Stanford University Press, 2014); Dan Zahavi, *Husserl's Phenomenology* (Stanford, CA: Stanford University Press, 2002).

9. The influence, however, should not be overstated. On Marcuse's critical distance from Heidegger even before his teacher's 1933 embrace of national socialism, see the crucial essay by John Abromeit, "Herbert Marcuse's Critical Encounter with Martin Heidegger, 1927–1933," in *Herbert Marcuse: A Critical Reader*, ed. John Abromeit and W. Mark Cobb (New York: Routledge, 2004), 131–151. The *Habilitationsschrift* is available in English as Herbert Marcuse, *Hegel's Ontology and the Theory of Historicity*, trans. Seyla Benhabib (Cambridge, MA: MIT Press, 1989). For other important writings see *Herbert Marcuse's Heideggerian Marxism*, ed. Richard Wolin and John Abromeit (Lincoln: University of Nebraska Press, 2005).

10. Howard Caygill, "Benjamin, Heidegger, and the Destruction of Tradition," in *Walter Benjamin's Philosophy: Destruction and Experience*, ed. Andrew E. Benjamin and Peter Osborne, Warwick Studies in European Philosophy (New York: Routledge, 1994), 1–31. See also, in the same volume, Andrew Benjamin, "Time and Task: Benjamin and Heidegger Showing the Present," 216–250.

11. General histories and critical studies of the Frankfurt school have deeply informed my own perspective. They include Seyla Benhabib, *Critique, Norm, and Utopia: A Study of the Foundations of Critical Theory* (New York: Colombia University Press, 1986); Susan Buck-Morss, *The Origin of Negative Dialectics; Theodor W. Adorno, Walter Benjamin and the Frankfurt Institute* (New York: Free Press, 1977); Martin Jay, *The Dialectical Imagination*, 2nd ed. (Berkeley: University of California Press, 1996); and Rolf Wiggershaus, *The Frankfurt School: Its History, Theories, and Political Significance*, trans. Michael Robertson (Cambridge, MA: MIT Press, 1994).

12. Elsewhere I have broadened this claim into a general methodological point: if one adopts a maximalist posture by viewing philosophical arguments as nothing more than ideologies in disguise, one dispenses with the very ideal of philosophical argumentation altogether. This

amounts to what Jürgen Habermas has (rightly) called a performative contradiction. For a compressed statement on this problem, see Peter E. Gordon, *Continental Divide: Heidegger, Cassirer, Davos* (Cambridge, MA: Harvard University Press, 2010), 357; see also Peter E. Gordon, "Heidegger in Black," *New York Review of Books*, October 9, 2014.

13. Of the prior literature that explores similar topics, I would like to make special mention of the excellent essay by Fred R. Dallmayr, "Phenomenology and Critical Theory: Adorno," *Cultural Hermeneutics* 3 (1976): 367–405; and also Marcia Morgan, *Kierkegaard and Critical Theory* (Lanham, MD: Lexington, 2012).

14. For readers who feel themselves drawn to Sartrean philosophy and especially to Sartre's model of phenomenological subjectivity, David Sherman's sympathetic treatment is an especially valuable resource; see Sherman, *Sartre and Adorno: The Dialectics of Subjectivity* (Albany: State University of New York Press, 2007), 10.

15. On Adorno and Nietzsche, see, e.g., Karin Bauer, *Adorno's Nietzschean Narratives: Critiques of Ideology, Readings of Wagner* (Albany: State University of New York Press, 1999). On Adorno and Schelling, see, e.g., the lucid discussion in Andrew Bowie, *Adorno and the Ends of Philosophy* (Cambridge: Polity, 2013), esp. 114–116, and passim. See also Peter Dews, "Adorno's Relation to Schelling," *British Journal for the History of Philosophy* 22, no. 6 (2015): 1180–1207.

16. The locus classicus for this argument is Jürgen Habermas, *The Philosophical Discourse of Modernity* (Cambridge, MA: MIT Press, 1985).

1. Starting Out with Kierkegaard

1. *JA*, 105.

2. For a summary of Adorno's early study of Kierkegaard, see Martin Jay, *The Dialectical Imagination*, 2nd ed. (Berkeley: University of California Press, 1996), 66–68; and Martin Jay, *Adorno* (Cambridge, MA: Harvard University Press, 1984), 30. Also crucial are Marcia Morgan, "Adorno's Reception of Kierkegaard: 1929–1933," *Sören Kierkegaard Newsletter* 46 (2003): 8–11; Robert Hullot-Kentor, "Critique of the Organic: Kierkegaard and the Construction of the Aesthetic," in *Things beyond Resemblance: Collected Essays on Theodor W. Adorno*

206 / Notes to Pages 13–15

(New York: Columbia University Press, 2006), 77–93; and Matt Waggoner, "Giving Up the Good: Adorno, Kierkegaard, and the Critique of Political Culture," *Journal for Cultural and Religious Theory* 6, no. 2 (2005): 63–83. Most important of all is Asaf Angermann's study, which brings an especially keen analytical eye to the theme of irony in Kierkegaard, drawing out the affinities between Kierkegaard's irony and Adorno's negative dialectic as two moments of critical leverage against Hegel's dialectic of reconciliation; see Angermann, *Beschädigte Ironie. Kierkegaard, Adorno und die negative Dialektik kritischer Subjektivität* (Berlin: Walter de Gruyter, 2013).

3. MD, 123.

4. Editor's afterword in *GS* 2:261, "*unfangreiche* [thick]" and "*verschlungene* [meandering]."

5. Walter Benjamin, "Kierkegaard: The End of Philosophical Idealism," originally published in the *Vossische Zeitung* (April 1933); trans. Rodney Livingstone in Walter Benjamin, *Selected Writings,* vol. 2, *1927–1934* (Cambridge, MA: Harvard University Press, 1999), 703–705, quote at 703.

6. Dedicated to the memory of Paul Tillich, "Kierkegaard's Doctrine of Love" first appeared in *Zeitschrift für Sozialforschung* 8 (1940): 413–429. "Kierkegaard noch einmal," *Neue Deutschen Heften* (1963), is reprinted in *GS,* 2:239–258.

7. For a comprehensive summary of Adorno's engagement with Kierkegaard, see Peter Sajda, "Theodor W. Adorno: Tracing the Trajectory of Kierkegaard's Unintended Triumphs and Defeats," in *Kierkegaard's Influence on Philosophy,* vol. 1, ed. Jon Stewart (Farnham, England: Ashgate, 2002), 3–48.

8. For a general complaint against reading philosophical debate as political allegory, see Peter G. Gordon, *Continental Divide: Heidegger, Cassirer, Davos* (Cambridge, MA: Harvard University Press, 2010), esp. 3–5 and passim.

9. In his author's afterword, Adorno writes, "die Wirkung des Buches war von Anbeginn überschattet vom politischen Unheil. Doch wurde es, auch als der emigrierte Autor längst ausgebürgert war, nicht verboten und stetig weiter verkauft. Vielleicht schützte es das Unverständnis der Zensoren. Zumal die Kritik der Existentialontologie, die es übt, mochte schon damals oppositionelle Intellektuelle in Deutschland erreichen." Adorno, "Notiz," in *GS,* 2:261–263, quote at 261. My translation in the text; emphasis added.

10. Sören Kierkegaard, *Gesammelte Werke,* ed. Hermann Gottsched and Christoph Schrempf with Wolfgang Pfleiderer (Jena, Germany: E. Diederichs, 1913–1925). For an excellent history of the Kierkegaard reception, see Heiko Schulz, "Germany and Austria: A Modest Head Start: The German Reception of Kierkegaard," in *Kierkegaard's International Reception,* vol. 1, *Northern and Western Europe,* ed. Jon Stewart (Burlington, VT: Ashgate, 2009), 307–420; see also Edward Baring, "A Secular Kierkegaard: Confessional Readings of Heidegger before 1945," *New German Critique* 42 (2015): 67–97.

11. Karl Kraus, quoted in Allan Janik, "Haecker, Kierkegaard and the Early *Brenner:* A Contribution to the History of the Reception of Two Ages in the German-Speaking World," in *Two Ages: The Present Age and the Age of Revolution. A Literary Review,* ed. Robert L. Perkins. *International Kierkegaard Commentary.* Vol. 14 (Macon, GA: Mercer University Press, 1984), 189–222, quote at 192.

12. For a careful examination of the important translator and interpreter Theodor Haecker, who translated Kierkegaard's *Two Ages* into German (as *Kritik der Gegenwart*), see Janik, "Haecker, Kierkegaard and the Early *Brenner.*"

13. Georg Lukács, "Das Zerschellen der Form am Leben: Sören Kierkegaard und Regine Olsen," in *Die Seele und die Formen. Essays* (Berlin: Fleischel, 1911).

14. Scott Spector, *Prague Territories: National Conflict and Cultural Innovation in Franz Kafka's Fin de Siècle* (Berkeley: University of California Press, 2000), 61–91, quote at 17–18.

15. Leena Eilittä, "Art as Religious Commitment: Kafka's Debt to Kierkegaardian Ideas and Their Impact on His Late Stories," *German Life and Letters* 53, no. 4 (2000): 501.

16. Max Brod, *Franz Kafka: A Biography* (New York: Schocken, 1963), 170–171 and passim.

17. For a summary of the reception of Kierkegaard's work in German philosophy and theology (with special emphasis on Karl Barth, Rudolf Bultmann, Martin Heidegger, and Karl Jaspers), see Wilhelm Anz, "Zur Wirkungsgeschichte Søren Kierkegaards in der deutschen Theologie und Philosophie," *Text und Kontext* 15, no. 15 (1983): 11–29.

18. See Peter E. Gordon, "Weimar Theology: From Historicism to Crisis" in *Weimar Thought: A Contested Legacy,* ed. Peter E. Gordon and John P. McCormick (Princeton, NJ: Princeton University Press, 2013), 150–178.

19. Paul Tillich, "Die Theologie des Kairos und die gegenwärtige geistige Lage," *Theologische Blätter* 13 (1934): 313. See also John Stroup, "Political Theology and Secularization Theory in Germany, 1918–1939: Emanuel Hirsch as a Phenomenon of His Time," *Harvard Theological Review* 80, no. 3 (1987): 321–368. On Emanuel Hirsch, see *Theologians under Hitler: Gerhard Kittel, Paul Althaus, and Emanuel Hirsch,* ed. Robert P. Erickson (New Haven, CT: Yale University Press, 1985).

20. For an exceptionally helpful survey, see Marcia Morgan, *Kierkegaard and Critical Theory* (Lanham, MD: Lexington, 2012).

21. See, e.g., the unpublished criticism of Tillich from 1944: "Theodor W. Adorno contra Paul Tillich: Eine bisher unveröffentlichte Tillich-Kritik Adornos aus dem Jahre 1944," ed. Erdmann Sturm, *Zeitschrift für neuere Theologiegeschichte* 2, no. 2 (1996): 251–299.

22. See, e.g., Tillich's classic early work, *Die religiöse Lage der Gegenwart* (Berlin: Ullstein, 1926), and his political declaration, *Die sozialistische Entscheidung* (Potsdam: A. Protte, 1933). A helpful guide is A. James Reimer, *Paul Tillich: Theologian of Nature, Culture and Politics* (Münster: LIT Verlag, 2004). See also Wilhelm Pauck and Marion Pauck, *Paul Tillich: His Life & Thought,* 1: Life (New York: Harper & Row, 1976).

23. *LD,* 3. For Adorno's more complex assessment of Tillich, recorded in the "Entwurf contra Paulum," see "Theodor W. Adorno contra Paul Tillich," 251ff. See also Theodor W. Adorno, *Metaphysics,* trans. Edmund Jephcott (Stanford, CA: Stanford University Press, 2001), 182n4. I owe these citations to Rolf Tiedemann, ed., *LD,* 211–212.

24. Theodor W. Adorno, quoted in MD, 124. Actually, notwithstanding this portrait of isolation, Horkheimer and Pollock also lived at Kronberg with Adorno. In the midst of writing the *Kierkegaard,* Adorno also sent small essays to Kracauer to be published in the *Frankfurter Zeitung;* he also continued to write music criticism.

25. Theodor W. Adorno, quoted in Robert Hullot-Kentor, "Foreword," in *KC,* xx.

26. Hullot-Kentor notes that "it appeared in bookstores on February 27, 1933, the day that Hitler declared a national emergency and suspended the freedom of the press, making the transition from chancellor to dictator." See Hullot-Kentor, "Foreword," xi.

27. Gershom Scholem to Walter Benjamin, October 24, 1933, in *The Correspondence of Walter Benjamin and Gershom Scholem, 1932–1940,* ed. Gershom Scholem, trans. Gary Smith and Andre Lefevre (New

York: Schocken, 1980), 84; originally published in German as *Walter Benjamin/Gershom Scholem Briefwechsel, 1930–1940* (Frankfurt am Main: Suhrkamp, 1980).

28. Benjamin, "Kierkegaard: The End of Philosophical Idealism," 703–705, quote at 704. For remarks on Benjamin's review, see DC, 94. For further insight concerning the impact of Adorno's Kierkegaard-book on Benjamin, see Max Pensky, *Melancholy Dialectics: Walter Benjamin and the play of Mourning* (Amherst, MA: University of Massachusetts Press, 2001), 140–149.

29. *KC*, 19 ("absurd"); *KC*, 22 (on Beethoven).

30. *KC*, 3, 4–5, 3, 5.

31. *KC*, 6, 7, 9–10.

32. *KC*, 32.

33. *KC*, 32.

34. *KC*, 35, 32.

35. *KC*, 41.

36. Olaf Peder Monrad, *Søren Kierkegaard. Sein Leben und seine Werke* (Jena, Germany: Eugen Diederichs, 1909), 30.

37. *KC*, 42; German at *GS*, 2:64.

38. *KC*, 44, 43. In connection with Adorno's remarks on the bourgeois interior, it may be worth reflecting on the art-historical significance of such spaces, as described by T. J. Clark, who writes the following of Picasso: "The world, for the bourgeois, is a room. . . . And no style besides Cubism has ever dwelt so profoundly on these few square feet, this little space of possession and manipulation. The room was its premise—its model of beauty and subjectivity." T. J. Clark, *Picasso and Truth: From Cubism to Guernica* (Princeton, NJ: Princeton University Press, 2013), 79. Many thanks to Jay Bernstein for this reference.

39. *KC*, 46.

40. Like the natural self, "the crowd" is for Kierkegaard "the untruth." *KC*, 52.

41. *KC*, 50. In German, "Fliehend von Verdinglichung gerade zieht er sich in die 'Innerlichkeit' zurück." *GS*, 2:74.

42. *KC*, 44.

43. Daphne Hampson, *Kierkegaard: Exposition and Critique* (New York: Oxford University Press, 2013), 210 ("unfair"), 174 ("misleading").

44. Marcia Morgan, *Kierkegaard and Critical Theory* (Lanham, MD: Lexington Books, 2012), viii.

45. *KC*, 39.
46. *KC*, 39.
47. *KC*, 44.
48. Jean Wahl, *Études kierkegaardiennes* (Paris: Fernand Aubier, 1938). Adorno's reviews can be found in *Journal of Philosophy* 36, no. 1 (1939): 18–19; and *Studies in Philosophy and Social Science* 8, nos. 1–2 (1940): 232–235.
49. Theodor W. Adorno to Walter Benjamin, March 4, 1938, in Theodor Adorno and Walter Benjamin, *The Complete Correspondence, 1928–1940*, ed. Henri Lonitz, trans. Nicholas Walker (Cambridge, MA: Harvard University Press, 2001), 251.
50. Theodor W. Adorno, "Wahl, *Études kierkegaardiennes*" (review), *Journal of Philosophy* 36, no. 1 (1939): 18–19, quote at 19.
51. Adorno, "Wahl, *Études* kierkegaardiennes" (review), *Studies in Philosophy and Social Science* 8, nos. 1–2 (1940): 233, 235.
52. KL, 423.
53. KL, 424.
54. KL, 426.
55. For a discussion, see, e.g., S. D. Chrostowska, "Thought Woken by Memory: Adorno's Circuitous Path to Utopia," *New German Critique* 40, no. 118 (2013): 93–117.
56. KL, 426.
57. KL, 428–429.
58. KL, 429; emphasis added.
59. "Finale," in *MM*, 153; emphasis added.

2. Ontology and Phenomenology

1. Rolf Tiedemann, editor's remarks in *GS*, 1:381–384. The manuscript is dated May 7, 1931; it was Adorno's *Antrittsvorlesung*. Tiedemann notes that from the correspondence between Adorno and Benjamin, we know that this lecture was supposed to be published, and with a dedication to Benjamin.
2. "Preface," in *ND*, 8; German text at *GS*, 6:8.
3. See Martin Jay, *Marxism and Totality: The Adventures of a Concept from Lukács to Habermas* (Berkeley: University of California Press, 1986), esp. 241–275; see also *HS*.
4. *AE*, 1; *GS*, 1:9.

5. AP, 25. On Marburg neo-Kantianism, see Michael Friedman, *A Parting of the Ways: Carnap, Cassirer, and Heidegger* (Peru, IL: Open Court, 2000); and Peter E. Gordon, *Rosenzweig and Heidegger: Between Judaism and German Philosophy* (Berkeley: University of California Press, 2003), esp. chap. 1. For general remarks on the language of philosophical crisis in the 1920s and 1930s, see Peter E. Gordon, *Continental Divide: Heidegger, Cassirer, Davos* (Cambridge, MA: Harvard University Press, 2010), 43–86; and Charles Bambach, *Heidegger, Dilthey, and the Crisis of Historicism* (Ithaca, NY: Cornell University Press, 1995). See also Moritz Föllmer and Rüdiger Graf, *Die "Krise" der Weimarer Republik: Zur Kritik eines Deutungsmusters* (Frankfurt am Main: Campus, 2005).

6. AP, 26.

7. AP, 24–25.

8. AP, 123.

9. AP, 123; *GS*, 1:330.

10. AP, 124.

11. Cf. *MM*, 247.

12. AP, 127, 126.

13. AP, 127.

14. AP, 128, 129, 131, 129.

15. AP, 130.

16. AP, 132.

17. AP, 132.

18. AP, 133.

19. AP, 133.

20. AP, 133.

21. See Rolf Tiedemann's editorial afterword in *GS*, 1:383.

22. NH, 111, 121.

23. NH, 111–112, 112.

24. NH, 113, 114.

25. NH, 115, 116.

26. *HS*, 19; emphasis added.

27. *MM*, 50.

28. NH, "possibility over reality," 116; "*Entwurf*," 116.

29. NH, 117, 120.

30. For an excellent summary of Adorno's complex idea of natural history, see Deborah Cook, *Adorno on Nature* (New York: Routledge, 2014), esp. 1–6.

31. NH, 118. For remarks on Adorno's affinities with Lukács, see DC, 85–86.

32. NH, 120.

33. NH, citing the German version in GS, 1:345–365; quote from 365.

34. NH, 121.

35. MD, 192.

36. Gilbert Ryle, "Review of Heidegger's *Sein und Zeit*," *Mind* 38 (1929): 355–370. The review merits close examination insofar as it anticipates Adorno's verdict that Heidegger's fundamental ontology remains subjectivistic or anthropocentric in character, caught in the kind of idealism for which Heidegger reproached Husserlian phenomenology. Thus Ryle: "I think, too, that it can be shown that the only reason why Heidegger's Hermeneutic of 'Dasein' takes or promises to take the form of a sort of anthropologistic Metaphysic (smelling a little oddly both of James and of St Augustine) is because Heidegger presupposes that the Meanings which his Hermeneutic is to unravel and illuminate must be in some way man-constituted. . . . And I must also say, in his behalf, that while it is my personal opinion that qua First Philosophy Phenomenology is at present heading for bankruptcy and disaster and will end either in self-ruinous Subjectivism or in a windy mysticism, I hazard this opinion with humility and with reservations since I am well aware how far I have fallen short of understanding this difficult work" (370).

37. MD, 190.

38. Theodor W. Adorno, *Berg. Der Meister des kleinsten Übergangs*, in GS, 13:321–494, quote from 367. In English as *Alban Berg: Master of the Smallest Link*, ed. Juliane Brand and Christopher Hailey (Cambridge: Cambridge University Press, 1991), 34.

39. "In 1968 he still labeled it the most important of his books for him next to *Negative Dialectics*." Bibliographical note, AE, 241.

40. Adorno, "Die Transcendenz des Dinglichen und Noematischen in Husserls Phänomenologie," GS, 1:17.

41. Theodor W. Adorno, "Résumé der Dissertation," GS, 1:375–377, quote from 376.

42. Fred R. Dallmayr, "Phenomenology and Critical Theory: Adorno," *Cultural Hermeneutics* 3 (1976): 369.

43. MD, 77.

44. Theodor W. Adorno, "Husserl and the Problem of Idealism," *Journal of Philosophy* 37 (1940): 5–18.

45. Rolf Tiedemann, "Editorische Nachbemerkung," *GS*, 5:385–386.

46. Horkheimer remained unconvinced of Adorno's efforts "to demonstrate the impossibility of categorial intuition." Nor did he accept the larger attempt to portray Husserl's work as the paradigm of bourgeois idealist philosophy. "Try as I might to immerse myself in your arguments," Horkheimer wrote, "I find myself unable to confirm your passionate belief that an attack on Husserl's phenomenology as the most advanced form of bourgeois philosophy is also to refute the most important intellectual motifs leading to idealism." Quoted in MD, 204.

47. The essay's original title was "Zur Philosophie Husserls"; see MD, 204.

48. An exception is the superb essay by Jared A. Miller, "Phenomenology's Negative Dialectic: Adorno's Critique of Husserl's Epistemological Foundationalism," *Philosophical Forum* 40, no. 1 (2009) 99–125. See also Sabine Wilke, "Adorno and Husserl as Readers of Husserl: Some Reflections on the Historical Context of Modernism and Postmodernism" in *Boundary 2* 16, nos. 2–3 (1989): 77–90.

49. Joanna Hodge, "Poietic Epistemology: Reading Husserl through Adorno and Heidegger," in *AH*, 85–86.

50. "Portions of an extensive manuscript produced in Oxford during my first years of emigration, 1934–1937, have been selected and reworked . . . the question I shall broach—by means of a concrete model—is the possibility and truth of epistemology in principle. *Husserl's philosophy is the occasion and not the point of this book.*" Preface to *AE* (1956), 1; emphasis added.

51. *AT*, 6.

52. See Simon Jarvis, *Adorno: A Critical Introduction* (New York: Routledge, 1998), esp. 154–155.

53. BC, 1–3.

54. *AE*, 3, 10, 4.

55. *AE*, 4, 26, 4.

56. For Adorno's claim regarding "immanent problems of form" in his aesthetic theory, see *AT*, 7.

57. *AE*, 27.

58. *AE*, 234; *GS*, 5:235, *Zur Metakritik der Erkenntnistheorie*.

59. An excellent summary of Heidegger's critique of classical phenomenology is Dermot Moran, "Heidegger's Critique of Husserl's and Brentano's Accounts of Intentionality," *Inquiry* 43 (2000): 39–66.

60. *AE*, 180; *GS*, 5:184.

61. *AE*, 228; *GS*, 5:228.

62. *AE*, 227; *GS*, 5:228; translation modified. Adorno further remarks, "If the variant, 'pure ego' is always supposed to remain a variant of 'my ego' and draw its evidence from self-experience, then it is necessarily bound to a determinate life of consciousness, *viz.*, that which is called 'I.' It is thus mundane or irrevocably referred back to the mundane. Otherwise, the loaded term, 'my' which Husserl repeatedly employs, is strictly incomprehensible." *AE*, 228.

63. *AE*, 14.

64. *AE*, 21; *GS*, 5:28.

65. *AE*, 44.

66. *AE*, 128; *GS*, 5:134.

67. *AE*, 130; *GS*, 5:135–136.

68. *AE*, 42.

69. *AE*, 196; *GS*, 5:199.

70. *AE*, 23.

71. *AE*, 89; *GS*, 5 96.

72. *AE*, 190; *GS*, 5:194. Earlier in the book Adorno expresses the same point thus: "Husserl's programme of philosophy as a rigorous science and its idea of absolute security are no exception. His Cartesianism builds fences around whatever *prima philosophia* believes it holds the title deeds of the invariable and *a priori* for, i.e., around what (in the French of the *Cartesian Meditations*) '*m'est spécifiquement propre, à moi ego.*' Thus *prima philosophia* itself becomes property [*Besitz*]." *AE*, 17; *GS*, 5:25.

73. *AE*, 190; *GS*, 5:194.

74. *AE*, 219; *GS*, 5:221.

75. *AE*, 29–30. On the transcendence of the thing-in-itself, see the recent defense of this view in Rae Langton, *Kantian Humility: Our Ignorance of Things in Themselves* (Oxford: Clarendon, 2011).

76. *AE*, 23.

77. *AE*, 10.

78. *AE*, 32; *GS*, 5:40.

79. *AE*, 32; *GS*, 5:40.

80. *AE*, 39; *GS*, 5:46.

81. *AE*, 197.

82. *AE*, 222; *GS*, 5:223.

83. *AE*, 141, 143; *GS*, 5:148.

84. Michael Rosen, *Hegel's Dialectic and Its Criticism* (Cambridge: Cambridge University Press, 1982), 164.

85. *AE*, 145n; emphasis added.
86. *AE*, 221; *GS*, 5:223.
87. On Günther Anders and "pseudo-concreteness," see Chapter 4 of the present volume.
88. *AE*, 37; *GS*, 5:44.
89. *AE*, 36, 15. Adorno's implied alternative of "undiminished experience," with its specific implications for sensuous happiness, raises the vexed question as to how such experience was to be conceived without reduction. On this topic, see Martin Jay, *Songs of Experience: Modern American and European Variations on the Universal Theme* (Berkeley: University of California Press, 2005), esp. chap. 8. See also Roger Foster, *Adorno: The Recovery of Experience* (Albany: State University of New York Press, 2012).
90. *AE*, 34.
91. *AE*; *GS*, 5:13.
92. *AE*, 186; *GS*, 5:190.
93. "Husserl's ontological, anthropological, and existential heirs are just as little justified in disowning the antecedent of their thought property. They are beholden to Husserlian method, and not to the method alone. This method was just so thoroughly covered over with bourgeois circumspection and critical responsibility that those disciples were simply unwilling to recall Husserl. That is true for Scheler as much as for Heidegger. It did seem in *Being and Time* that Kierkegaard's concept of existence had undone the posture on the part of the 'observer' in which the phenomenologist felt himself vindicated. But one may count among the surprising results of more recent studies of Husserl that some of the principle themes of *Being and Time* are already assembled in the works of the teacher, though academically scored. Common to both, to begin with, is that no assertion is bound by 'the things themselves.' Just as the confrontation with any Husserlian concept with its object can be quashed by alluding to the fact that the concept obtains in the *époché* alone and not 'naively' in the world of facts [*Fakten*], so any more drastic interpretation of Heideggerian theses about anxiety, care, curiosity, and death were obviated even before the 'conversion' *(Kehre)*. For it is supposed to be a question of pure ways of being of existence *(reine Seinsweisen des Daseins)*. However striking and close to experience Heidegger's pronouncements may be, they simply do not connect to the reality of society." *AE*, 187–188.

94. *AE*, 189; *GS*, 5:192. My translation; Domingo uses "bootstrap" for *Wesenzopf*, but the reference here is presumably to Münchhausen's hair braid.

95. *AE*, 234; *GS*, 5:234.

96. This comparison is also noted in Martin Jay, *Adorno* (Cambridge, MA: Harvard University Press, 1984).

97. *AE*, 234; *GS*, 5:235.

98. *AE*, 33; *GS*, 5:40. Adorno writes elsewhere: "In the end, however, the question of being dissolves the ontico-ontological difference *(Differenz)* on the side of the sheer concept, while solemnly protesting to be beyond the difference." *AE*, 36.

99. *AE*, 20, 21.

100. *AE*, 25.

101. *AE*, 39; *GS*, 5:47.

102. *AE*, 39; *GS*, 5:47.

103. In the concluding portion of the Husserl book Adorno offers a less dialectical distinction between "advanced" and "restorative elements." "Those are advanced," he writes, "in which thought 'means beyond itself' [*hinausmeint*; Adorno's quote from Husserl, *Logical Investigations*] under the compulsion of its contradictions. This may occur by phenomenology turning, however much in vain, to a reality not immanent to consciousness. Or by phenomenology bumping up against the primitive idealistic rock while pursuing its own contradictions, and falling into aporia which can no longer be avoided unless the idealistic beginning itself were abandoned." *AE*, 212–213.

104. Martin Heidegger, *Sein und Zeit* (Tübingen: Niemeyer Verlag, 1967), §6, Die Aufgabe einer Destruktion der Geschichte der Ontologie, 19–27; in English in *BT*, 41–49.

105. Martin Heidegger, *Kant and the Problem of Metaphysics*, 5th ed., trans. William Taft (Bloomington: Indiana University Press, 1997).

106. *AE*, 189; *GS*, 5:193.

107. This programmatic statement can also be found in the 1940 essay "Husserl and the Problem of Idealism," where Adorno fastens his attention on the specific problem of categorial intuition *(kategoriale Anschauung)* in Husserlian phenomenology. The idea of a categorial intuition, claims Adorno, embodies the central paradox of idealism. On the one hand, a categorial intuition *qua* intuition must appear as something "pre-given objectively" and as such it is analogous to a sense per-

ception of a given *Sachverhalte*—that is, a given state of affairs. On the other hand, these *Sachverhalte* are "merely ideal laws like the principles of mathematics." In Adorno's opinion these two poles of immediate givenness and logical necessity cannot cohere in a single doctrine. Categorial intuition is therefore "the *deus ex machina* in Husserl's philosophy, by which it tries to reconcile the founder's contradictory motives, namely, his desire to save the absolute objectivity of truth and his acceptance of an imperative need of positivistic justification." This paradox is not unique to phenomenology; it afflicts all forms of idealism that wish "*to break through the walls of idealism with purely idealist instruments.*" Adorno, "Husserl and the Problem of Idealism," 14, 17. For a lucid account of the problem of categorial intuition in Husserlian phenomenology, see Robert Sokolowski, "Husserl's Concept of Categorial Intuition," *Philosophical Topics* 12, suppl. (1982): 127–141.

108. *ND,* 10.

109. *AE,* 233; *GS,* 5:234: "Husserl's concept of contingency is, like that of accident in the entirety of bourgeois thought, the expression of the impossibility of reducing the real to its concept, the fact to its essence, or in the final instance the object to the subject."

110. For more on Adorno's interpretation of Husserlian phenomenology as a "failed outbreak," see Roger Foster, *Adorno: The Recovery of Experience* (Albany: State University of New York Press, 2012).

111. *AE,* 25.

3. The Jargon of Authenticity

1. MD, 273.

2. "Gold Assay," in *MM,* 152.

3. For further discussion of Adorno's assessment of anti-Semitism, see Jack Jacobs, *The Frankfurt School, Jewish Lives, and Antisemitism* (New York: Cambridge University Press, 2004).

4. For a critical reconstruction, see the excellent essay by Anson Rabinbach, "The Cunning of Unreason: Mimesis and the Construction of Anti-Semitism in Horkheimer and Adorno's *Dialectic of Enlightenment,*" in *In the Shadow of Catastrophe: German Intellectuals between Apocalypse and Enlightenment* (Berkeley: University of California Press, 2001), 166–198.

5. *MM,* 152.

6. Søren Kierkegaard, *The Present Age,* trans. Walter Kaufmann (New York: Harper and Row, 1962), 65.

7. MD, 430.

8. MD, 430, 431.

9. MD, 434.

10. "Author's Note," in *JA,* xix.

11. *JA.*

12. MD, 433.

13. See, e.g., Theodor W. Adorno, *The Stars Down to Earth: The* Los Angeles Times *Astrology Column* (New York: Routledge, 1994) and "Theses on Occultism," in *MM,* 238–244.

14. The book that Adorno cites in *Jargon* is Otto Friedrich Bollnow, *Neue Geborgenheit; das Problem einer Überwindung des Existentialismus* (Stuttgart: Kohlhammer, 1955).

15. Theodor W. Adorno to Herbert Marcuse (December, 15, 1964), quoted in MD, 432.

16. Victor Klemperer, *LTI: Notizbuch eines Philologen* (Leipzig: Reclam, 1946).

17. Victor Klemperer, quoted in Peter E. Gordon, "Heidegger in Purgatory," in Martin Heidegger, *Nature, History, State (1933–1934),* ed. Gregory Fried and Richard Polt (London: Bloomsbury, 2013), 102.

18. Theodor W. Adorno, "Notiz" (written later, in June 1967); reprinted in *GS,* 6:525.

19. *JA,* 3–4 (German ed., 415–416).

20. *JA,* 31.

21. *JA,* 31, epigraph to the title page.

22. *JA,* 4–5.

23. *JA,* 25, 21.

24. *JA,* 12.

25. *JA,* 12, 65.

26. On criticism of the Buber-Rosenzweig Bible translation by Kracauer and others, see Peter E. Gordon, *Rosenzweig and Heidegger: Between Judaism and German Philosophy* (Berkeley: University of California Press, 2003), esp. 238 and passim; see also Martin Jay, "Politics of Translation: Siegfried Kracauer and Walter Benjamin on the Buber-Rosenzweig Bible," *Leo Baeck Institute Yearbook* 21, no. 1 (1976): 3–24.

27. *JA,* 4. For full details of Kracauer's possible identity, see Martin Jay, "Taking On the Stigma of Inauthenticity: Adorno's Critique of Genuineness," *New German Critique* 97 (2006): 15–30, esp. 24.

28. *JA*, 33.

29. *JA*, 9; emphasis added.

30. *JA*, 10.

31. *JA*, 45.

32. On this theme, see the excellent essays collected in Alexander Stephan, ed., *Americanization and Anti-Americanism: The German Encounter with American Culture after 1945* (New York: Berghahn, 2005).

33. Theodor W. Adorno, "On the Fetish Character in Music and the Regression of Listening," in *The Essential Frankfurt School Reader*, ed. Andrew Arato (London: Continuum, 1978), 270–299; see esp. 278.

34. *DE*, 135.

35. *JA*, 55, 44; the German word *Schänke* is an old-fashioned term for "tavern."

36. *JA*, 17.

37. "Baby with the bathwater," in *MM*, 43–45. In the later tradition of critical theory this warning against the objectivistic reduction of intersubjective meaning assumes new theoretical importance for the Habermasian theory of communicative action. See, e.g., the remarks on "context-transcending" meaning in Jürgen Habermas, *Between Facts and Norms: Contributions to a Discourse Theory of Law and Democracy*, trans. William Rehg (Cambridge, MA: MIT Press, 1998), 19.

38. For a different reading of Adorno's views on this theme, see Alexander Garcia Düttmann, *So ist es: Ein philosophischer Kommentar zu Adornos "Minima Moralia"* (Frankfurt am Main: Suhrkamp, 2004).

39. *JA*, 153.

40. *JA*, 42–43.

41. On Carnap's critique of Heidegger in his well-known 1932 paper, "Overcoming Metaphysics through a Logical Analysis of Language," see Peter E. Gordon, *Continental Divide: Heidegger, Cassirer, Davos* (Cambridge, MA: Harvard University Press, 2010), esp. 99; see also Michael Friedman, *A Parting of the Ways: Carnap, Cassirer, and Heidegger* (Peru, IL: Open Court, 2000).

42. Adorno quotes from Martin Heidegger, *Hölderlin und das Wesen der Dichtung* (Munich, 1937), 6.

43. *JA*, 114.

44. *JA*, 121.

45. *JA*, 116.

46. *JA*, 116, 37.

47. For a subtle analysis of Adorno's critique of the category of authenticity, see Jay, "Taking On the Stigma of Inauthenticity." As Jay notes, despite Adorno's critique of "authenticity," there was still conceptual space in his writing for related notions of the "genuine [*Echtheit*]."

48. *JA*, 125.

49. "Outside of the tautology all we can see here is the imperative: pull yourself together. It is not for nothing that in Kierkegaard, the grandfather of all existential philosophy, right living is defined entirely in terms of decision. All his camp followers are in agreement on that, even the dialectical theologians and the French existentialists. Subjectivity, Dasein itself, is sought in the absolute disposal of the individual over himself, without regard to the fact that he is caught up in a determining objectivity." *JA*, 128.

50. See *DE*, esp. chap. 1, "The Concept of Enlightenment."

51. "Heidegger has praise for the 'splendor of the simple.' He brings back the threadbare ideology of pure materials, from the realm of handicrafts to that of the mind—as if words were pure, and, as it were, roughened materials." *JA*, 50.

52. "In spite of its eager neutrality and distance from society, authenticity thus stands on the side of the conditions of production, which, contrary to reason, perpetrate want: When Heidegger finally calls 'homelessness' the 'third essential characteristic of this phenomenon' . . . he conjures up the Ahasuerian element. He does this by means of the demagogically proven technique of allusion, which keeps quiet about that to which it expects secret consent. The pleasure of mobility becomes a curse for the homeless. . . . In philosophy . . . the rootless intellectual carries the yellow mark of someone who undermines the established order." *JA*, 113.

53. *JA*, 47.

54. "Theory sanctions death. The partisan of authenticity commits the same sin of which he accuses the *minores gentes,* the lesser people of the They. By means of the authenticity of death as he flees from it. Whatever announces itself as 'higher' than mere empirical certainty, in this attitude, falsely cleanses death from its misery and stench—from being an animalistic kicking of the bucket. This cleansing occurs in the same manner as a Wagnerian love- or salvation death. All this is similar to the integration of death into hygiene, of which Heidegger accuses the inauthentic." *JA*, 156.

55. "Death is sublimated because of a blinded drive for self-preservation; its terror is part of the sublimation. In a life that is no longer disfigured, that no longer prohibits, in a life that would no longer cheat men out of their dues—in such a life men would probably no longer have to hope in vain, that this life would after all give them what it had so far refused. For the same reason they would not have to fear so greatly that they would lose this life no matter how deeply this fear had been ingrained in them." *JA,* 155.

56. *JA,* 129.

57. Friedrich von Schiller, quoted in *JA,* 164–165.

58. *JA,* 165.

59. For an excellent discussion of Adorno's interpretation of Beckett, see EH, especially chap. 5, "A Topography of Nothingness: Adorno on Beckett."

60. "Editorisches Nachwort," in *GS,* 7:537–544; citing 544.

61. *AT,* 250.

62. A reference on the just-completed essay appears in a letter, Theodor W. Adorno to Gershom Scholem, December 2, 1960, in Theodor W. Adorno and Gershom Scholem, *Briefwechsel, 1939–1969: "Der liebe Gott wohnt im Detail,"* ed. Asaf Angermann (Berlin: Suhrkamp, 2015), 231. Theodor W. Adorno, "Versuch, das Endspiel zu verstehen," first published in *Noten zur Literatur II* (Frankfurt am Main: Suhrkamp Verlag, 1961); *GS,* 11:281–321; reprinted in English as "Trying to Understand *Endgame,*" trans. Michael J. Jones, *New German Critique* 26 (1982): 119–150; subsequently reprinted in *AR,* 319–352. Hereafter, citations are from *AR.*

63. "Take Beckett. I like *Waiting for Godot* very much. I go so far as to regard it as the best thing that has been done in the theatre for thirty years. But all the themes in Godot are bourgeois—solitude, despair, the platitude, incommunicability. All of them are a product of the inner solitude of the bourgeoisie." Jean-Paul Sartre, *Sartre on Theater,* ed. Michel Contat and Michel Rybalka, trans. Frank Jellinek (New York: Pantheon, 1976), 51.

64. A similar sentiment, directed against Sartre, appears in Adorno's essay "Engagement," where he notes that both Kafka and Beckett "arouse the fear which existentialism merely talks about. By dismantling appearance, they explode from within the art which committed proclamation subjugates from without, and hence only in appearance. The

inescapability of their work compels the change of attitude which committed works merely demand." "Engagement," in *GS*, 11, *Noten zur Literatur*, 409–430, quote from 426. In English as "Commitment" in *Notes to Literature*, vol. 2, trans. Shierry Weber Nicholsen (New York: Columbia University Press, 1992), 76–94, quote from 86.

65. Adorno, "Trying to Understand *Endgame*," 330, 347.

66. See Lambert Zuidervaart, *Adorno's Aesthetic Theory: The Redemption of Illusion* (Cambridge, MA: MIT Press, 1991), esp. 152–177.

67. Adorno, "Trying to Understand *Endgame*," 330.

68. Adorno, "Trying to Understand *Endgame*," 330.

69. Adorno, "Trying to Understand *Endgame*," 330, 343, 325, 328.

70. Jean-Paul Sartre, *Nausea*, trans. Lloyd Alexander (New York: New Directions, 1975), 114.

71. Adorno, "Trying to Understand *Endgame*," 346.

72. Adorno, "Trying to Understand *Endgame*," 348; *GS*, 11:319.

73. Adorno, "Trying to Understand *Endgame*," 348; *GS*, 11:319.

74. Adorno, "Trying to Understand *Endgame*," 348; *GS*, 11:319.

75. *MM*, 247; emphasis added.

76. Adorno, "Trying to Understand *Endgame*," 331; emphasis added.

77. Adorno, "Trying to Understand *Endgame*," 331.

78. For an account of Hölderlin's reception in postwar Germany, see Robert Ian Savage, *Hölderlin after the Catastrophe: Heidegger, Adorno, Brecht.* (Rochester, NY: Camden House, 2008), 96.

79. JB, 356.

80. Theodor W. Adorno, "Parataxis. Zur späten Lyrik Hölderlins," in *Noten zur Literatur* (Frankfurt am Main, 1974); reprinted in English as "Parataxis: On Hölderlin's Late Poetry," in Nicholsen, *Notes to Literature*, vol. 2, 109–149, quotation on 133. Also in *GS*, 11:447–491. Hereafter, citations are to the English edition unless otherwise noted.

81. Adorno, "Parataxis," 114.

82. Adorno, "Parataxis," 119; *GS*, 11:459.

83. Adorno, "Parataxis," 119; *GS*, 11:459.

84. Adorno, "Parataxis," 119–120; *GS*, 11:458.

85. Adorno, "Parataxis," 140–141; *GS*, 11:482.

86. Adorno, "Parataxis," 141; *GS*, 11:459.

87. Adorno, "Parataxis," 126.

88. Martin Heidegger, "The Question concerning Technology," in *Basic Writings,* ed. David Farrell Krell (San Francisco: HarperPerennial, 1993), 308–341.

89. Friedrich Hölderlin, "Patmos," in *Selected Poems and Fragments,* trans. Michael Hamburger (London: Penguin, 1998), 242–243.

4. Negative Dialectics

1. *LD,* 67.
2. Adorno referred to *Negative Dialectics* as "my chief philosophical work, if I may call it that. . . . Henceforth my work will be concentrated, far more strongly than for years now, on artistic matters." Theodor W. Adorno to Helene Berg (July 1966), quoted in MD, 434; "fat child" from MD, 436.
3. "Preface," in *ND,* xix.
4. Lorenz Jäger, *Adorno: A Political Biography,* trans. Stewart Spencer (New Haven, CT: Yale University Press, 2004), 67.
5. Jean Beaufret, *Dialogue avec Heidegger,* quoted in Danilo Scholz, "Tout seul dans le pays de l'heideggérianisme. Adorno conférencier au Collège de France," in *L'Angle mort des années 1950. Philosophie et sciences humaines en France,* ed. Giuseppe Bianco and Frédéric Fruteau de Laclos (Paris: Publications de la Sorbonne, 2016), 143. Scholz offers a superb analysis of Adorno's Paris lectures and provides very helpful contextualization. As Scholz explains, the lectures were taken to be directed against Heideggerians on the French left, such as Kostas Axelos, Lucien Goldmann, and Henri Lefebvre.
6. See the promotional notice for Adorno's Paris lectures reproduced in Theodor W. Adorno Archiv, ed., *Adorno: Eine Bildmonographie* (Frankfurt am Main: Suhrkamp, 2003), 254.
7. "Preface," in *ND,* xx.
8. For a reconstruction and critique of this idea see Michael Rosen, *Hegel's Dialectic and Its Criticism* (London: Cambridge University Press, 1982), esp. 153–178. For a more sympathetic reconstruction, see Brian O'Connor, *Adorno's Negative Dialectic: Philosophy and the Possibility of Critical Rationality* (Cambridge, MA: MIT Press, 2004).
9. Axel Honneth, *Pathologies of Reason: On the Legacy of Critical Theory,* trans. James Ingram (New York: Columbia University Press, 2009), 85.
10. See "Idealism as Rage," in *ND,* 33–35; *GS,* 6:33–35.
11. My English here is based on the older translation of Adorno, *Negative Dialectics,* trans. E. B. Ashton (New York: Continuum, 1973), 23;

citing the German from *ND,* in *GS,* 6:33–34. This is not the place to comment on the striking resemblance between Adorno and Levinas—a resemblance that has been explored with great precision in a book by Hent de Vries. Despite the vigor with which Lévinas developed his critique of idealism as a philosophy of domination, Adorno had already developed the rudiments of a remarkably *similar* critique as early as his inaugural lecture in 1931. In "The Actuality of Philosophy," Adorno diagnosed the crisis of the contemporary philosophical discipline as due to its failure to grasp the totality of reality. The pretension to grasp the whole of reality in thought would necessarily founder insofar as "autonomous reason" could never be "adequate to" its object. The task for a new species of philosophy would be to allow for the persistence of an "irreducible" reality: "philosophy which no longer makes the assumption of autonomy, which no longer believes reality to be grounded in the *ratio,* but instead assumes always and forever that the law-giving of autonomous reason pierces through a being which is not adequate to it and cannot be laid out rationality as a totality—such a philosophy will not go the entire path to the rational presuppositions, but instead will stop there where irreducible reality breaks in upon it." AP, 37–38.

12. On the theme of self-preservation in *Dialectic of Enlightenment,* see Josef Früchtl, "The Struggle of the Self against Itself: Adorno and Heidegger on Modernity," in *AH,* 138–154, esp. 146.

13. "Dialectics and the Solidified," in *ND,* 48–50.

14. *ND,* 38.

15. In the original, this is "Durchgeführte Kritik an der Identität tastet nach der Präponderanz des Objekts"; in the Redmond translation, "The thorough-going critique of identity gropes for the preponderance [*Praeponderanz*] of the object." Most of the secondary literature on Adorno in English prefers the concision of the term "primacy" instead of the cognate "preponderance." Later in the paragraph Adorno uses the term "Vorrang," and here the translation as "primacy" is more accurate. *ND,* 184; *GS,* 6:184.

16. BC, 47.

17. On the "preponderance [*Vorrang*] of the object," see *ND,* 184–187.

18. *ND,* 184–187; modified with reference to the original.

19. Theodor W. Adorno, "The Idea of Natural History," *Telos* 60 (1984): 115, 116.

20. Karl Löwith, *Heidegger: Denker in dürftiger Zeit* (Frankfurt am Main: Fischer, 1953).

21. Karl Löwith, "Preface to the Second Edition," in *Heidegger: Thinker in a Destitute Time,* in *Martin Heidegger and European Nihilism,* ed. Richard Wolin, trans. Gary Steiner (New York: Columbia University Press, 1995), 31.

22. Günther Anders, "On the Pseudo-Concreteness of Heidegger's Philosophy," *Philosophy and Phenomenological Research* 8, no. 3 (1948): 337–371.

23. Elisabeth Young-Bruehl, *Hannah Arendt: For Love of the World* (New Haven, CT: Yale University Press, 1982), 155.

24. See, e.g., Günther Anders, *Über Heidegger,* ed. Gerhard Oberschlick (Munich: Beck, 2001).

25. Anders, "Pseudo-Concreteness," 349, 362; emphasis in the original.

26. Anders, "Pseudo-Concreteness," 367, 357; emphasis in the original.

27. Anders, "Pseudo-Concreteness," 357. The critique of Heidegger's concept of "thrownness" also plays a central role in Ernst Cassirer's assessment in *The Myth of the State.* For this critique see Peter E. Gordon, *Continental Divide: Heidegger, Cassirer, Davos* (Cambridge, MA: Harvard University Press, 2010), esp. chap. 6.

28. "Disappointed Need," in *ND,* 80–83.

29. "Disappointed Need," in *ND,* 80–83.

30. *HF,* 102, 125, 126.

31. For helpful remarks on the meaning of the term "concrete" for Adorno, see the editorial remarks in *HF,* 329n8.

32. Martin Heidegger, *Sein und Zeit* (Tübingen: Niemeyer, 1967), 1.

33. "Meaning of Being," in *ND,* 93–94.

34. "No-Man's Land," in *ND,* 85–86.

35. "Lack as Gain," in *ND,* 83–84.

36. On Benjamin's concept of aura, see Miriam Bratu Hansen, "Benjamin's Aura," *Critical Inquiry* 34, no. 2 (2008): 336–375.

37. Walter Benjamin, "The Work of Art in the Age of Its Mechanical Reproducibility," in *Selected Writings,* vol. 4, *1938–1940,* ed. Michael Jennings and Howard Eiland (Cambridge, MA: Harvard University Press, 2006), 256.

38. "Existence is sanctified without the sanctifying factor [*Existenz wird geweiht ohne das Weihende*]. Of the eternal idea in which entity was to share, or by which it was to be conditioned, nothing remains but the

naked affirmation of what is anyway—the affirmation of power." *ND*, 131; *GS*, 6:136. The claim that Heidegger's philosophy abjures a critical perspective and ends by merely affirming what already exists "anyway" is repeated elsewhere; see, e.g., Theodor W. Adorno, "Why Philosophy?," trans. Margaret D. Senft-Howie and Reginald Freeston, in *AR*, 51: "But the much overstated trend of neo-ontology against idealism ends, not in a dynamic restatement of its aims and purpose, but in resignation. Thought has allowed itself to become, as it were, intimidated, and *no longer possesses the self-confidence to go beyond the mere reproduction of what is anyway*. In contrast to such resigned attitudes, idealism at least retained an element of spontaneity" (emphasis added).

39. "Lack as Gain," in *ND*, 83–84. See also Adorno's later remark: "In spite of such affected humility not even theological risks are undertaken. The attributes of being do indeed resemble, like the absolute idea of old, the ones transmitted by the deity. But the philosophy of being guards itself from the existence of such. So archaistic the whole, so little does it wish to reveal itself to be unmodern. Instead it participates in modernity as the alibi of the existent, of that to which being transcended [zu dem Sein transzendierte] and yet which is supposed to be sheltered therein." "Lack as Gain," in *ND*, 84.

40. *ND*, 131; *GS*, 6:136.

41. *ND*, 131.

42. *ND*, 136; *GS*, 6:136. In connection with this argument Adorno cites Löwith's remarks about the difficulty of distinguishing between the "higher" and "vulgar" modes of historicity and time. See Löwith, *Heidegger, Denker in dürftiger Zeit*, 49.

43. *ND*, 131; *GS*, 6:136.

44. For a full treatment of the philosophical relationship between Adorno and Sartre, see David Sherman, *Sartre and Adorno: The Dialectics of Subjectivity* (Albany: State University of New York Press, 2007).

45. "The most recent attempt to break out of conceptual fetishism—out of academic philosophy, without relinquishing the demand for commitment—went by the name of Existentialism. Like fundamental ontology, from which it split off by entering into political commitments, existentialism remained in idealistic bonds." *ND*, 49.

46. *ND*, 50, 49.

47. Theodor W. Adorno, "Engagement," lecture given for Radio Bremen, March 28, 1962. First published as "Engagement oder künstlerische

Autonomie," *Die Neue Rundschau* 73 (1962); reprinted in *GS,* 11:409–430. Reprinted in English as "Commitment," in Adorno, *Notes to Literature,* vol. 2, trans. Shierry Weber Nicholsen (New York: Columbia University Press, 1992), 76–94. Citations hereafter are to the English translation.

48. In this respect, Adorno finds Sartre's plays more effective in their social criticism than Brecht, whose plays romanticize the degraded conditions they ostensibly condemn: "Those whom Brecht considers classics denounced the idiocy of rural life, the stunted consciousness of those who are oppressed and in poverty. For him, as for the existential ontologist, this idiocy becomes ancient truth." Adorno, "Commitment," 85.

49. Adorno, "Commitment," 80.

50. Karl Jaspers, *Die Schuldfrage* (Heidelberg: Lambert Schneider, 1946). For an interpretation, see Anson Rabinbach, "The German as Pariah: Karl Jaspers's *The Question of German Guilt,*" in *In the Shadow of Catastrophe: German Intellectuals between Apocalypse and Enlightenment* (Berkeley: University of California Press, 2001), 129–165.

51. "Engagement," in *GS,* 11, *Noten zur Literatur,* 409–430, quote from 424; translation modified from "Commitment."

52. *ND,* 58–61.

53. On the debate between Heidegger and Sartre that portrays Sartrean (humanistic) existentialism as a misprision of fundamental ontology, see Ethan Kleinberg, *Generation Existential: Heidegger's Philosophy in France, 1927–1961* (Ithaca, NY: Cornell University Press, 2005).

54. Adorno was not alone among the Frankfurt school critics of Sartre. See, e.g., Herbert Marcuse's interpretation, which takes up some of the same charges of pseudo-concreteness and uncritical affirmation of given reality. "No philosophy," Marcuse wrote, "can possibly comprehend the prevailing concreteness. Heidegger's existential ontology remains intentionally 'transcendental': his category of *Dasein* is neutral toward all concretization. Nor does he attempt to elaborate *Weltanschauung* and ethics. In contrast, Sartre attempts such concretization with the methods and terms of philosophy—and the concrete existence remains 'outside' the philosophical conception, as a mere example or illustration. His political radicalism lies outside his philosophy, extraneous to its essence and content. Concreteness and radicalism characterize the style of his work rather than its content. And this may be

part of the secret of its success. He presents the old ideology in the new cloak of radicalism and rebellion. Conversely, he makes destruction and frustration, sadism and masochism, sensuality and politics into ontological conditions. He exposes the danger zones of society, but transforms them into structures of Being. His philosophy is less the expression of defiance and revolt than of a morality which teaches men to abandon all utopian dreams and efforts and to arrange themselves on the first ground of reality: Existentialism 'dispose les gens à comprendre que seul compte la réalité, que les rêves, les attentes, les espoirs permettent seulement de définir un homme common rêve deçu, comme espoirs avortées, comme attentes inutiles . . .' Existentialism has indeed a strong undertone of positivism: the reality has the last word." Herbert Marcuse, "Existentialism: Remarks on Jean-Paul Sartre's *L'être et le néant*," *Philosophy and Phenomenological Research* 3, no. 3 (1948): 335–336.

55. *ND*, 130–131.

56. *ND*, 130–131.

57. Martin Heidegger, *Being and Time*, trans John Macquarrie and Edward Robinson (San Francisco: Harper & Row, 1962), 67, 68 and passim.

58. "Nominalistic Aspect," in *ND*, 131–132; *GS*, 6:131–132; here I borrow from the old translation by Ashton.

59. "If subjectivity dissolves solidified preordained substances by its—in Kant's term, functional—essence, its ontological affirmation assuages the fear of these. Subjectivity, the functional concept *kat' hexochên* [Greek: what is preeminent, what leads], becomes something absolutely solid, as was already by the way presupposed in Kant's doctrine of the transcendental unity." *ND*, old translation, 127.

60. "Existence Authoritarian," in *ND*, 132–133; old translation, 127.

61. New translation, *ND*, 133; old translation, 128.

62. Heidegger, *Being and Time*, 72, 472. For a study of the general theme of reification, see Rüdiger Dannemann, *Das Prinzip Verdinglichung, Studie zur Philosophie Georg Lukács* (Frankfurt am Main: Sendler, 1987). On the connections between Lukács and Heidegger, see Axel Honneth, *Reification: A New Look at an Old Idea* (Oxford: Oxford University Press, 2012).

63. "Protest against Reification," in *ND*, 96–99; *GS*, 6:98. A further problem, Adorno notes, is that Heidegger himself subscribes to a reified model of the "matter-at-hand"—i.e., the basic field of appear-

ances that is supposed to be the object of phenomenological description. "If Heidegger had emphasized the aspect of the appearance [*Erscheinens*] against its complete reduction to thought, that would be a salutary corrective on idealism. But he isolates therein the moment of the matter-at-hand [Sachverhalt], gets hold of it, in Hegel's terminology, just as abstractly as idealism synthesized it. Hypostasized, it ceases to be a moment, and becomes in the end what ontology, in its protest against the division between the concept and the existent, least of all wished to be: reified." "On Categorical Intuition," in *ND*, 87–90.

64. "Protest against Reification," in *ND*, 99; *GS*, 6:99.

65. "Protest against Reification," *ND*, 96–99; *GS*, 6:99.

66. *DE*, 191.

67. "False Need," in *ND*, 99–100; quotation modified.

68. "False Need," in *ND*, 99–100; quotation modified.

69. "Philosophically, the anamnesis of suppressed nature, in which Hölderlin tries to separate the wild from the peaceful, is the consciousness of non-identity, which transcends the compulsory identity of the Logos." Theodor W. Adorno, "Parataxis: On Hölderlin's Late Poetry," in Adorno, *Notes to Literature*, vol. 2, 109–152, quote from 141.

70. "False Need," in *ND*, 99–100.

71. "False Need," in *ND*, 99–100.

72. "Being," *Thesei* [Greek: thesis], in *ND*, 90–92; emphasis added.

73. Compare this claim to that which is found in *The Philosophy of the New Music* (1948) where Adorno suggests a kinship between phenomenology and the music of Stravinsky: "In both cases, distrust of what is not original—ultimately, the suspicion of the contradiction between real society and its ideology—is seduced to the hypostatization of what 'remains,' of what would be left after discarding all that is supposedly merely added in, as the truth. In both cases, the mind is caught up in the delusion that in its own sphere—that of thought and art—it could escape the curse of being merely mind, merely reflection, and not being itself. In both, the unmediated contradiction between thing and intellectual reflection becomes absolute, and therefore what is produced by the subject is invested with the dignity of the natural." Theodor W. Adorno, *The Philosophy of New Music*, trans. Robert Hullot-Kentor (Minneapolis: University of Minnesota Press, 2006), 107.

74. "Copula," in *ND*, 107–111; emphasis added.

75. Iain Macdonald, "Ethics and Authenticity: Conscience and Non-Identity in Heidegger and Adorno, with a Glance at Hegel," in *AH*, 6–21.

76. On the question of Heidegger's stand on realism, see Peter E. Gordon, "Realism, Science, and the Deworlding of the World," in *A Companion to Phenomenology and Existentialism*, ed. Hubert Dreyfus and Mark Wrathall (Oxford: Blackwell, 2006), 425–444.

77. Gordon, "Realism, Science, and the Deworlding of the World," 438.

78. The full passage betrays Heidegger's own conflicted thoughts on subjectivity: "The world is something 'subjective,' presupposing that we correspondingly define subjectivity with regard to this phenomenon of world. To say that the world is subjective is to say that it belongs to the Dasein so far as this being is in the mode of being-in-the-world." Martin Heidegger, *The Basic Problems of Phenomenology*, trans. Albert Hofstadter (Bloomington: Indiana University Press, 1982), 168.

79. "Disenchantment of the concept is the antidote of philosophy. It keeps it from growing rampant and becoming an absolute to itself." This is from the section "Disenchantment of the Concept," in *ND*, 23–24; *GS*, 6:24.

80. *ND*, 111.

81. "Disenchantment of the Concept," in *ND*, 23–24; *GS*, 6:23–24. Beyond its significance for the critique of past philosophical systems, the notion of the concept's bid for autarky also had a political meaning. As Martin Jay observed, Adorno felt that a "utopian social order" would be one that wholly recognized the nonidentical without aiming to incorporate it into the "myth of total reason." See Martin Jay, *Adorno* (Cambridge, MA: Harvard University Press, 1984), 68, 100.

82. "Its mediated nature through the non-conceptual survives in it by means of its significance, which for its part founds its conceptual nature. It is characterized as much by its relation to the nonconceptual—as in keeping with traditional epistemology, where every definition of concepts ultimately requires non-conceptual, deictic moments—as the contrary, that the abstract unity of the onta subsumed under it are to be separated from the ontical." "Disenchantment of the Concept," in *ND*, 23–24; *GS*, 6:23–24.

83. "Disenchantment of the Concept," in *ND*, 23–24; *GS*, 6:23–24.

84. "Disenchantment of the Concept," in *ND*, 23–24; *GS*, 6:23–24: "Disenchantment of the concept is the antidote of philosophy. It keeps it from growing rampant and becoming an absolute to itself."

85. "Disenchantment of the Concept," in *ND*, 23–24; *GS*, 6:23–24.

86. An unfortunate truth about Adorno, however, is that he only rarely emerges from the work of immanent critique to spell out just what the preponderance of the object in a materialist sense would entail. But his materialism remains at least compatible with an affirmation of the irreducible subjectivity of the human being. I therefore agree entirely with Ute Guzzoni, who writes, "While the problem in Adorno consists in the fact that there are only a few occasions where he looks beyond the spell of identity and alienated existence, the difficulty in Heidegger originates from the fact that the question of thing and world—that is, of a non-objectifying thinking—becomes more and more central in his later works, while *humans themselves* and their actual relation to things increasingly fade into the background." Guzzoni, "'Were Speculation about the State of Reconciliation Permissible . . .': Reflections on the Relation between Human Beings and Things in Adorno and Heidegger," in *AH*, 124–137.

5. Kierkegaard's Return

1. Theodor W. Adorno, quoted in Rolf Tiedemann, "Editorisches Nachwort," in Theodor W. Adorno, *Nachgelassene Schriften*, vol. 7, *Ontologie und Dialektik* (Frankfurt am Main: Suhrkamp, 2002), 422; see also MD, 437. For the full exchange, see Theodor W. Adorno and Gershom Scholem, *Briefwechsel, 1939–1969: "Der liebe Gott wohnt im Detail,"* ed. Asaf Angermann (Berlin: Suhrkamp, 2015), 409 and passim.

2. Gershom Scholem, "Appendix: Correspondence from the Spring of 1931 concerning Historical Materialism," in *Walter Benjamin: The Story of a Friendship* (New York: Schocken, 1988), 227–234.

3. Adorno, quoted in Tiedemann, "Editorisches Nachwort," 422; see also MD, 437.

4. *ND*, 207.

5. BC, 16.

6. Theodor W. Adorno, "Zu Subjekt und Objekt," in *GS*, 10:741–758, *Kulturkritik und Gesellschaft*, part 2; quote from 752–753; English translation in *AR*, 147. See also the quotation and comment in BC, 20.

7. *HS*, 10, 11.

8. *LD*, 21; emphasis added.

9. *LD*, 20.

10. Theodor W. Adorno, "Interest in Freedom Split," in *ND*, 213–215; *GS*, 6:213–215.

11. On this theme, see Steven Vogel, *Against Nature: The Concept of Nature in Critical Theory* (New York: State University of New York Press, 1996); see also Deborah Cook, *Adorno on Nature* (New York: Routledge, 2014), which begins with Adorno's early lecture on natural history and concludes with an especially nuanced defense of Adorno's conception of the diversity of nature against certain romantic strains in deep ecology; see esp. 155–162. See also Nishin Nathwani, "Adorno's Dialectical Conception of Nature," undergraduate senior honors thesis, Harvard University, June 2015.

12. *ND*, 112; emphasis added.

13. This idea pays homage, of course, to a complex inheritance that connects Adorno to Schelling's critique of idealism. On Adorno and Schelling, see, e.g., the lucid discussion in Andrew Bowie, *Adorno and the Ends of Philosophy* (Cambridge: Polity, 2013), esp. 114–116 and passim.

14. *ND*, 12.

15. "A philosophy that lets us know this, that extinguishes the autarky of the concept, strips the blindfold from our eyes. That the concept is a concept even when dealing with things in being does not change the fact that on its part it is entwined with a nonconceptual whole. Its only insulation from that whole is its reification—that which establishes it as a concept." *ND*, 12.

16. "Disenchantment of the concept is the antidote of philosophy. It keeps it from growing rampant and becoming an absolute to itself." *ND*, 24; *GS*, 6:24.

17. *LD*, 74; emphasis in the original.

18. Following the older translation of Adorno's *Negative Dialectics*, trans. E. B. Ashton (New York: Continuum, 1973), 104. New translation, "Copula," in *ND*, 107–111; *GS*, 6:107–111; emphasis added.

19. Martin Heidegger, *BT*, 251.

20. Martin Heidegger, *Basic Problems of Phenomenology*, rev. ed. (Bloomington: Indiana University Press, 1988), 166; emphasis added, translation modified.

21. Theodor W. Adorno, "Parataxis: On Hölderlin's Late Poetry," in *Notes to Literature*, vol. 2, trans. Shierry Weber Nicholsen (New York: Columbia University Press, 1992), 117; see also Adorno's polemic against

the "abstraction" that governs Heidegger's readings of Hölderlin, a polemic that occasions once again a reference to Günther Anders's notion of the "pseudo-concreteness" of Heidegger's work, 123–124.

22. On Adorno's interpretation of Hölderlin's poetry, and the polemic against Heidegger's Hölderlin-interpretation, see the excellent essay by Jeffrey Bernstein, "From Tragedy to Iconoclasm: The Changing Status of Hölderlin in Adorno's Early and Late Conceptions of History," *Epoché* 15, no. 1 (2010): 137–161.

23. *ND*, 107–111.

24. *ND*, 149. For a powerful interpretation of this passage see JB, 342–343.

25. JB, 342–343.

26. *LD*, 141.

27. *LD*, 176; emphasis in the original. The claim is also made earlier in the lectures; for example, "Existentialism promotes what exists anyway, the bare existence of mankind, to the level of a mentality that the individual must choose, as if he had any other choice. If Existentialism teaches more than such tautologies, it regresses to the reinstatement of a subjectivity existing for itself as the only substantial reality." *LD*, 174.

28. "Time itself, and thus transiency, is both absolutized and transfigured as eternal by the existential-ontological drafts. The concept of existence as the essentiality of transience, the temporality of temporal things, keeps existence away by naming it. Once treated as the title of a phenomenological problem, existence is integrated. This is the latest type of philosophical solace, the type of mythical euphemism—a falsely resurrected faith that one might break the spell of nature by soothingly copying it." *ND*, 131.

29. *ND*, 131; *GS*, 6:136.

30. Theodor W. Adorno to Walter Benjamin, December 17, 1934, in Theodor Adorno and Walter Benjamin, *The Complete Correspondence, 1928–1940*, ed. Henri Lonitz, trans. Nicholas Walker (Cambridge, MA: Harvard University Press, 2001), 66. The postwar essay was published as "Notes on Kafka," in Theodor W. Adorno, *Prisms*, trans. Shierry Weber Nicholsen and Samuel Weber (Cambridge, MA: MIT Press, 1981), 243–271; originally "Aufzeichnungen zu Kafka," *Die Neue Rundschau* 64 (1953); reprinted in *Prismen*, in *GS*, vol. 10, *Kulturkritik und Gesellschaft*.

31. Adorno to Benjamin, December 17, 1934, 66.

32. *MM*, 247.

33. The original German can be found in *Adorno-Benjamin Briefwechsel, 1928–1940*, ed. Henri Lonitz (Frankfurt am Main: Suhrkamp Verlag, 1994), 74; letter dated December 17, 1934.

34. Adorno and Benjamin, *Complete Correspondence*, 66.

35. Adorno, "Notes on Kafka," 245, 268, 259.

36. Franz Kafka, "Die Sorge des Hausvaters," in *Ein Landarzt. Kleine Erzählungen* (Munich: Wolff, 1919); reprinted in Kafka, *Sämtliche Erzählungen* (Frankfurt am Main: Fischer Verlag, 1969), 139–140; here using the translation in Kafka, *The Complete Stories*, ed. Nahum Glatzer (New York: Schocken, 1971), 427–429.

37. Kafka, *Complete Stories*, 428–429.

38. Adorno, "Notes on Kafka," 262–263.

39. Kafka, *Complete Stories*, 429.

40. Adorno to Benjamin, December 17, 1934, 93; emphasis added.

41. Adorno, "Notes on Kafka," 269.

42. *MM*, 240.

43. Adorno, "Notes on Kafka, 269; emphasis added.

44. Theodor W. Adorno, "Aufzeichnungen zu Kafka," in *Prismen*, in *GS*, vol. 10, *Kulturkritik und Gesellschaft*, 284.

45. Adorno, "Notes on Kafka," 269.

46. This may seem an overstatement, since Adorno clearly believed that aesthetic experience and memory (as in Proust's memory of village names) can serve as something like a "metaphysical experience" even in the absence of religion. Thus Adorno: "What metaphysical experience would be, to those who eschew the reduction of this to presumably religious primal experiences, is closest to how Proust imagined it, in the happiness promised by the names of villages like Otterbach, Watterbach, Reuenthal, Monbrunn." But Adorno immediately retracts the promise of such experiences with a warning that they are "antinomic"—i.e., they also encourage an uncritical acceptance: "Whoever meanwhile naïvely enjoys this sort of experience, as if they held what it suggests in their hands, succumbs to the conditions of the empirical world, which they wanted to escape from." Adorno's warning, then, would seem to turn us away from naive or immediate happiness (even in the realm of aesthetics) and turns us once again toward an "inverse theology." Adorno, "Happiness and Waiting in Vain," in *ND*, 366–368.

47. For a remarkably subtle exposition and critique of Adorno's emphasis on the nonidentical object as the figure of "transformative hope," see Lambert Zuidervaart, *Social Philosophy after Adorno* (Cambridge: Cambridge University Press, 2007), esp. 70–72.

48. Adorno, "Notes on Kafka," 254.

49. Hans Jonas, *Der Gottesbegriff nach Auschwitz: Eine jüdische Stimme* (Frankfurt am Main: Suhrkamp, 1987).

50. Adorno's own postscript, in *GS*, 2:261–263, explains that the lecture was originally delivered before an assembly of the philosophy faculty at Johann Wolfgang Goethe University in 1963 and was then first published in the *Neue deutsche Hefte* that same year. The postscript does not explain that this version, of course, lacked the inscription to Tillich's memory; in 1963 Tillich was still alive. The dedication to Tillich only appeared at the head of the lecture when the dissertation was published for a third time in Germany in 1966; in this edition the lecture was included as supplementary material. The relevant edition is Theodor W. Adorno, *Kierkegaard: Konstruktion des Ästhetischen. mit zwei Beilagen* (Frankfurt am Main: Suhrkamp, 1966).

51. For a treatment of "late style" in Adorno, see Peter E. Gordon, "The Artwork beyond Itself: Adorno, Beethoven, and Late Style," in *The Modernist Imagination: Essays in Intellectual and Cultural History*, ed. Warren Breckman, Peter E. Gordon, A. Dirk Moses, Samuel Moyn, and Elliot Neaman (New York: Berghahn, 2008), 77–98.

52. Theodor W. Adorno, "The Essay as Form," in *AR*, 91–111.

53. KN, 244.

54. KN, 244, 245.

55. KN, 248–249, 247.

56. See the summary in *DI*, 64.

57. KN, 250.

58. Axel Honneth, "Performing Justice: Adorno's Introduction to *Negative Dialectics*," in *Pathologies of Reason: On the Legacy of Critical Theory*, trans. James Ingram (New York: Columbia University Press, 2009), 82; emphasis added.

59. On experience and Adorno's appeal to the Proustian memory of happiness, see Martin Jay, *Songs of Experience: Modern American and European Variations on the Universal Theme* (Berkeley: University of California Press, 2005), 335.

60. KN, 251, 252.

61. KN, 257, 258.
62. "Kierkegaard's Protest gegen die Philosophie war auch der gegen das verdinglichte Bewußtsein, in dem, nach seinem Wort, die Subjektivität ausgegangen ist: er nahm gegen die Philosophie auch deren Interesse wahr." *ND*, 123; *GS*, 6:129.
63. On the affinities between Beethoven's "late style" and Adorno's own thought, see Gordon, "Artwork beyond Itself."
64. *AT*, 116; *GS*, 7:177.
65. *AT*, 116; *GS*, 7:177.
66. *AT*, 116; *GS*, 7:177.
67. *AT*, 197; *GS*, 7:293–294.
68. *AT*, 197; *GS*, 7:293–294.
69. Cf. Albrecht Wellmer's important suggestion that "Adorno rehabilitates the category of the sublime in the spirit of Beckett." Wellmer, "Adorno, Modernity, and the Sublime," in *The Actuality of Adorno: Critical Essays on Adorno and the Postmodern*, ed. Max Pensky (Albany: State University of New York Press, 1997), 117.

Conclusion

1. Theodor W. Adorno, "Offenbarung oder autonome Vernunft," originally a discussion with Eugen Kogon in Münster, broadcast by Westdeutscher Rundfunk on November 20, 1957, was first published in *Frankfurter Hefte* 13 (1958): 392–402 (which consists of position papers by Adorno and his interlocutor Kogon) and 484–498 (a discussion between the speakers). Reprinted in English as "Reason and Revelation," in *Critical Models: Interventions and Catchwords*, trans. Henry Pickford (New York: Columbia University Press, 1998), and subsequently reprinted in Eduardo Mendieta, ed., *The Frankfurt School on Religion: Key Writings by the Major Thinkers* (New York: Routledge, 2005), 167–173; the Mendieta edition will be cited herein.
2. Adorno, "Reason and Revelation," 169.
3. Adorno, "Parataxis: On Hölderlin's Late Poetry," in *Notes to Literature*, vol. 2, trans. Shierry Weber Nicholsen (New York: Columbia University Press, 1992), 148; my emphasis.
4. Hent de Vries, *Minimal Theologies: Critiques of Secular Reason in Adorno and Levinas*, trans. Geoffrey Hale (Baltimore, MD: Johns Hopkins University Press, 2005). For an excellent analysis of the com-

parison to negative theology, see James Gordon Finlayson, "On Not Being Silent in the Darkness: Adorno's Singular Apophaticism," *Harvard Theological Review* 105, no. 1 (2012): 1–32.

5. Adorno, "Reason and Revelation," 173.

6. Theodor W. Adorno, *Mahler: A Musical Physiognomy,* trans. Edmund Jephcott (Chicago: University of Chicago Press, 1996), 9.

7. *MM,* 247.

8. *DE,* 22.

9. [Hans-Jürgen Krahl], quoted in Jürgen Habermas, "Theodor Adorno: The Primal History of Subjectivity—Self-Affirmation Gone Wild," in *Philosophical-Political Profiles,* trans. Frederick Lawrence (Cambridge, MA: MIT Press, 1985), 105. On Krahl, see MD, 486. What I have characterized in this book as "the philosophy of bourgeois interiority" as diagnosed by Adorno bears certain affinities with what Habermas has called the paradigm of "the philosophy of consciousness," which, according to Habermas, has finally reached a point of exhaustion. But the resemblance should not deter us from also recognizing the points of substantive disagreement between Adorno and Habermas. For a full discussion of the philosophy of consciousness (including critical remarks on Adorno's continued allegiance to this paradigm), see Jürgen Habermas, *The Philosophical Discourse of Modernity: Twelve Lectures,* trans. Frederick G. Lawrence (Cambridge, MA: MIT Press, 1990), especially 106–130, 296.

Index

Adorno's affinity with, 12, 27, 30–36, 156–157, 183–193, 197; Adorno's biographical mirroring of, 14, 32, 182, 192; and aesthetics, 6, 21–26, 31, 174, 189–192; and authenticity, 86, 91, 94, 100; and Barth, 17, 30; and Beckett, 112; and Benjamin, 189–190; and bourgeois interiority, 1, 14, 26, 31–32, 127, 152, 160–161, 186, 190–191, 197; and Brenner Kreis, 16; and consciousness, 30, 194; and constitutive subjectivity, 39, 42, 126, 142–145, 152, 186; contrast to existentialism, 33–34, 183–187; and critical resistance, 30–36; and death, 34–35; and decision, 18, 20, 100, 139–140; and dialectic, 12, 24, 31, 190–191, 197; and German idealism, 39; German reception of, 13, 15–18, 29–30; and Hegel, 12, 23–24, 31–32, 39–40, 124, 184–186; and Heidegger, 20, 29–30, 33–34, 42, 76, 86, 94, 100, 142–146, 160–162; and history, 23–26, 31–32; and hope, 33–36, 188; and idealism, 10, 20, 39, 42, 129, 142–146, 152, 184–187; and identity theory, 24, 185–186; and ideology, 29–31, 181–191 passim; and *intérieur,* 25–28, 111–112, 129; and inwardness, 20, 24–28, 32, 186, 189–190; and jargon of authenticity, 91; and Jaspers, 29–30, 110, 144–145, 182–183; and Kafka, 16, 174–175, 180; and love, 31–36; and Lukács, 16; and

materialism, 21–31 passim, 157, 160, 174–175, 191; and meaning, 142–143; and mirror, 27–28, 32, 68, 152, 189; in modernity, 194–195; and negative dialectic, 35–36, 189; and nominalism, 142–146; and nonidentity, 24, 185–186; and Regine Olsen, 16; and politics, 183–184; and publicness, 26, 33, 85–86, 184; and reification, 26–27, 91, 161, 183–188 passim; and seriousness, 34–35, 192; and skepticism, 10; and subjectivity, 24–28, 42, 91–92, 102, 110, 126, 142–145, 161, 184–192, 197; and the sublime, 191–192; and theology, 34, 86, 142–143, 174–175, 181–182, 188, 195–197; on time, 17, 23, 25–26; and utopia, 33; and Wahl, 29–30; as world historical figure, 183

Kierkegaard, Søren, works: "Concluding Unscientific Postscript," 30; *Either/Or,* 23, 25; *Fear and Trembling,* 175; *The Present Age,* 86; *Stages on Life's Way,* 21; "Wie wir in Liebe Verstorbener gedenken," 34; *Works of Love,* 31–32

"Kierkegaard noch einmal," 14, 182–188

Klee, Paul, 177

Kleinberg, Ethan, 227n53

Klemperer, Victor, *LTI—Lingua Tertii Imperii,* 89

Kogon, Eugen, 194

Kracauer, Siegfried, 13, 19, 94, 208n24

Krahl, Hans-Jürgen, 198